The UFFIZI Gallery

BONECHI

THE UFFIZI

Editorial project and conception: CASA EDITRICE BONECHI.
Editorial management: Alberto Andreini.
Graphic design and cover: Maria Rosanna Malagrinò, Andrea Agnorelli.
Editing: Costanza Marsili Libelli.
Make-up: Bernardo Dionisio.

New updated edition.
Texts: Luciano Berti, Caterina Caneva, Maria Grazia Ciardi Dupré dal Poggetto, Mina Gregori.
Foreword: Annamaria Petrioli Tofani.
Catalogue entries: Alberta Bencini, Rita Bianucci, Giovanna Giusti, Eliana Pilati,
Claudio Pizzorusso.

© by CASA EDITRICE BONECHI, Via Cairoli 18/b - Florence - Italy
Tel. +39-55-576841 - Fax +39-55-5000766
E-mail: bonechi@bonechi.it   -   Internet: www.bonechi.it

Translation: Anthony Brierley.

Printed in Italy by Centro Stampa Editoriale Bonechi.

ISBN 88-476-0278-5

Warning

The Uffizi Gallery is a living reality and therefore continually subject to transformation and
changes. It may happen that during a visit to the museum variations are encountered
compared to the indications included in the present volume.

Works which have undergone restoration, and are shown in their present condition, are
marked with an asterisk.

CONTENTS

The catalogue entries were compiled by Alberta Bencini, Rita Bianucci, Giovanna Giusti, Eliana Pilati and Claudio Pizzorusso.

FOREWORD

Annamaria Petrioli Tofani
Director of the Gallery

Many changes have taken place at the Uffizi since 1982 and since 1995 - the years in which the previous editions of this monograph were published - changes which have necessitated numerous modifications and updating of the illustrative apparatus of this guide. The work itself, with an appealing approach to the subject and with a wealth of information, provides a comprehensive survey of one of the most fascinating episodes in the history of museology and collectionism.

Important work has been done on the architectural structure of the gallery, which is exposed to the daily wear and tear of many thousands of visitors and so demands constant maintenance and functional adaptation. The upkeep, which is carried out with rigorous respect for the building, one of the great masterpieces of sixteenth-century architecture, guarantees the preservation and optimum visibility of invaluable and extremely fragile works of art. In 1996 the three monumental Corridors forming the Gallery proper were completely reorganized. This initiative succeeded in restoring them to their original historical use for the exhibition of paintings and the prestigious appearance that had been given them by the Medici, which had been completely lost in the course of the centuries. Restructuring has also been carried out, with new museographical criteria, on the Leonardo Room (1991), the Lippi Room (1997), the five rooms that follow the Tribune - where the non-Florentine Renaissance paintings have been displayed, from Dürer and Memling to Mantegna - and the entire series of rooms from 25 to 34, that is, the rooms where it is possible to admire the famous masterpieces of Michelangelo, Raphael, Andrea del Sarto, Pontormo, Rosso Fiorentino, Titian, Parmigianino, Veronese, Tintoretto, Lorenzo Lotti, and so on, not to mention all that has been done in all the other sectors in the way of improving air-conditioning, security and the illumination of the paintings.

The structural modifications have been accompanied by a progressive reorganization of the works exhibited in the rooms. This has been necessary not only to rationalize certain areas of the historical itinerary which in the course of time had lost their original meaning, but also to accommodate various particularly prestigious additions notwithstanding the dramatic shortage of space which is an endemic malaise of this museum. Among the positive events which in recent years have marked the life of the Uffizi, the collections have in fact increased significantly, both in the field of ancient art and as regards some sectors of the 20th century. It is enough to recall the acquisition in 1989 of about a hundred works successfully retrieved by Rodolfo Siviero following their dispersion during the last war, including those by artists of the calibre of Masaccio, Masolino, Memling, Bronzino, Veronese, Rubens and Tiepolo, works it would obviously be unthinkable of withholding from public enjoyment; or the donations arriving through the Association of the Friends of the Uffizi which have recently enriched various sections of the collections, from the archeological section to Baroque painting and contemporary art; or the definitive arrival at the Uffizi of both the paintings formerly in the Feroni Collection, to which a fine exhibition was dedicated last year, as well as the large group of works bequeathed to the Italian State by the heirs of Alessandro Contini Bonacossi, works which only recently have finally reached their designated destination in the architectural complex of our museum. As for the significant acquisitions in the sector of self-portraits, it will be enough to recall the splendid self-portrait of Giorgio Morandi donated by Lamberto Vitali and the equally remarkable one of Giacomo Balla donated by the artist's daughters

There has been intense activity in the field of restoration, activity which has again made possible the previously unimaginable critical interpretation and aesthetic appreciation of some of the masterpieces for which this museum is famous throughout the world. The restoration of many works of art has often been essential in order to arrest dangerous processes of decay which were seriously compromising their state of preservation. The results have convinced us of the need to renew many illustrations in this volume. This is the case, for want of recalling at least some of the most important examples, with the three great altarpieces of the *Enthroned Madonna* by Cimabue, Duccio di Buoninsegna and Giotto, the *Adoration of the Magi* and *Coronation of the Virgin* by Lorenzo Monaco, the great altarpieces by Filippino Lippi, many of the paintings by Pollaiolo and Botticelli, the *Baptism of Christ* by Verrocchio and Leonardo, and the *Portrait of Leo X* by Raphael; and again, the paintings of Perugino and Andrea del Sarto, Pontormo and Rosso Fiorentino, the *Madonna of the Long Neck* by Parmigianino, the *Venus of Urbino* and the portraits of the Duke and Duchess of Montefeltro by Titian. These and other operations were supplemented in the years between 1993 and 1995 by the salvaging of more than two hundred works which in various ways were damaged as a result of the terrorist bombing of 27 May 1993, an event of unprecedented brutality which wreaked death and destruction and dramatically altered the life and programmes of the museum. Although some of the wounds inflicted on the collections are sadly irreversible (including the total destruction of two canvases by Bartolomeo Manfredi and one by Gherardo delle Notti), the highly-reputed diligence of the many restorers who work in Florence and habitually aid our daily work has reduced the damage to a minimum.

In conclusion, we can say that the history of the Uffizi in the last few years has been full of events, both for the better and, unfortunately, for the worse. In 1988 we witnessed the move to another site of an entire institution, the State Archive, which for over a century had extended its own collections and had come to occupy about two-thirds of Vasari's building, therefore preventing any possibility of developing the museum. If and when it is possible, in a future we are unable to foresee at the present time, to extend the itineraries of the Gallery of the Uffizi to spaces that have thus been made available - which would make possible, among other things, a greatly-desired recovery from our deposits of works of great interest that would be perfectly worthy of being included in the permanent display - it will also necessitate a new edition of the present book.

Annamaria Petrioli Tofani

FOUR CENTURIES OF HISTORY

Luciano Berti
former Director of the Gallery

The four hundred years of the Uffizi Gallery are certainly a long and eventful history even to summarize, especially considering that the gallery is the oldest in the world, the one with perhaps the most exemplificative range of museum experiences possible. Founded in the Mannerist age, it subsequently passed through the Baroque and neoclassical periods, the 19th and 20th century up to the present time; now, the same institution faces the imminent prospect of the century ahead, as far as we are able to predict at any rate. I have said before, in this context, that if in 1881 it was difficult to imagine the Gallery in 1981, it is surely a more arduous leap of the imagination now to envision the Uffizi in the year 2081.

But let us go back to that history which has been lived through, a history which has been comprehensively described in the books of Bencivenni-Pelli (1779) and Gotti (1872), and by myself in the extended 'Profile' which prefaced the great 'General Catalogue' of 1979.

The Gallery was founded in 1581, with ambitious intent yet without any public inauguration or declaration, on the wishes of that taciturn, introverted, but culturally refined Grand-duke, Francesco I de' Medici, the son of Cosimo I. The Florentines had witnessed the completion of the great edifice, planned by Cosimo and designed by Vasari, the year before, 1580, when Parigi and Buontalenti (who had succeeded Vasari as architects) joined up the return wing of the majestic building of the Uffizi, which overlooked the Arno at its southern end, to the Loggia dei Lanzi.

The Uffizi, as its name suggests (offices), had been built to house various magistracies (the building was originally known as the Palazzo dei Magistrati) in a modern bureaucratic centre adjacent to Palazzo della Signoria. That the open gallery on the top floor began to be used as a museum instead — which everyone now knows as the 'Uffizi' — was a great turning-point, although its future importance can hardly have been intuited by contemporaries. Not by accident, however, was Vasari's building a 'container' for the Gallery, for the structure appeared almost predestined to house it. The Uffizi's fascination as a museum is in fact closely bound up with its fascination as a monument, the ingenious architectural and urbanistic achievement of Giorgio Vasari, in effect his greatest masterpiece.

The huge construction — resembling a deep theatrical enclosure, or an immense courtyard — is characterized by the compact arrangement of architectural elements both horizontally and vertically: columns and pilasters in the ground-floor arcade, then small square windows set between brackets, rather like a mezzanine but actually admitting light to the gallery below; solemn balconied large windows on the first floor; then the upper loggia with its parapet and columns; and finally, at the top, the great overhang of the roof extending along the three sides of the building. At the end, towards the River Arno, the light almost passes right through the building due to the great central arch and the larger windows.

Thus, adjacent to the old, severe and broader Piazza della Signoria, a

smaller secluded long square with refined Renaissance 'decor' was created, a passage from the heart of the city which brought light and air from the river. The Uffizi does communicate a feeling of movement which is felt inside the Gallery, with its long corridors and the views from the numerous windows, either towards the inner square and Palazzo Vecchio, or towards the city and the River Arno to the south.

Dynamic, and no longer crystallinely static like the buildings of the early Renaissance, the Uffizi was also dynamic in the process of its construction, which was rapid in spite of considerable intrinsic difficulties. Vasari wrote that it was "because its foundations are in the river, and it almost stands on air", alluding not only to the treacherous terrain on which it was founded, but also to the daringly open framework of the facade which he built in characteristic Florentine pietra serena. Vasari also incorporated into the building the church of San Piero Scheraggio, which stood near the present entrance to the Gallery, a Romanesque basilica whose remains and successive layers, as far down as the vestiges of a Roman building, were brought to light in the restoration of 1971 (Bemporad). Five years after building had begun in 1560, most of the construction was complete; and in only five months in 1565, the year of Francesco de' Medici's marriage to Joanna of Austria, the Emperor's daughter, the extraordinary Corridor was built which linked Palazzo Vecchio to the Uffizi (with an overbridge) and via Ponte Vecchio to the new residence of the Medici dukes at Palazzo Pitti — another dynamic invention which connected the two most important centres of Medici power,

Portrait of Cosimo I dei Medici, by Agnolo Bronzino

Self-portrait of Giorgio Vasari

Francesco I dei Medici as a boy portrayed by Agnolo Bronzino.

On a wall of the Room of Leo X, Giorgio Vasari painted the papal procession in Piazza della Signoria (1515). Note, between the Loggia dei Lanzi and Palazzo della Signoria, the "Baldracca" quarter, which would later be demolished to make space for the Palazzo degli Uffizi.

and the two parts of the city divided by the river. The Gallery was supposed to have extended along this same route, and since the last century it has indeed occupied the kilometric length of the Vasari Corridor to the point where it meets the illustrious and no less imposing museum complex of Palazzo Pitti.

We have already mentioned that there was no official inauguration or public announcement of the foundation of the Uffizi Gallery. In April 1581 an informer of the Duke of Urbino, a certain Fortuna, told his sovereign that Francesco I had begun to house a collection of antiques on the top floor, and that the Gallery would be "a stupendous thing". At the same time the account-books of the painter Alessandro Allori record expenses for the elegant and vivacious grotesques which were being frescoed on the ceiling of the first corridor by a team of decorators.

In 1583 the same Fortuna was writing that the Grand-duke would stroll "through the splendid Gallery where he had assembled most of his excellent paintings and sculptures", and where he had already had portraits of illustrious men displayed. We can already recognize the development of characteristics which would survive in the museum to this day. Along the eastern wing, with Francesco and later with the brother who succeeded him, Ferdinando I, the main rooms were set up. The Medici Theatre (1586), which housed impressive stage performances organized by Buontalenti, occupied two floors where the present Gabinetto Disegni e Stampe is, and had its Ricetto with monumental facade (still visible) at the end of the first Vasarian stairway; three of the Theatre's large wooden roof trusses were uncovered in the new (1978) Botticelli Room.

In 1584, again on the initiative of the ingenious Buontalenti, the lavish octagonal Tribune was built, to this day the highpoint of the Gallery. The room was designed following a complex cosmological symbolism.

At the top an external weathercock, linked to an inner pointer, symbolizes Air; the dome studded with mother-of-pearl refers to the Heavenly Vault and to Water; the red of the wall hangings (restored to that colour in 1970) symbolizes Fire. Other elements refer to the Medici family and to Florence. Hanging on the walls were paintings by Raphael, Andrea del Sarto, Pontormo, etc.; lower down was an ebony cabinet with 120 drawers full of medals and other valuables, and on top small statues and trinkets interspersed with shelves supporting bronzes by Giambologna; on the lower part of the walls, finally, there were other small paintings, bas-reliefs and inlaid arms. In the centre of the room stood a precious chest (now lost) shaped like a small temple; it was later (1649) replaced by a splendid table with semi-precious stone inlay which was returned here in the restoration of 1970. In the recent rearrangement it was sought, as far as possible, to recreate the original appearance of the rooms; thus, the Tribune today redisplays various paintings which appeared in the first inventory of the Uffizi of 1589.

The Tribune of the Uffizi became famous throughout the world as a model of what museums should be like, a sort of ideal for every great collector. In 1772 the painter Zoffany was commissioned by the Queen of

The building of the Uffizi in two drawings by G.A. Dosio and Giorgio Vasari the Younger.

Detail of three large windows on the first floor of the Gallery.

The total restoration (Bemporad) of Vasari's building returned the structure to its former airy splendour.

England to paint a view of it (today at Windsor Castle), a view which Zoffany made even more sumptuous by including in it masterpieces that were actually at the Pitti.

Next to the Tribune is a small room, frescoed on the ceiling with allusions to the scientific instruments that were once conserved in it. More scientific material was in the nearby Terrazza delle Carte Geografiche with its magnificent large maps of the Florentine and Sienese territories (the two regions comprising the Grand Duchy) frescoed on the walls. Beyond the Tribune the Armoury, created by Ferdinando, occupied the next four rooms, again with allusions (to battles in this case) painted on the ceilings. At the end of this first corridor was the 'Gabinetto di Madama' (corresponding to the present Room of the Miniatures) where the Grandduchess kept her own treasures, and where 'idols' (antique bronzes) and miniatures were also preserved. These were the oldest rooms of the Uffizi, full of precious objects in addition to the picture collections, and although today they are necessarily arranged to display paintings, they nevertheless retain an evocative sixteenth-century atmosphere — warm, secluded and

PRIMO INTERMEDIO DELLA VEGLIA DELLA LIBERATIONE DI TIRRENO FATTA NELLA SALA DELLE COM DIE DEL SER.^mo GRAN DVCA DI TOSCANA IL CARNOVALE DEL 1616. DOVE SI RAP.^ta IL MONTE D'ISCHIA CON IL GIGANTE TIFEO SOTTO.

The Medici Theatre with a performance of 1616 in an engraving by Jacques Callot.

fanciful in the pictorial decoration of the ceilings.

On the western side of the Uffizi were various laboratories for the minor arts, and the Foundry (or Pharmacy) where perfumes, medicines (considered prodigious and given by the Grand-duke to important guests) and even poisons were distilled. At the end of this wing, above the terrace of the Loggia dei Lanzi, a hanging garden had been created with a greenhouse (or 'loggetta', which was unfortunately demolished in 1840), and a small fountain designed by Buontalenti and Giambologna, now (1973) partly rebuilt. The Medici children would come here in the late afternoon to listen to music being played in Piazza della Signoria by a famous band, the Franzosini.

The Gallery, therefore, contained many different types of collection: ancient and modern statues and busts, historical portraits, classical paintings, refined objects of decorative art, scientific instruments and maps, etc.; it was also multi-faceted, according to the taste for *Wunderkammer* (the collection of every kind of wonderful thing), as well as a reflection of the Manneristic dualism between nature and art due to the continuous metamorphic transition from one to the other.

The discerning Medici family, however, needed to find some justification for their hoarding of treasures, in a city where art hitherto had been offered prevalently for public pleasure, in churches or as urban decoration. Thus, in 1591 it was written that "here (in the Gallery, the works) are kept properly", that is, they were safer than they would have been out in the open or elsewhere; and that "the Grand-duke has provided that the officials who look after these things are courteous to whosoever wishes to see them...". The Gallery was not yet public, but was at least hospitable, at least — we may assume — for qualified scholars and visitors of a certain standing.

The "last Medici", considered decadent by later historiographers, nevertheless contributed greatly to the expansion of the Gallery. The collections of single members (from Cardinal Leopold to Grand Prince Ferdinando and Cosimo III himself) sooner or later found their way into the Uffizi, starting with the famous 'Urbino inheritance' (the dowry of Vittoria della Rovere) which yielded paintings by Titian, Raphael and Barocci, and the diptych by Piero della Francesca.

Ferdinando II had the ceilings of the second and third corridors completed, dedicating them to Florentine glories in every field. In the west wing Cosimo III created the Vestibule (of the present exit on Buontalenti's staircase), which was decorated throughout with archeological pieces and ancient inscriptions, the Room of the Porcelains (now the Veronese Room), the Room of the Self-Portraits (now the Tintoretto Room), which was covered from top to bottom with the extraordinary collection started up by Cardinal Leopold, followed by the Room of the Medals (now the Rubens Room) containing some 30,000 pieces. In the meantime other rooms were prepared for Cardinal Leopold's great col-

The portico of the Uffizi visible in a detail of the "Oreficeria", painted by Alessandro Fei in the Studiolo of Palazzo Vecchio around 1570.

The frontispiece of the inventory designed by Benedetto De Greyss shows a striking image of the three corridors of the Gallery in a single view (1748-65).

lection of drawings (which became the nucleus for the present Gabinetto Disegni e Stampe), and for the bronzes; later, other collections of miniatures and works in semi-precious stone, etc. were accumulated, and the collection of ancient marbles was enriched with exceptional pieces like the *Hermaphrodite, Cupid and Psyche,* the *Medici Venus* and the *Wrestlers.* Already in 1689 the corridors contained about 102 busts and 72 statues; the first official restorer of these archeological pieces was the sculptor Ferrata, who took up residence in Palazzo Vecchio in order to gain easy access to the museum through the communicating passageway.

Erudite cataloguing of the collections also started at this time, for the medals with the Englishman Fitton, with Noris (abbot and later cardinal) and with Vaillant. There was also an attempt to create a Florentine specialist in Sebastiano Bianchi, and A. F. Gori devoted himself to studying ancient inscriptions and Etruscology. In 1731 the first tome of the 'Museum Florentinum' appeared, a lavish publication illustrating the collections of the Gallery promoted by a group of nobles under the direction of Senator Filippo Buonarroti, a descendant of Michelangelo.

But what would happen when, as was now foreseeable, the Medici dynasty died out? Other instances of dynastic decline had denuded other Italian cities of their artistic treasures. The last surviving Medici, Anna Maria Ludovica, Electress Palatine, resolved the dilemma with the famous convention of 1737, in which — with the passing of Tuscany to the Lorraine family — it was arranged, as far as works of art were concerned, that "nothing of what is for the adornment of the State, for the use of the public, and for attracting the curiosity of foreigners, shall be taken away from the capital and the state of the Grand Duchy". At this point, works of cultural importance associated, as we would say today, with the 'territory' of Florence, with public enjoyment, and with touristic interest, were covered by this act, an act which won the Electress Palatine the supreme recognition of Florence for having saved its Gallery. An 18th-century portrait of the Electress appears in the entrance on the ground floor.

Moved more by ideals of 'good government' than by those of the 'fine arts', the Lorraine family nonetheless carried out a far-reaching reform of the Uffizi, of which the new (and still present-day) entrance on the east side was representative, with its pleasant staircases and vestibules of eighteenth-century, almost neoclassical taste, with pink and light green decoration, and the vigorous bust of Pietro Leopoldo (1789), the work of Carradori. There were innovations, notable increases, as well as one or two blunders, like the liquidation of the Medici Armoury (1775) or the reduction of the maiolica collection. The scientific instruments were transferred to a new museum created specially for them (La Specola).

The 18th century saw the passion for archeology prevail, that mixture of history and aestheticism: Etruscan collections were bought, the 'Niobe

An old engraving shows a wall of the Room of the Inscriptions with the celebrated bas-relief of the Ara Pacis, transferred to Rome in 1938.

Group' was transferred from Villa Medici in Rome and set up in a splendid new room in the west wing designed by G. M. Paoletti, a worthy neoclassical *pendant* to the Manneristic Tribune. The collection of paintings was enlarged with works by 'primitive' artists, like the *Thebaid*; an exchange (1793) with the Gallery of Vienna was extremely advantageous, bringing Dürer's *Adoration of the Magi* and Titian's *Flora*. In 1793 a section was also created for French paintings of the 17th and 18th centuries, bought in a Paris oppressed by the Revolution. The best from the grand-ducal possessions was again sifted out: Leonardo, Titian, Cellini's great bust of Cosimo I on Elba; exchanges were made, like those to obtain Barocci's *Madonna del Popolo* from Arezzo, and Simone Martini's *Annunciation* from Siena. Another renovated room was at the end of the first corridor, the Room of the Gems and Semi-precious Stones (now the Room of the Miniatures), sumptuously designed (1782) by the architect Zanobi del Rosso.

There was also a whole administrative, scientific and didactic reorganization. In August 1762 a serious fire broke out in the west wing of the Gallery as a result of the negligence of the Keeper Bianchi, who had been the first author of a guide to the Uffizi (1759). In 1775 the office of Director was instituted and entrusted to a cultured administrator, Bencivenni-Pelli, who was assisted by an exceptional ancient and modern art historian, Luigi Lanzi. In 1779 Pelli wrote the first documented history of the Gallery in two volumes, and in 1782 Lanzi compiled his first critical Guide. The museum of the Uffizi was modernized throughout: from 1793 the Royal Guards were charged with the surveillance of the Gallery,

View of the first corridor of the gallery, around 1980.

The second corridor, which connects the two wings of the building, like the others contains precious classical sculptures.

both at the entrance and inside, and in 1795 name-cards were put up next to the paintings for the information of visitors.

In 1793 Tommaso Puccini succeeded Pelli as director of the museum. In 1796, with great trepidation, he was obliged to receive the visit of General Bonaparte, whose rapacious ambitions were directed particularly at the *Medici Venus*, a statue he later succeeded in obtaining. In 1799 Puccini was again under pressure, when orders arrived from Paris to empty the Tribune of the Niobe group, Etruscan vases and ancient bronzes. Puccini's defence was both skilful and arduous, but he was aided by the above-mentioned testament of the Electress Palatine, which had established that the Uffizi were popularly and universally considered the heritage not of a dynasty but of Florence, a source of the city's wealth and prestige. The works of art preyed upon by France, especially in the Pitti, were given back in 1815, with an exhibition at the Accademia and to the great joy of the people. Sadly, the courageous Puccini did not live to see the works returned as he died in 1811. His portrait hangs, deservedly, among those of the historic Jovian and post-Jovian series in the third corridor.

The recent history of the Gallery, which covers another two centuries, is less documented but no less important. In the 19th century increasing specialization led to the transfer elsewhere of the Egyptian Museum and most of the archeological exhibits, the section for the Gallery of Modern Art and a collection of paintings for Lucca; sculptures and minor arts went to the Bargello, and the paintings of Beato Angelico to San Marco.

In the 17th bay of the eastern corridor, a fresco dated 1581 is an example of a fantastic, decorative grotesque by Alessandro Allori and his school. In the centre, a winged woman (Liberality) scatters gold coins; on the long sides the Rape of Europe has been represented on the left, and Cupid between Venus and Mars on the right. Four small ovals in the corners contain pretty landscapes.

Even so, in 1850 a general identification of the deposits listed 2817 paintings, and later many others entered the museum with the suppression of religious institutions carried out by the nascent Kingdom of Italy. The collection of paintings was substantially enlarged, and with exceptional pieces especially from the 14th and 15th centuries; it obtained the Feroni collection, and in 1900 the collection of Santa Maria Nuova, with the spectacular triptych by Hugo Van der Goes. In 1974 the museum received the Contini-Bonacossi donation, now displayed at the Meridiana

The great stairway (1780) by Zanobi del Rosso which leads to the floor of the Gallery.

Gallery of Palazzo Pitti, and in 1988 an important group of works from the Minister Siviero. The directors were eager to extend the representativeness of the Gallery, which in any case had never been Tuscan alone, but Italian and international as well, and among the new acquisitions there were two paintings by Chardin, one by El Greco and two by Goya. Under the Fascist regime the Uffizi was deprived of the reliefs of the *Ara Pacis*, which were transferred to Rome, and Raphael's *Muta* was moved to Urbino.

The Gallery, even by the standards of the most advanced museographical conceptions, needed space. In 1866 the Vasari Corridor became part of the museum (being rearranged in 1972 to display over 700 paintings), and in 1890 various other rooms were obtained from the space formerly occupied by the Medici Theatre. In 1964 plans were drawn up for the 'grand Uffizi', which was to extend throughout Vasari's building, the architectural part being entrusted to Nello Bemporad. Following the dispersion of works of art in the Second World War, which witnessed the adventurous transportation of works as far as the German border, the present reorganization has taken place under the successive directorships of Salvini, Becherucci and Berti (1969-1987), and has been accomplished throughout the Gallery with renovations and new rooms. There

The entrance to the Gallery with the white marble bust of Francesco I dei Medici, the work of Domenico Poggini, and the 17th-century porphyry bust of Ferdinando I dei Medici.

The square of the Uffizi as seen by Rossi Melocchi (d. 1820): note Donatello's Judith under an arch of the Loggia dell'Orcagna on the right.

are presently around 1700 paintings on display, and another 1000 are carefully stored in the new deposits created in 1978. A comprehensive General Catalogue of the Gallery was published in 1979.

Linked to the Gallery is a Didactic Section and a Research Office. Sensational restorations have been carried out, including those of Michelangelo's *Tondo Doni* and Botticelli's *Primavera* and *Birth of Venus*. A philological "Studies and Research" series was begun in 1984. In 1981-82, on the occasion of the fourth centenary of the Gallery, an International Studies Conference and a series of Florentine exhibitions entitled "The City of the Uffizi" were held. An appeal by the directors to assemble the donated self-portraits of twentieth-century masters yielded 230 new acquisitions (Chagall presented his personally in 1976). In 1950 the Gallery had received about 100,000 visitors; in 1980 it reached a peak of 1,335,000.

In 1988 the State Archive, which had been at the Uffizi since 1852, was transferred to its new headquarters in Piazza Beccaria, thus making available for the Gallery all the rooms on the first and ground floors, which meant a triplication of available space. As a result of this, the "Uffizi Project" was launched, and although the execrable bombing of Via dei Georgofili on 27 May 1993 succeeded in causing substantial damage to the entire west wing of the Gallery (fortunately with a minimal loss of art objects), which has necessitated extensive repair work, it has in no way impeded the continuation of this project, which has already involved the occupation of a series of rooms on the first floor, presently used for exhibitions. Since 1978 the director of the Uffizi has been Anna Maria Petrioli Tofani.

THE 13TH AND 14TH CENTURIES

Caterina Caneva

The history of Italian and particularly Tuscan art in the thirteenth and fourteenth centuries is the history of an evolution from forms ideologically and technically independent of the Byzantine tradition to the more humanly concrete and spatially defined forms of western art.

Architecture and sculpture had already made this leap, starting from the prophetic year 1000, when the new social order of free communes and the new value placed on human work, together with the circulation of new cultural ferments throughout Europe, caused a widespread reawakening of new forms of creativity. The immediate consequence of this social revival was an unusual fervour in the practice of architectural construction: in various European regions, cities with their new cathedrals and the abbeys of the most important religious orders document the search for and conquest of daring, grandiose technological solutions. Sculpture came to integrate the religious message in the same way.

View of the third room

Painting, on the other hand, during the eleventh and twelfth centuries remained stylistically and iconographically tied to the Byzantine tradition, which flattened images and froze figures in solemn, repetitive poses to the extent that they were confined within a transcendent sphere where for men only reverent contemplation was possible and there was no space for any dialogue. Even during these centuries, however, in the context of these repeated formulas that were by now almost devoid of any message, we find tentative and perhaps unconscious instances of dissent. Mosaic and fresco painting were still the most commonly used techniques during this period, although painting on wood, in which colours were applied in tempera, was more and more widely adopted. Generally speaking, however, modes of pictorial expression evolved imperceptibly. Even within mosaic and fresco cycles, for example, dramatic and popularesque elements that introduced a more concrete sense of reality became more common during the course of the twelfth century. In the same way painting on wood continued in its conquest of human values, portraying actions and sentiments that could be fully understood, particularly with the help of a progressively defined sense of space. In the first decades of the thirteenth century, in Tuscany, instances of radical innovation in pictorial representation appeared in the work of the Berlinghieri, who were active in Pisa and Lucca, and particularly in the art of Giunta Pisano (doc. 1229-54). The subjects, given their almost exclusively ecclesiastical destination, appear again and again: Crucifixes in which Christ is presented as "Triumphans" (according to the most widespread Byzantine iconography), but also and increasingly often as "Patiens"; Enthroned Madonnas and Child; large figures of saints (especially Saint Francis) surrounded by small scenes depicting episodes from their lives. To this phase, which witnessed the gradual emergence of a dramatic significance in the narration and a more concrete spatial setting aided by a more studied use of colour and outline, belong some works displayed in the second room of the Uffizi dedicated to thirteenth-century painting which culminated with Giotto.

This is highly significant evidence of how much Tuscan artists, with intense intellectual and formal rigour, were breaking away from tradition up until the appearance of the great innovators Cimabue and Giotto, regarded even by the earliest artistic historiographers as the "fathers" of Italian art. See, for example, the *Crucifix with Stories of the Passion* of the late twelfth/early thirteenth century, which was freed from heavy repaintings during a restoration in around 1960. The small side stories, although executed according to traditional schemes, make use of bright colours and a lively, descriptive movement that is reminiscent of miniature painting. The other *Crucifix*, of a later date, which presents the iconography of the "Christus patiens", also breaks away from Byzantine models (still present in the figure of Christ), eliminating the traditional eurhythmy in the stories in favour of a less refined but more concrete structure, with scanty yet precise references to the surroundings. Note also in the paintings of the *Madonna and Child*, both dating from the second half of the thirteenth century and of medium-size dimensions (for tabernacles or private altars), the general structure remains Byzantine but in both works and in different ways technical and expressive innovations are beginning to emerge.

Other works in this room, on the other hand, show the strong influence of re-elaborations effected in the mosaics of the Baptistery in Florence by several local artists who worked there alongside the Venetian masters. In this decorative enterprise, begun in 1225, the Tuscans, including Coppo di Marcovaldo and Cimabue, gave a highly personal contribution that is recognizable by its vigour and intense dramatic force. The same can be said of the Master of the Bardi Saint Francis, so called from

WORKSHOP OF
BONAVENTURA BERLINGHIERI
(Second half of 13th C.)

Madonna and Child with Saints and
Crucifixion

Tempera on wood, 103x122 overall
Dated variously to the second half of the
13th century

The painting represents one of the earliest surviving examples of the "Eleusa" Virgin, the "Affectionate Mother", an iconographic model that was first used for portable household altars although it subsequently became increasingly popular and widespread until the end of the fourteenth century, being well suited to the emotional tendency expressed by Gothic art. Bonaventura Berlinghieri instils a liveliness into the figures and objects with a refined, almost miniaturist technique. There is, however, a clear reference to Byzantine models which allow the artist to express his lyrical mysticism.

 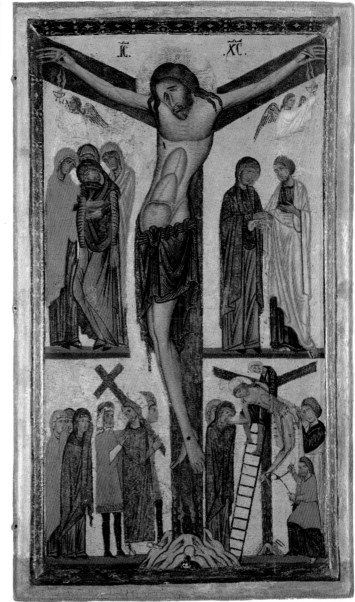

the work executed in Santa Croce, who is represented at the Uffizi with a *Saint Francis Receives the Stigmata*.

The disintegration of the Byzantine tradition in the second half of the 13th century was experienced as a process of rapid acceleration of quite revolutionary significance, this time affecting painting in particular. A whole series of factors combined to spur artists on towards a structural reform of the pictorial event, to which Cimabue was the first to apply a personal solution. These factors included a flourishing mercantile policy put into effect by the Italian communes which encouraged craft production in the same way as industrial production; trade with other European regions resulting from this policy, with a consequent exchange of culture; and lastly a new philosophy propounded by Saint Thomas, but also by Saint Francis, by which art too, aspiring to beauty through time and experience of the world, finds its rightful and indeed noble place. "Beauty", in this vision, is nothing other than the sign of God in the creation (Argan), just as nature (which the artist can therefore also be religiously inspired by) is its faithful mirror.

Tuscany was at the forefront of this evolutionary process that affected all the arts — poetry, architecture, painting and sculpture. This was not entirely due to particularly favourable geographical and economic circumstances, but was also because various important people were active in the region at this time, like Nicola and Giovanni Pisano, Arnolfo, Giotto, and the latter's master Cimabue (doc. 1272-1302), active in Rome in 1272 and in 1301 in Pisa. Initially close to the exasperated style of Coppo di Marcovaldo, at whose side, as we have said, he worked on the mosaics of the Baptistery, in later contacts with Roman artists, who were also in an advanced stage of renewal (due to the presence in Rome of a strong classical substratum), and in cultural exchanges occurring in the great hotbed of the Basilica of Assisi (which drew to it artists of various cultural background), he found the material that could be reworked into a rigorous intellectual and artistic vision now fully oriented in a western direction.

The *Santa Trinita Madonna* of the Uffizi, originally from the church of Santa Trinita, executed between 1260 and 1280, is already a totally new image, although it does retain some elements of the tradition such as the rigidly frontal pose and the golden highlights on the robes of the Virgin and Child. But the large throne lightened by precious inlays now has a new spatial dimension, and in the faces of the divine figures, as in the garments of the angels and the prophets looking on from the loggia-crypt below, the chiaroscuro introduces a concrete physicalness, a different softness and roundness. Also included in this conquest of human values, both concrete and spiritual, made by Cimabue, are the *Crucifixes* of Arezzo and Santa Croce in Florence (now partially destroyed by the flood of 1966) and the frescoed stories of Assisi, which in the *Crucifixion* reach a new and perturbing dramatic force.

Departing from the innovations absorbed during his apprenticeship with Cimabue, whom he followed as an assistant in Rome and Assisi, Giotto di Bondone (1267?-1337) took that technical, formal and ideological revolution that had been so slowly prepared in the course of almost two centuries even further. Through the frescoes in the Upper Basilica of San Francesco in Assisi, those of the Scrovegni Chapel in Padua (1304-6) and the Peruzzi and Bardi Chapels in Santa Croce in Florence (1314-27), as well as the altarpieces and paintings on wood, the great Master to whom Dante himself paid homage ("Cimabue thought he held the field / In painting, and now Giotto is the cry, / The other's fame obscured".) created a style that surpassed the Byzantine tradition by making direct contact with the Latin classical world, a world that provided the means to conquer space, nature and the slow narration of human and divine events. Strongly involved with the religiousness of his

PISAN SCHOOL

Crucifix with Stories of the Passion

Tempera on wood, 377x231
Late 12th C. - early 13th C.

This painting, one of the oldest in the gallery, was for many years given a general attribution to the Italian school of the twelfth century. Later, a close study of the clear, bright colours used in the small stories revealed the influence of miniature painting and the Byzantine taste of the composition, although with personal touches in the amusing narration which in places verges on the grotesque.
The work is seen as significant evidence of the early influence of Pisan-Oriental art in Florence.

Pisan school, Crucifix with Stories of the Passion: detail.

age, Giotto gave to each of the scenes he painted (both the life of Saint Francis in Assisi and episodes from the New Testament in the Scrovegni Chapel) the feeling of a human story unfolding within a fabric woven by God, though not because of this removed from the concrete sense of nature and reality. A withered tree growing on a barren hillside or a spring gushing from out of the rocks are images charged with highly symbolic meaning in the episodes depicted, but they are not separate from reality and therefore give full credibility to scenes in which the characters, in spite of their classical monumentality, act in a natural way. With Giotto the technical innovations of chiaroscuro and the research into perspective revolutionized the structure of the image, as can be seen in the *Ognissanti Madonna* (1300- ca. 1303), now at the Uffizi. The gold background and the obvious lack of proportion between the Virgin and the other figures are lingering vestiges of the Byzantine tradition, but the throne, with its oblique sides and elusive steps, and the complex and elaborate colour tones confer a total physicalness and humanity to the celestial creatures which for centuries had been incorporeal and immobile in their timeless atmospheres, making any contact with the worshippers impossible.

The third large altarpiece on display in this room introduces a theme that will continue in the next room dedicated to Sienese painting. This is the *Rucellai Madonna* (1205) by Duccio da Buoninsegna (ca. 1255-1319), the first famous Sienese artist. His clear affinity with Cimabue has in the past caused the work to be attributed to the Florentine master, but in this large work (as in the later *Maestà* of Siena) the characteristics of Duccio and the subsequent Sienese school are already apparent. Indeed, from the establishment in Siena of a Byzantine neo-Hellenistic current, and from the presence of French illuminated manuscripts, local painters developed a style which, while taking account of Florentine innovations, emphasized chromatic and linear values rather than volumetric and spatial ones. The result was a search for eurhythmy, for formal elegance accompanied by a refined use of colour that was not darkened by chiaroscuro. In this work by Duccio note the Virgin's even profile and the golden hem of her cloak that constructs the form yet at the same

GIOTTO
(Vespignano, Vicchio di Mugello, 1267 - Florence, 1337)

Ognissanti Madonna ∗

Tempera on wood, 325x204
ca. 1300-1303

According to a recent theory this work, attributed to Giotto from the time of Ghiberti, was painted for an altar to the right of the now demolished rood-screen in the church of Ognissanti. The inclusion of six saints alludes to the name of the church, which was dedicated to all saints. The altarpiece was probably replaced around 1360 by Giovanni da Milano's polyptych, now partially conserved at the Uffizi.
In this painting, which for reasons of style can be placed between the frescoes of Assisi and those of the Scrovegni Chapel in Padua, Giotto breaks away from the Byzantine tradition and draws instead on classical art and culture. The ample spatial structure is now confidently three-dimensional, as we can see from the perspective given to the throne and the staggered positions of the angels.

CIMABUE (Cenni di Pepo)
(Florence, records until 1302)

Santa Trinita Madonna *

*Tempera on wood, 385x223
1260-1280*

Cimabue is regarded as one of the great architects of the modernization of Italian painting and is traditionally seen as Giotto's teacher.
This Madonna, which is similar in structure to the same artist's Madonna at the Louvre and Duccio's Rucellai Madonna, still shows the influence of the Byzantine tradition. There is, however, an unprecedented tension in the profiles and in the attempt to create spatial depth, which is rendered by superimposing the figures and in the concave structure at the base of the throne behind the figures of the prophets Jeremiah, Abraham, David and Isaiah. The architectural structure of the throne becomes a sort of robust spatial scheme which creates a three-dimensional effect, while the edges of the painting seem to compress and hold in the bodies. There is an intense vitality in the figures and the same dramatic force that characterizes all Cimabue's work. The work is unanimously dated to Cimabue's maturity, around the time of the Assisi frescoes.

DUCCIO DI BUONINSEGNA
(Siena, ca. 1255 - 1319)

Rucellai Madonna *

*Tempera on wood, 450x290
1285*

The Rucellai Madonna is an extremely important work belonging to Duccio's early period.
This painting, which was for long attributed to Cimabue, recalls in the faces of the angels and the Child the Maestà of Santa Trinita, but the delicate spirituality, the lightness of the bodies and the decorative liveliness, create a pensive Madonna, a fragile Child, and angels absorbed in aristocratic contemplation. It is less dramatic than Cimabue's Madonna, but no less moving or emotionally charged.

Badia Polyptych, details of the angels in the cusps

GIOTTO
(Vespignano, Vicchio di Mugello, 1267 -
Florence, 1337)

Badia Polyptych

Tempera on wood, 91x334
ca. 1301

In 1801 the work was brought from the
convent of the Badia Fiesolana to Santa
Croce, where it remained until 1957. It is
almost certainly by Giotto, except for the
angels in the roundels of the cusps and,
partially, Saint Nicholas and Saint John the
Evangelist, which may have been painted
by the Saint Cecilia Master.

AMBROGIO LORENZETTI
(Siena, doc. 1319-1347)

Presentation in the Temple

*Part of a triptych, tempera on wood,
257x168
1342*

Attributable to Lorenzetti inasmuch as
payments relative to 1339 and 1340 are
documented, this work is also signed and
dated. It is the central part of a triptych,
whose side panels with Saints Crescentius
and Michael Archangel are now lost.
Ambrogio Lorenzetti's poetic imagination is
very apparent in this Presentation in the
Temple, in which the figures, painted with a
meticulous, analytical care, stand out against
an elegant, finely decorated architectural
structure.

MASTER OF THE BARDI SAINT FRANCIS
(active in Florence between 1240 and
1270)

Saint Francis Receives the Stigmata

Tempera on wood, 81x51
1240-1250

This is a portable Franciscan diptych which critics variously associated with the Luccan school of the Berlinghieri. In actual fact the work seems to characterize admirably a period of Florentine art represented by the master mosaicists of the cupola of the Baptistery and Coppo di Marcovaldo.

Characteristic of this master, who may reasonably be considered pre-Giottesque, was a direct and vehement insistence on the significance of the scene. Note, for example, the naturalness of the surroundings, with the hill and the temple rising above and almost holding up the kneeling saint as if to emphasize his bodily weight. This concreteness, a quality at the heart of Florentine painting from these very early times, might explain why Vasari attributed the work to Cimabue.

AMBROGIO LORENZETTI
(Siena, doc. 1319-1347)

Four Stories from the Life of Saint Nicholas

*Two panels each containing two scenes,
tempera on wood, 96x35
ca. 1330*

The panels represent four episodes from the life of the saint: Saint Nicholas offering the endowment to three poor young women, Saint Nicholas elected bishop of Myra, Saint Nicholas bringing back to life a boy strangled by the devil, and lastly Saint Nicholas ridding Myra of famine.
Ghiberti wrote that Ambrogio Lorenzetti was also a philosopher, a man of letters and a scholar of the ancient world, and this is confirmed by the intellectual character of his work; his ideal was a mental beauty that emerged from a balance between colour and volume, between line and mass.

PIETRO LORENZETTI
(Siena, ca. 1280-1348?)

Beata Umiltà Altarpiece

*Tempera on wood, 128x57 (centre),
45x32 (each panel), diam. 18
(each roundel of the predella)
ca. 1341*

Almost unanimously attributed to Pietro Lorenzetti, this composite work portrays in its centre the large figure of the Beata Umiltà, the founder of the Florentine Vallombrosan convent of the Nuns of Faenza who died in 1310.
The stories in the side panels depict episodes from the life of the Beata. The roundels contain the deposed Christ, two mourners, Saint Benedict, Saint Paul, Saint Peter and Saint John Gualberto.

time retains its decorative function. The angels, painted in delicate colours, renounce Giottesque spatial solidity and instead rise into the air with an elegance that is at once concrete and incorporeal.

The cultured tendency, of difficult mediation between Florentine innovations and local traditions, continued in the Sienese school of the 14th century, sensitive *ante litteram* to the new elegance of transalpine Gothic.

Simone Martini (ca. 1284-1344), active not only in Siena (*Maestà* in the Palazzo Pubblico), but also in Naples, Pisa, Assisi and finally in Avignon, was considered by the Sienese critical tradition the most important master of his time. A far cry from the bare spirituality of Giotto, whose revolutionary significance he acknowledged, Simone seemed enchanted by the elegance of French Gothic, by the profane splendour of court life and the fabulous knightly ideal.

No historical story emerges from his painting, but rather a fine poem in which the characters, endowed with an aristocratic beauty, perform according to canons of well-selected realism, in fabulous settings perspectively defined by precious colours. The pertinent examples of this production, in addition to the above-mentioned *Maestà*, are the *Saint Louis of Toulouse* (now in Naples), the *Stories of Saint Martin* (in Assisi), the fresco of *Guidoriccio da Fogliano* (Palazzo Pubblico, Siena). But all the modulations dear to Simone are also contained in the *Annunciation* of the Uffizi, co-executed in around 1333 with his brother-in-law Lippo Memmi: the splendour of the colours and the gold, and the linear elegance that gives the scene, already animated by the timorous shying away of the Virgin at the Angel's impetuous arrival, the tone of a courtly tribute with aristocratic overtones.

Preferred by the earliest Florentine critics, the brothers Pietro and Ambrogio Lorenzetti are represented at the Uffizi by highly significant works that show the two artists to be even more directly involved with Giotto's innovations. Pietro (ca. 1280-1348?) took note of them during a visit to Assisi and it was like a confirmation of how far he had already gone previously in developing a chromatic and linear severity.

Pietro's later long stay in Florence was ideal for the formulation of a kind of perfect synthesis between the characteristics of the apparently antithetical Florentine and Sienese schools. The *Beata Umiltà Altarpiece* of around 1341 is particularly significant in this context. With the liveliness of a popular story it gives spatial credibility to the stories of the saint, yet preserves the Sienese school's taste for pure, sharp colours, juxtaposed with "natural refinement".

Ambrogio (doc. 1319-1347) was both more modern and more characteristically Sienese. He too spent a long time in Florence, carefully assimilating Giotto's lesson with the help of another speculative capacity: he absorbed its plastic meaning and moral rigour and inserted them into a personal framework in which space was given to fantastic flourishes and a freer search for poetic values.

Two of his most famous works are here in the Uffizi: the *Stories from the Life of Saint Nicholas* of around 1330 and the *Presentation in the Temple* of 1342. In the former, the narration reaches levels of quaint naturalism in the rendering of details, while the human figure is introduced into a setting devoid of symbolic connections in which it can move freely.

In the later *Presentation in the Temple*, the rich, colourful scene with its delicate details blends spatially with the complex, elegant structures of the building. In his most important work, the fresco with *Allegories of Good and Bad Government* in the Palazzo Pubblico of Siena, Ambrogio continues his research aimed at placing human actions in a setting of correct spatial proportions, like a natural stage on which the new civil and religious ideals are inserted.

SIMONE MARTINI
(Siena, ca. 1284 - Avignon, 1344)

LIPPO MEMMI
(?, ca. 1290 - ?, ca. 1347)

Annunciation and Two Saints

Tempera on wood, 184x210
1333

The work, signed and dated, is the result of the combined efforts of Simone Martini and his brother-in-law Lippo Memmi, to whom the Saint Ansanus and another saint, presumably Margaret, can probably be ascribed.

Simone Martini was the initiator of an artistic style that would dominate the art of the fourteenth century, the flamboyant Gothic, a style which imbues the figures with a supreme abstraction, immerses them in gentle yet vivid colours, and delineates them with a purity that is at the limit of reality. In this work the shying away of the Madonna at the appearance of the angel becomes a spiritual element, while the gold of the background enhances the transcendence of the vision.

PIETRO LORENZETTI
(Siena, ca. 1280-1348?)

Madonna and Child Enthroned
with Angels

Tempera on wood, 145x122
Variously dated 1315 and 1340

In this work, as in all his Madonnas,
Pietro Lorenzetti emphasizes the
immediately human dimension of the
relationship between Mother and Child,
a rapport which the other figures
portrayed are drawn to share in.
With this radiant, solemn version of the
subject, the artist reveals his ability to
apply colour in such a way as
to produce an entirely volumetric
solidity, an ingenious discovery that
surpasses the traditional classicism
of the Florentines.

The third room of the Uffizi dedicated to painting contains an almost complete panorama of the fourteenth-century Florentine school. It would be reasonable to say that painting in Florence during this century was dominated by the figure of Giotto. The influence of Giotto was felt early on and continued for a considerable time because of the master's rich and extremely well-attended workshop in which generations of artists, the authors of altarpieces and fresco cycles for the most important churches in Florence, received their artistic training. These artists elaborated Giotto's achievements up until the turn of the fifteenth century.

One of the very first artists to adhere to Giotto's teaching, as represented by the *Stories of Saint Francis in Assisi*, was the Saint Cecilia Master (active ca. 1300-1320), an anonymous painter whose name derives from the altar frontal of the Uffizi, in which the stories of the saint are vividly and meticulously portrayed with an agreeable vulgarization of the Giottesque style. Other artists in Florence were particularly influenced by Giotto's style as it appeared in Padua, where the master's forms became more classical and full-bodied and the colours richer and more elaborate. Among these artists we find Giottino (rec. ca. 1320-1369), Giotto's grandson, whose *Pietà of San Remigio*, now at the Uffizi (ca. 1360-65) stands as one of the highest achievements in 14th-century painting. It is an articulate, harmonious composition of figures beautifully arranged against a traditional gold background. The soft chiaroscuro and delicate use of colours help to bestow upon the scene a melancholy pathos that is utterly human, a quality produced as a result of attentive reflection on developments that had taken place in the meantime in the Sienese school, and particularly in the art of Ambrogio Lorenzetti.

An even more direct relationship linked Giotto to several other artists who remained in his workshop for a considerable time. Taddeo Gaddi (ca. 1300-1366), the most faithful pupil and later Giotto's partner, worked there for twenty-four years. His most important work was the fresco decoration of the Baroncelli Chapel in Santa Croce with *Stories from the Life*

View of the fourth room.

SAINT CECILIA MASTER
(active in Florence ca. 1300-1320)

Saint Cecilia altar frontal

Tempera on wood, 85x181
ca. 1304

The painting, in the form of an altar
frontal, shows Saint Cecilia enthroned in
the middle of the composition and eight
stories of her life at the sides.
The influence of Giotto is very apparent.
The Saint Cecilia Master was in fact a
contemporary, who, inspired by Giotto's
art, followed him to Assisi and helped paint
various scenes from the life of Saint
Francis.
He applied the solid pictorial structure and
the clear-cut chromatic planes
characteristic of Giotto, but we notice a
tendency towards softer, more pinkish
tones, while the more delicate lateral
scenes show traces of a pleasant narrative
style that is not at all Giottesque.

BERNARDO DADDI
(Florence, ca. 1290 - 1348)

Madonna and Child with Saints Matthew
and Nicholas

Tempera on wood, 144x194
1328

This triptych with half-length figures and
cusps containing roundels with busts of
the Redeemer and two angels is signed and
dated on the base; it is the painter's first
dated work.
This painting shows Daddi to be already a
mature painter very close to Giotto,
particularly the Giotto of the Paduan
frescoes, and therefore contemporary with
and similar to the Saint Cecilia Master.

JACOPO DEL CASENTINO
(?, ca. 1290 - Florence, after 1358)

Madonna Enthroned with Angels and Saints

Tempera on wood, 39x42
1320-1330

This work is a precious portable tabernacle
with shutters. In the central panel is the
enthroned Madonna and Child, four Angels
and Saints on the left and the Crucifixion
on the right. It is the only signed work by
this painter and as such represents a basis
for reconstructing his entire artistic
production.
Like Bernardo Daddi and his workshop,
Jacopo del Casentino seems to have played
an important part in the spread of this type
of small altar and small tabernacle for
private worship since he and his circle
were responsible for many works of the
period belonging to this genre.

of San Silvestro (1332-38), in which he revealed his far from slavish
adherence to Giotto's style, a specific interest in architecture and a delicate use of colours.

Bernardo Daddi (ca. 1290-ca. 1348) was also active for a long time at
Giotto's side. In the frescoes of the Pulci Chapel in Santa Croce (ca. 1330)
he showed a marked propensity towards the elegance of Sienese art. The
result is a pleasant, vivaciously narrative painting in which the slim figures are lightened by soft colours and no longer firmly bound to their
backgrounds. The Uffizi houses the artist's triptych of 1328 (his first
dated work), the great dismembered *San Pancrazio Polyptych* (ca. 1336)
with its bright colour scheme that already reveals a tendency towards the
refinement of the Gothic style, and the small panel with the *Madonna
and Child Enthroned* of 1334, an example of a small portable altar used
for private worship, a genre in which Bernardo, like his contemporary
Jacopo del Casentino, specialized.

Around the middle of the century a Lombard master who had trained
in the north on the local examples of Giotto's first followers worked for
some time in Florence. He grafted his robust style on the local school
which set out to become a learned academy. This was Giovanni da
Milano (ca. 1325-post1369), the author of the frescoes in the Rinuccini
Chapel in Santa Croce (1365) and a *Pietà* now at the Galleria dell'Accademia. The Uffizi houses the dismembered *Ognissanti Polyptych* (ca.
1360), a work belonging to the mature years of this artist whose attention to formal elegance and refined details showed his openness to profane influences; however, the bold shading of the forms dampens these
effects, subduing them to the level of a realism of distinctly Lombardic
origin.

Despite the vivifying contribution of this great master, the second half
of the fourteenth century saw the local school engaged in a weary and
by now academic faithfulness to traditional formulas, apart from a revival
of the Master's early style attempted by the last Giottesque artists. Andrea
di Cione, called Orcagna (ca. 1320-1368), painter, sculptor and architect,
belonged to this phase. Orcagna showed the greatest technical ability,
knowledge of composition and correct formal interpretation of Giotto's
inventions, reaching the highest level attained in this part of the century.
Beside him worked his brothers Jacopo and Nardo di Cione, who are also

represented in the Uffizi collections.

By Andrea, in collaboration with Jacopo, is the fine triptych with *Saint Matthew and Stories from his Life* (1367-70), originally placed on a pilaster in the church of Orsanmichele. Recently restored, it has been redisplayed with the original wings, which give due emphasis to the statuary figure of the Saint and at the same time confer the right angle to the lateral architectural structures. There is a *Crucifixion* by Nardo di Cione, one of the finest works by the Florentine artist who was also the author of the frescoes in the small cloister of Santa Maria Novella and in the Strozzi Chapel of the same church.

BERNARDO DADDI
(Florence, ca. 1290 - 1348)

San Pancrazio Polyptych

Tempera on wood
165x85 (central panel)
127x42 (each side panel)
31x17 (each cusp panel)
50x38 (each predella panel)
diam. 20 (each roundel)
1336-1340

The San Pancrazio Polyptych is Bernardo Daddi's most structurally complex work. It was dismembered at an early date and some parts of it are now missing. The enthroned Madonna surrounded by angels is portrayed in the central panel, while six saints are depicted in the six side panels. In the predella, inside rectangular panels with multifoiled arched frames, the following scenes are represented: Joachim being banished from the temple, Joachim and the Shepherds, the Meeting at the Golden Gate, the Birth of the Virgin, the Presentation of Mary in the Temple, the Annunciation and the Birth of Christ. The third from last panel representing the Marriage of the Virgin was unfortunately sold in 1815.
The work belongs to a period of the artist's full stylistic activity; the painting is rendered with an elegant, flowing rhythm and sharp, lively colours that are a distinctly Gothic in taste.

BERNARDO DADDI
(Florence, ca. 1290 - 1348)

Madonna and Child Enthroned with Angels
and Saints *

Tempera on wood, 56x26
1334

This painting, a small cuspidate altarpiece
depicting the Madonna and Child with
eight Angels and Saints Peter and Paul, is
signed and dated.
The piece reveals all the qualities of this
painter, who was particularly devoted to
works destined for the private worship of
rich noble and well-to-do families: the
symmetrical, harmonious composition, the
refined setting, the gentle chiaroscuro and
the soft colours blending in with the gold
are all characteristics that confirm
Bernardo Daddi as an artist of a delicate,
intimate painting rather than large, solemn,
historico-religious representations.
In this work note the stage-like
architecture of the throne, whose almost
towering cusp takes up the shape of the
whole composition, and the ample yet
almost weightless mass of the Virgin in the
highly traditional arrangement of angels
and saints that had been in vogue since the
thirteenth century.

TADDEO GADDI
(Florence, ca. 1300 - 1366)

Madonna and Child Enthroned with Angels
and Saints

Tempera on wood, 154x80
1355

This painting and the small Berlin triptych
of 1353 are the only signed and dated
works by Taddeo Gaddi that have survived,
works that are therefore highly important
for establishing a point of reference for this
master's late style. The figures of Saint Mary
Magdalen and Saint Catherine are seen
standing on each side of the Virgin. The
coat of arms of the Segni family appears on
the base of the throne.
Taddeo Gaddi worked with Giotto for
twenty-six years. He was responsible for
popularizing the master's style and laid the
foundations on which the painting of the
second half of the fourteenth century was
built.
Like other contemporary artists, Gaddi
attempted to fuse the two great cultural
sources represented by Giotto and
Ambrogio Lorenzetti; the result is a nobly
oratorical style, with little emphasis on the
narrative dimension, and a dissolving of
Giottesque drama into a dignified yet
academic oratory. A serene monumentality
pervades the entire composition.
The work is highly important for our
understanding of Taddeo Gaddi's late style
for it seems to reflect a period of
uncertainty, perhaps of crisis, towards
Giottesque models.

NARDO DI CIONE
(Florence, ca. 1320 - 1365-66)

Crucifixion *

Tempera on wood, 145x71
ca. 1350-1360

This is one of the most important works
produced in Florence around the middle of
the fourteenth century. It was probably the
central panel of a tabernacle and in the
predella contains half-length figures of
various saints: Saint Jerome, James the Less,
Saint Paul, James the Great and Saint Peter
the Martyr. The elegant twisted columns
have been restored on the basis of the
authentic ones.

Crucifixion: detail of the predella
before restoration.

ORCAGNA (Andrea di Cione)
(Florence, ca. 1320 - 1368)

JACOPO DI CIONE
(Florence, ca. 1330 - 1398)

Saint Matthew and Stories from his Life

*Tempera on wood, 291x165
ca. 1367-70*

This triptych, which has survived substantially intact, portrays the standing figure of Saint Matthew and stories from his life. The work was commissioned to Orcagna in 1367 by the Arte del Cambio for a pilaster in the Church of Orsanmichele. When Andrea fell ill the following year, it was his brother Jacopo who undertook to complete the work.
Note the four roundels above the lateral cusps containing gold coins on a red background, symbol of the Arte del Cambio.

GIOTTINO (Giotto di Stefano)
(Florence, ca. 1320-1330 - post 1369)

Pietà of San Remigio

*Tempera on wood, 195x134
ca. 1360-1365*

The San Remigio Pietà is a masterpiece of fourteenth-century Florentine painting. In addition to the traditional figures of the Pietà there also appear here, as an iconographical innovation, Saint Benedict and San Remigio presenting the two patrons: an aged Benedictine nun and a young lady dressed in the latest fashion.
Giottino, a highly singular artist, belonged to the generation that succeeded Giotto's. In this work the cross stands now against the abstract gold background as the only symbol of the Passion. The emotional intensity is accompanied by the use of a subtle combination of radiant and contrasting colours. What Giotto conveys is the sense of a meditated drama, in which each figure is characterized and set off by his own particular gesture, expression or attitude.

THE 15TH CENTURY

Maria Grazia Ciardi Dupré dal Poggetto

The rooms presently dedicated to late Gothic and early Renaissance Florentine painting contain works that come mainly from the city's churches, rather than from the Medici collections.

This fact, which in the gallery is neither clear nor adequately made known, is of fundamental importance for anyone wishing to explore the basic principles of an historical, cultural and social upheaval and grasp its often vital connections with the artistic production of the time.

In the sixteenth century — especially when the Medici dukedom's role of power and representativeness became established — the 'Gallery' was the mirror of the Medici dynasty, in other words of one of the nerve centres of European artistic patronage.

The phenomena which characterized the fifteenth century in Florence were essentially three: first, Florence's experience of late Gothic culture; second, the *renovatio* which intensified with the rise of Humanism and later on with the Renaissance; and third, the spread of the Renaissance.

By 'spread', I mean two fairly complex developments: one was its acceptance, first in Italy, in cultural environments originally extraneous to it, and later abroad, in the sixteenth century; the other was its adaptation to the historical evolution of the Florentine environment, which during the fifteenth century passed from a political situation associated with an aristocratic republic to a pseudo-Signoria — that of the Medici — to which the hereditary succession was entrusted.

Let us examine the first problem: what were the main features and tendencies of the late Gothic period in Florence, normally called International Gothic.

This style is represented in the Uffizi by the Florentine artists emerging in those years, such as Lorenzo Monaco. Gentile da Fabriano, who was not Tuscan but came here to work, is also present here with two masterpieces.

The works on display, although limited in number, are highly significant, providing us with the means to reconstruct an important and certainly fascinating historical and artistic style.

They are Lorenzo Monaco's *Coronation of the Virgin* and *Adoration of the Magi*, and Gentile da Fabriano's *Quaratesi Polyptych* (to which the Saint Mary Magdalen, Saint Nicholas of Bari, Saint John the Baptist and

Saint George belonged) and *Adoration of the Magi* (which came from the chapel of Palla Strozzi in Santa Trinita). All these works were executed within a single decade, from 1414 to about 1424-25.

When one considers that in those same years Brunelleschi was building the Foundling Hospital and vaulting the cupola in the cathedral of Santa Maria del Fiore, that Donatello had already sculpted his Saint John the Evangelist and Saint Mark and modelled the Saint George, and that the *Madonna and Child with Saint Anne and Five Angels* by Masolino and Masaccio dates from 1424, it is not difficult to understand that the paintings in rooms 5/6 of the Uffizi represent not only the continuity of the Gothic tradition, but also a conscious response to the assertion of an artistic vision that was different and boldly innovative. From the very first years of the fifteenth century, indeed, Florence had witnessed the development of a characteristic 'International Gothic' style which, although having certain similarities with what was being produced in Europe at the same time, revealed those differences which it is only reasonable to expect from a socio-political situation that was totally different from those existing in other European countries.

At this time Florence was a city that had accumulated extensive territory in Tuscany with the annexation of Arezzo and Pisa, and had evolved from a Commune into a Republic. In Italy this situation was paralleled only in Venice, since elsewhere the transition from Commune to Signoria, and at times to a landed Signoria as in the case of the Visconti of Milan, had already taken place.

In France, on the other hand, the formation of a national state had been consolidated with Charles V, despite the fact that vast territories were held by powerful vassals. This would later lead to an inevitable power clash, but between the end of the fourteenth century and the beginning of the fifteenth the situation was still controlled by the close bonds of kinship which united the king of France with the brothers Jean de Berry and Philip of Burgundy and with Louis of Anjou.

The power, wealth and magnificence of these great feudal dynasties was equalled elsewhere only by the imperial family of the Holy Roman Empire, in this period represented by the House of Luxembourg, which had established its capital at Prague in Bohemia, and from which the three *Stories of Saint Benedict* displayed in the Uffizi, which actually belong to the Venetian cultural and artistic area, have wrongly been seen to have descended.

Intense artistic activity in France and Bohemia spread through Europe, including Italy, at least through those prevalently northern areas of Italy like Piedmont and Lombardy that were linked by political relations, and the Venetian republic, whose solidly aristocratic structure gave it a social foundation in common with the monarchy and feudal aristocracy of France or the centre of the Holy Roman Empire.

Over these strictly aristocratic foundations a unitary figurative vision was expressed in Europe which partly justifies the label 'International Gothic' given to this final period of the Middle Ages. The Middle Ages, indeed, can be considered finished with the establishment of the Italian Renaissance, which broke European cultural unity.

Although the Uffizi has no painting of the European International Gothic, Gentile da Fabriano is highly representative of European artistic tendencies, even though the artist himself never actually crossed the Alps. Before coming to Florence, he had worked not only in Venice but also in Brescia, then under the rule of the Visconti, a family related to the House of Valois and the Holy Roman Empire.

Gentile da Fabriano's relations with the cities of northern Italy were due to the fact that as a native of the Marches he gravitated naturally towards the Adriatic basin and therefore towards Venice.

Gentile's Florentine works — i.e. the *Adoration of the Magi* and the

Beato Angelico, Thebaid: detail.

BEATO ANGELICO
(Fra' Giovanni da Fiesole)
(Vicchio di Mugello, ca. 1400 - Rome 1445)

Thebaid

Tempera on wood, 80x216
ca. 1420-1430

Art scholars have attributed the painting to various artists: some have ascribed it to the activity of Starnina, others to Pietro Lorenzetti, while as early as 1940 Longhi believed it to be by Angelico. From the traditional attribution to Gherardo Starnina, a key figure in the introduction of the

International Gothic style into Florentine artistic circles, in more recent times it has been convincingly argued (Bellosi) that Angelico was the author of this extraordinary painting.
A painting of this subject was recorded as the work of Angelico in the inventory drawn up at the death of Lorenzo the Magnificent, in 1492. The young Angelico reveals here his affinity with the style of Lorenzo Monaco, in whose circle at Santa Maria degli Angeli he had been an apprentice. Certainly there must have been previous versions, other Thebaids, fragments identified in the painting of the Esztengon Museum, attributable to Mariotto di Nardo, and another formerly in the Davenport Bromley Collection. The very high pictorial quality of the painting transcends the archaicity of the compositional structure, and some details, like the presence of the small clouds in the sky, reveal that the work of the Uffizi cannot date from before the third decade of the Quattrocento (whereas Starnina had died in 1413).
The conception itself of the Thebaid shows that it was executed on the commission of one of the Mendicant Orders: it unfolds, in fact, in the form of a story of the life of a saint, the life in the desert of the anchorites and the whole space is animated by episodes and by the movement of small figures. In the foreground, the sea with sailing vessels and sea monsters against the background of the rocky landscape, moulded in the style of Ghiberti, with tiny dwellings scattered here and there.

Quaratesi Polyptych — are closely linked to the Northern world and to the aristocratic, 'courtly' culture of the transalpine passes. What impresses us in them at first sight is the portrayal of a noble, rich, immensely elegant world, in which the lavish brocade costumes and the measured harmony of gestures and expressions are worthy of the courts of France, Burgundy, Anjou and Prague.

Having inserted Gentile da Fabriano into the European circuit, we may reasonably affirm that thanks to Palla Strozzi and the Quaratesi family, the magnificent patrons of his Florentine paintings, Florence has perhaps the most important painting on wood of the International Gothic: the *Adoration of the Magi*. This painting bears all the hallmarks of the highly refined sensitivity and culture of International Gothic, to whose composition, as the great Italian art scholar Pietro Toesca has demonstrated, Lombardy itself had given an important contribution. We are talking here about a culture which, although on the one hand was associated with the abstract, exaggerated refinements of court etiquette, on the other hand rediscovered nature, everyday life, and an impalpable yet real light.

This relationship with reality is particularly revealing in the representation of countryside, in the woods and in the gardens growing with roses and carnations, in other words, in those places characteristic of feudalism. The society reflected in it is that of a noble, opulent, magnificent court, a life of subtle, rarefied rituality. In the realm of this twilight world Gentile da Fabriano used his pictorial skills to magnificent effect: delicate tints on which the light leaves tiny points of gold; shadows breaking up into as many shades of a darker tone; a line of exquisite elegance surrounds the figures and traces the gestures and movements that gracefully unwind, blending into the landscape with the soft line of the hills. Even when there is a gold background instead of a landscape, as in the *Quaratesi Polyptych* — housed at the Uffizi in a fragmentary state — the figures seem to be able on their own to convey the sense of a surrounding atmosphere.

Let us come now to contemporary Tuscan artists. These artists are the

LORENZO MONACO (Piero di Giovanni)
(Siena? ca. 1370 - Florence ca. 1425)

COSIMO ROSSELLI
(Florence 1439 - 1507)

Adoration of the Magi *

Tempera on wood, 115x170
1421-22

The painting has always been identified as "the painting for the altar of Sant'Egidio" of which there exist payments made to Lorenzo Monaco in 1421-22. Readapted in the second half of the 15th century, when the Madonna and Prophets were added by Cosimo Rosselli, the work was originally surmounted with three cusps in which Lorenzo Monaco had painted two prophets and God the Almighty in the act of blessing. The figures of Lorenzo Monaco, as for that matter in the whole of the International Gothic style, seemed moved by an incessant linear flow, swaying figures, charged with draperies that often finish in ornamental motifs: even the landscape and the buildings are subordinated to this prevailing linearity.

The theme of the Adoration of the Magi was very dear to Lorenzo Monaco, who also executed a remarkable drawing on the "Journey of the Magi", and gave him the opportunity to develop in the presence of the procession, a refined Gothic movement. We can observe in it the elegant, richly dressed company and the greyhound held by a servant with a hunting horn on his shoulder (in Lorenzo Monaco there is an emphasis on the exotic, on a fantastic, oriental touch), but there is also a tangible quiver of drama in the content of the scene, in which the whole procession stands off in admiring and reverent wonder towards the figure of the Virgin.

Coronation of the Virgin: central cusp before restoration.

LORENZO MONACO (Piero di Giovanni)
(Siena? ca. 1370 - Florence, 1425)

Coronation of the Virgin *

*Tempera on wood, 450x350
1414*

This is the only signed and dated work by Lorenzo Monaco. Unfortunately the central part of the painting was sawn to provide space for a tabernacle, thus eliminating a large part of the figure of a musician angel, which recent restoration has reconstructed on the basis of a similar one in the other Coronation by the same artist in London.

Lorenzo Monaco, one of the key figures of the Florentine artistic revival, was also a miniaturist, the art he learned at the Convent of Santa Maria degli Angioli which allowed him to earn a reputation as the greatest exponent of the so-called Scuola degli Angioli. Close to Agnolo Gaddi and Spinello Aretino, after 1400 he was engaged prevalently in activity as a painter, developing and modernizing the iconography of a pious nature that enjoyed so much fortune with his successors.

Gentile da Fabriano, Adoration of the Magi: detail.

GENTILE DA FABRIANO
(Fabriano, ca. 1370 - Rome, 1427)

Adoration of the Magi

Tempera on wood with haloes and friezes forged in iron, 173x220
1423

The work, signed and dated in Gothic lettering, was executed for the Cappella di Palla di Noferi Strozzi in Santa Trinita during the artist's stay in Florence between 1422 and 1425. In the cusps of this complex and stage-like composition are Christ and the Annunciation with figures of prophets and cherubs; floral decorations grace the lateral pilasters, while the predella contains various religious scenes representing the Nativity, the Flight into Egypt and the Presentation in the Temple.
It is a spectacular work, an unequivocal affirmation of a "courtly" painting designed to fascinate and dazzle the upper echelons of Florentine society. Gentile da Fabriano's erudition is particularly apparent in this Adoration of the Magi. The artist shows he is familiar with Oriental facial features and costumes, and the strange fauna and flora of these far-off and exotic countries; he also knows the sacred stories down to the last details, as well as the ceremonies of a hunting party.
Executed during the artist's Florentine period, this painting, almost a monument to the refinement of international Gothic, reveals a latent tension, a repressed aspiration that is visible in the figures of the reclining prophets, while the brilliant colours, highlighted by a profusion of gold and glittering decoration, boldly proclaim Gentile da Fabriano's northern background.

heirs of a very different culture, a Giottesque culture, in which substantially classical ideals of nature prevail: the exaltation of the presence of man in a geometrically constructed space. The main ingredients are the composition and volume of the bodies obtained through line, chiaroscuro, and dense contrasting colours, without those shadings that might confuse the outlines with the surrounding atmosphere.

The Giottesque tradition at the end of the fourteenth century is represented by the son of one of Giotto's most important pupils, Agnolo Gaddi. His *Crucifixion* of the Uffizi is a good example of the tendencies which characterized the Florentine environment in the late fourteenth century.

The leading figures representing the International Gothic style in Florence were Lorenzo Ghiberti in sculpture, particularly the period of his first door for the Baptistery (now the north door), executed between 1405 and 1425, and Lorenzo Monaco in painting. The influence of these artists was responsible for the creation of a late Gothic Florentine school that flourished during the first half of the fifteenth century. Siena was also an important centre of International Gothic, and how could it be otherwise, for this city had contributed more than any other to the European formation of this style.

In sculpture the Sienese were represented by one of the greatest sculptors of all time, Jacopo della Quercia; in painting by a group of artists who were less famous than their Florentine counterparts only because Florence's excessive cultural influence tended unjustly to dwarf that of neighbouring Siena. In actual fact, artists like Sassetta and Giovanni di Paolo were among the greatest exponents of the style even at a European level.

There is, among the works on display in the Gallery, a polyptych of the *Madonna and Child with Saints* by Giovanni di Paolo, a painting which shows characteristics typical of both the Sienese school and the artist himself, even though its late dating — 1445 — also reveals its close attachment to a glorious tradition that at the time was drawing to a close. The elongated figures, imbued with a profound abstraction, stand out in an unreal way against the gold background, in a boundless isolation charged with melancholy. Jacopo della Quercia, on the other hand, represented the international tendency, projecting himself towards Burgundy. These tendencies, identified with the Tuscan tradition on the one hand and European links on the other, also existed in Florence from the beginning of the century.

Lorenzo Monaco, for example — an artist who was born in Siena but was trained in Florence — produced a high formal synthesis in which the Giottesque emphasis on volume was polished and articulated by the flowing line developed by Simone Martini that was spreading throughout Europe. Nature, particularly its decorative plant and animal life, as well as the works of man, were excluded from this formal abstraction. Using a compact compositional structure, the artist focused his attention on the religious figures, who thus acquire a much more immanent presence compared to that of Gentile da Fabriano's figures. This is very apparent in both the *Coronation of the Virgin* and the *Adoration of the Magi*.

In Florence the new age of the Renaissance began in painting with a rather subdued work, devoid of any rhetoric: the *Madonna and Child with Saint Anne and Five Angels* executed by Masolino and Masaccio in 1424. The structure of this work is simple, yet extraordinarily monumental. The succession of planes is compact and follows an upward direction, thus creating a pyramid shape. The composition can certainly be attributed entirely to Masaccio, who executed only the Madonna and Child and the two angels (the upper right-hand one, and the one looking down from on high). A sense of great dignity and power emanates from the faces, from the expressions and from the solidity of the bodies.

Despite the presence of a strong chiaroscuro, the painting is bright due to the use of a dense colour paste which absorbs the light and so heightens the tones. The light comes very distinctly from the left, and the figure of the Madonna casts a light but very visible shadow on the floor. The base and the throne are drawn according to precise points of reference which produce the effect of perspective.

This masterpiece of the youthful activity of Masaccio — already so innovative at such a young age — allows us to identify the stylistic point of departure for Beato Angelico.

Of all the great Florentine painters of the fifteenth century, Beato Angelico is the only one who can be regarded as Masaccio's direct pupil. To demonstrate this, we need only compare Angelico's *Madonna and Five Angels* of Pontassieve and the *Madonna and Child with Saint Anne and Five Angels* by Masaccio and Masolino. Angelico, however, immerses the pure geometric volumes of his figures into a crystalline, perfect light which is the pure essence of colour, transposing the chiaroscuro onto the chromatic plane. In his *Coronation of the Virgin*, Paradise seems to have come down to Earth, certain of the final resurrection, in a hallowed space blazing with a radiant light and golden rays. Impressed on the faces of the men and women populating this scene is a dignity that derives from their consciousness of reality and from their harmonious acceptance in living it.

The long protection which Cosimo il Vecchio dei Medici offered to Angelico in particular and to the Convent of San Marco — run by Dominican monks, to whose order he belonged — earned Angelico a privileged position at the very centre of Florentine artistic life. His influence not only on painting but also on manuscript illustration was deeply felt, and his art was an important stimulus in Ghiberti's stylistic devel-

MASACCIO (Cassai Tommaso)
(San Giovanni Valdarno, 1401 - Rome, 1428)

MASOLINO
(San Giovanni Valdarno, 1383? - 1440)

Madonna and Child with Saint Anne and Five Angels *

Tempera on wood, 175x103
1424-25

This work, formerly in the Church of Sant'Ambrogio, is mentioned by Vasari, but it is not known whether it formed part of a triptych or was independent.
The distinction of hands proposed by Longhi, who attributed the Virgin and Child and the angel at top left to Masaccio and the whole of the rest of the painting to Masolino, has been accepted by almost all critics.
The work certainly dates from after 1422, and probably between 1424 and 1425, a period in which Masolino, before leaving Florence for Hungary, was constrained to find a companion to assist him in honouring commitments previously undertaken. The astonishing new talent of Masaccio is already apparent in this jointly executed work: a plastic, almost rounded mass stands out here, a fullness of ordinary people dominates, morally responsible for its humanity, the hands are real, touching, holding and making clear, precise gestures, and the Child — a vital and robust putto — has broken with the canons of traditional beauty.

MASACCIO (Cassai Tommaso)
(S. Giovanni Valdarno 1401 - Rome 1428)

Madonna and Child *

Tempera on wood, 24.5x18.2
Post 1426

The small painting was published by Longhi for the first time in 1950 as a work by Masaccio
and the attribution was broadly accepted by most scholars. On the back is a shield emblem
with six red stars on a yellow field, divided in half by a black band with a gilded cross in the
centre, surmounted by a cardinal's hat. It represents the coat of arms of Antonio Casini, cardinal
from 24 May 1426, a date that would be a term *post quem* for the work, which compares
stylistically with the Pisa polyptych. Despite the painting's small size, evidence of its use for
private devotion, Masaccio combines the archaic preciosity of the gilded border in cubic letters
in the cloak with an entirely laical solidity typical of his major works.

BEATO ANGELICO (Fra' Giovanni da Fiesole)
(Vicchio di Mugello, ca. 1400 - Rome, 1455)

Coronation of the Virgin

Tempera on wood
112x114
1430-40

Anonimo Gaddiano (early sixteenth century) called this Coronation of the Virgin, the same subject of which exists in a painting by Angelico now at the Louvre, "Paradise".
The work lacks a rigorous perspective framework, but this fails to reduce the spatiality of the representation which is obtained through a highly complex compositional design. By means of a progressive diminishing of the figures Angelico aims to create a concave space formed by the assembled cohorts of Angels and Saints, in the middle of which the figures of the Virgin and Christ crowning her appear to rise upwards. Angelico attempts here to lay the foundations for a modern religious art, already of Renaissance design, but profoundly mystical in tone. The radiant colours and the alabastrine transparency of the faces are irrefutable foretastes of the luminous and chromatic refinements of Domenico Veneziano and Piero della Francesca.

opment. The influence of Beato Angelico was also fundamental for painters like Domenico Veneziano and Piero della Francesca.

The *Santa Lucia dei Magnoli Altarpiece*, painted by Domenico Veneziano between 1440 and 1445, marked an extremely important turning-point in the history of the Italian Renaissance. Within the Uffizi, moreover, it represents a perfect synthesis of the new vision of the Florentine Renaissance. Because the artist was not a Florentine by birth, he probably arrived at this highly significant result because he was able to envisage the unfolding of artistic developments with a certain degree of detachment.

The central theme of the Santa Lucia dei Magnoli altarpiece is the *Trinity* of Santa Maria Novella painted by Masaccio around 1426, astonishing evidence of the universal dimensions rapidly reached in Florentine Renaissance painting. However, in the *Santa Lucia dei Magnoli Altarpiece* Domenico gave expression to a more intimate, more personal and at the same time more civic expression of the universal values of the Renaissance. The architecture is not classical, but rather that of a Florentine Romanesque church extended with the addition of an arcade and three niches, designed by a 'modern' architect like Brunelleschi or Michelozzo. The figures are people that one might have met in the streets of Florence. All this, however, is cast into a perfect existence bordering on utopia, which is no different from the perfection of Angelico's paradises, even if it is expressed in an essentially secular fashion.

As with Angelico, this perfection is produced with perspective and light. Perspective is the mathematical domain of space inhabited by man; the clear, crystalline light suggests a perfect atmospheric situation: it reveals a humanity not sublimated by an eternal youth but, since life is transitoriness, marked by the various ages of the figures and moulded by reason, which should be understood as intellect and will. The filter of reason assumes a slightly heavy emphasis compared to the spontaneous adhesion to nature characteristic of Beato Angelico. To colour, Domenico now adds line, a line which perfectly defines the figures, their gestures, and their space. The perspective construction is not only a definition of the real depth in which the actions take place (as it was in Beato Angelico and as it had been — apart from the *Trinity* of Santa Maria Novella — in Masaccio), but a geometric series of crossed lines.

It is a well-known fact that all these aspects of Domenico Veneziano's painting, except the linear emphasis, were inherited and brought to sublime and universal expression by Piero della Francesca.

Born in Sansepolcro, but receiving his training in Florence, Piero della Francesca pursued his artistic activities far from the Tuscan capital. The diptych with the *portraits of Federigo da Montefeltro* (then count, not duke) *and his wife Battista Sforza*, for example, came from Urbino with the inheritance of the Della Rovere family. No one, until this moment, had succeeded in condensing the universe into a portrait, nor had man's relationship with nature been the reason for exaltation and sublimation. The nature which appears behind the two heads and which dominates the two allegorical scenes on the reverse — the triumphs of the Virtues of the Duke and Duchess — is nature created by God (the valleys, the lake, the hills, the fog...) as well as by man (the city, the castle, the boats...). If the geometry of the forms and objects, the mathematical certainty of the space, constitutes its rational and universal aspect, the colour on the other hand represents its 'particular' aspect, i.e. that which is characterized by specific qualities. The light, in emphasizing the volumetric reality of the forms, also reveals the chromatic cloak that covers them. There is no need, therefore, for either the drawing or the chiaroscuro to exalt the two persons portrayed, for it is their virtues and their power, obtained with peace and with the consent of their subjects, that bring them into the foreground.

DOMENICO VENEZIANO
(Venice, ca. 1400 - Florence, 1461)

Santa Lucia dei Magnoli Altarpiece

Tempera on wood, 209x216
ca. 1440-50

The work represents the Madonna and Child enthroned between Saints Francis, John the Baptist, Zenobius and Lucia, while the predella, formed of five panels showing episodes from the lives of the saints, is now housed in a dismembered state in the museums of Washington, Cambridge and Berlin. The author is indicated by a written inscription at the bottom of the painting. The painting induces a sense of peaceful solemnity, due to the symmetrical and regular composition in which the space is determined by an architectural structure several layers deep: the portico, a low exedra and the tops of the trees in the background. Domenico Veneziano creates a structure that with its pastel shades is exposed to as much light as possible, but he links it to the regular forms of the

colourful inlaid floor and the entire architectural construction.
The figures, arranged in a perspective fashion, maintain their firm independence in space, are solemnly and monumentally positioned, like the Baptist, in whom the influence of Andrea del Castagno is undeniable.
Lastly, note that the iconographical device of the arched portico replaces the traditional triptych.

PIERO DELLA FRANCESCA
(Borgo San Sepolcro, ca. 1410-20 - 1492)

Portraits of the Duke and Duchess of
Urbino *

Diptych, tempera on wood
47x33 each panel
ca. 1465-70

Piero della Francesca places these
medallion-style profile portraits of
Federigo da Montefeltro and his wife
Battista Sforza, boldly standing out
against the Urbino landscape, in mid-
air, without the traditional support of
a window or curtain.
The two panels are also painted on
the back, in an almost miniaturistic
style, with allegorical scenes
illustrating the virtues of the two
protagonists. In one, the carriage of
Federigo and the four Cardinal Virtues
advances theatrically on a surface of
false rocks and against a background
of faraway hills; the other panel shows
a similar scene with Battista Sforza

CLARVS INSIGNI VEHITVR TRIVMPHO
QVEM PAREM SVMMIS DVCIBVS PERHENNIS
FAMA VIRTVTVM CELEBRAT DECENTER
SCEPTRA TENENTEM

and the Theological Virtues.

Piero della Francesca, who wrote a treatise on the theory of painting, "De Prospectiva Pingendi", explores the faces of the noble couple, motionless and frozen in the foreground, with a disconcertingly meticulous eye for detail. He mercilessly makes visible even the most unpleasant details with a technique not far removed from Flemish portrait painting, to which even the clear landscape in the distance conforms.

Piero della Francesca's earliest contacts with Flemish art were made in Ferrara, where in 1449 the artist worked with Rogier van der Weyden. Later, at the court of Federigo da Montefeltro, he quickly became the leading personality of that humanistic circle.

This is how the portraits of the Duke and Duchess, with their unusual close-up profiles, came about. Well-versed in geometry, Piero also tested his ability to put a distant and well-illuminated landscape in proportion with the figures.

E MODVM REBVS TENVIT SECVNDIS ·
NIVGIS MAGNI DECORATA RERVM ·
VDE GESTARVM VOLITAT PER ORA ·
NCTA VIRORVM ·

Piero della Francesca, portrait of Federigo da Montefeltro: detail of the back.

These two portraits could not have been executed anywhere other than Urbino, a small city ruled by a learned, wise, 'virtuous', humanist condottiere of fortune, who in his 'city palace' had built the most perfect representation of the civilization of the Renaissance.

In Florence, a metropolis full of ideas, restlessness, political struggles and religious tension, the new civilization which the city had created would develop an extraordinary variety of sometimes sharply contrasting tendencies.

A painting like *The Battle of San Romano*, the only one left in the Uffizi of three large works that once decorated one of the ground-floor rooms of Palazzo Medici-Riccardi, is perhaps the most striking reflection of this reality.

The work contrasts radically not only with Masaccio, Angelico, Domenico Veneziano and other Florentine painters of the early fifteenth century, but also with the other two founders of the Renaissance, Filippo Brunelleschi and Donatello.

The *Battle of San Romano* expresses various themes which are in marked contrast to the exciting conventions of the Renaissance. Man's reality, which only here and there an unexpected light succeeds in revealing, is immersed in darkness. Man creates war, a chaotic and absurd mass which perspective rationalizes only as anonymous fragments, leav-

PAOLO UCCELLO (Paolo di Dono)
(Florence, 1397-1475)

The Battle of San Romano

Tempera on wood
182x220
ca. 1456

The painting, signed at bottom left, represents an episode of the battle of San Romano, possibly the unseating of Bernardino della Ciarda, a battle which the Florentines, under the command of Niccolò di Tolentino and Micheletto di Cotognola, won on 1 June 1432 against the Sienese led by Bernardino della Ciarda. The painting forms part of a series of three works; the other two paintings, of a similar subject, are housed at the Louvre and at the London National Gallery respectively.

The extraordinary modernity of this painter can be grasped by making a simple comparison: he is the only artist, together with those of the Cubist movement, to prove that the more improbable things are the more real they become. Here, in the battle of San Romano, the historical event is constructed not for itself, but rather according to the structure of the space. The painting, one of the most abstract plays of colour and form in Italian painting, powerfully evokes the excitement and nightmare of medieval warfare: in the bristling lances, the armoured, dehumanized warriors, in the play of encounters and entanglements, and the unusual and indeed utterly unreal colours. Paolo Uccello had no hesitation in painting red and green horses, for colours are a quality of perspective planes and space, not of things.

Notice the remarkable geometrical and visionary effects that Paolo Uccello creates here, offering up a whole complex repertoire of positions, clashes and unusual angles, where the fighters are automatons and the horses mechanical.

Filippo Lippi, Coronation of the Virgin: detail.

ing everything else as a heap of unusable scraps. Perspective therefore reveals the absurd, irrational dimension of the world that man has built, although it exalts the abstract, primordial value of geometry.

In the midst of the numerous contradictions that made the Florentine environment of those years 'unique', one painter emerged — Filippo Lippi — who created a stylistic formula which proved enormously successful. Once the heated debates that had pitted Donatello against Brunelleschi and Paolo Uccello against other painters had died down, this stylistic formula had the merit of generating and propagating those artistic ideals that were destined to become the common patrimony of Florentine society.

From Masaccio Filippo Lippi inherited the awareness that man's control over space and over the environment was obtained through the use of chiaroscuro and through the construction of a setting — which for Lippi could be imaginary — with the aim of emphasizing the human figure as the dominant element.

This is apparent in the *Coronation of the Virgin*, formerly in Santo Spirito (1441-47), and above all in the *predella* of the altarpiece of the *Madonna and Child with Saints* commissioned by the Barbadori family, again for the same church, although now at the Louvre (remember that Filippo Lippi was an Augustinian friar, and therefore perfectly at

FILIPPO LIPPI
(Florence, ca. 1406 - Spoleto, 1469)

Coronation of the Virgin

Tempera on wood
200x287
1441 (commissioned) - 1447 (paid for)

This work, restored between 1975 and 1978, is surmounted by three saints and the
Annunciation, which do not belong to the original.
Standing at the two sides of the composition are Saints Ambrose and John the Baptist. The
two figures of Carmelite monks on the left are traditionally identified as the self-portrait of
Lippi, the one in the foreground wearing a contemplative, almost bored expression, and the
person who commissioned the work, Francesco Maringhi, procurator of the church of
Sant'Ambrogio, who died in 1441. The monk on the right, Domenico Maringhi, is the chaplain
of Sant'Ambrogio, who supervised the execution of the painting.
The light descends from the golden, curly-haired heads of the angels. The artist has given
individual expression to each single face, and to the various textures of the veils and other
fabrics, textures he emphasizes with a lively chiaroscuro technique. The faces, so expansive in
the light, appear broad and almost compressed by the thin line at the edge of the painting.
It is a work of considerable artistic value, acknowledged by critics and celebrated for the
splendour of the colours, the strange crowding of the figures and the fantastic irrationality of
the space, all linked, however, to delicate observations of the tiniest details.

FILIPPO LIPPI
(Florence, ca. 1406 - Spoleto, 1469)

Annunciation, Saint Anthony Abbot and
Saint John the Baptist

*Two polyptych panels, tempera on wood
57x24 each
ca. 1450*

These polyptych or altarpiece panels have
for long been overlooked by art critics.
They have, however, especially in the figure
of the Virgin, a poetical grace and delicacy
of line that should not be underestimated.
These panels are generally dated to the end
of the period in which Lippi was still under
the influence of Beato Angelico.

FILIPPO LIPPI
(Florence, ca. 1406 - Spoleto, 1469)

Madonna and Child with Four Saints

*Tempera on wood
196x196
1440-45*

The work shows traces of a dynamism
that appears to derive from the
contemporary presence of Donatello.
Here, Lippi uses a light that is physical and
real, and groups the forms in a more
classical compositional arrangement. The
figures are fairly static, and not unjustly
has an unexpected angularity in the poses
been noticed, almost a hint of Andrea del
Castagno. In the Virgin's plump hands and
in the typically newborn proportions of
the Child, however, Lippi again reveals,
over and above the solemnity of the
scene, his openness towards a humanity
observed with love and sympathy.

FILIPPO LIPPI
(Florence, ca. 1406 - Spoleto, 1469)

Madonna and Child with Angels

Tempera on wood
95x62
ca. 1445

This extremely well-known and even popular work has always been considered as one of the highest and most lyrical expressions of Lippi's art. It is certainly a late composition, a distinct foretaste of themes that would be developed by Botticelli, Pollaiolo and Leonardo: the tension and incisiveness of the line, the typology of the faces and the tender melancholy expressed by the persons portrayed. It has been said that this work represents not a mother with her child, but rather abstract figures absorbed in a vaster contemplation of private thoughts and feelings.

home in Santo Spirito). In these works he is still visibly linked to monumental, even cumbersome forms, in a space that has become abstract to the point that it can be filled entirely with figures, as is the case for example in the *Coronation of the Virgin*.

If we compare this painting with the one by Angelico previously examined, we are immediately aware of fundamental differences. Even though Lippi was inspired by Angelico's work, the profound diversity of these two paintings is striking evidence of the unending dialectic which characterized the Florentine environment of those years.

The importance of Lippi in the development of Florentine painting is not so much by virtue of the works executed before the fifth decade — although they are undoubtedly the most interesting and most original — but the ones executed subsequently.

A characteristic example is the altarpiece with the *Madonna and Child with Four Saints*, in which the figures are arranged against a complex architectural construction with three niches and a part of it jutting out at right angles to accommodate the throne with the Madonna and Child. If Lippi's point of departure is Masaccesque, his point of arrival is marked by the intuition — in its own way ingenious — that it was possible to combine monumental, plastic forms with a line of beauty drawn from classical art, both directly and through Donatello.

Lippi's figures appear as a symbol not only of power, but of elegance and grace. These ideals were more in keeping with a cultured and refined society like the Florentine one, which towards the middle and in the second half of the century increasingly freed itself from political and civil responsibilities.

Lippi's paintings portray human beings who are not engaged in real actions or placed in a direct relationship with nature. Immersed in a timeless environment, lit by a grey, filtrated light, the figures which Lippi painted have inspired, detached poses and expressions, made abstract by vague reflections.

See the above-mentioned altarpiece with Saints Francis, Damian, Cosmas and Anthony of Padua, in which the figures are portrayed with symmetrical poses and with an elegant, undulating movement that is expressed by the drapery and gestures. These touches are accentuated and charged with a more refined elegance in the altar panels with the *Annunciation, Saint Anthony Abbot and Saint John the Baptist*, which are later works.

The importance of Lippi's late period is revealed by the celebrated *Madonna and Child with Angels*, in which the painter produces a classical balance between plasticity and line. The extremely fine and elegant line softens the profiles and lessens the compactness of the forms. The landscape is filtered through dense hatching and toned-down colours, reminiscent of a Chinese print. It is a mental re-evocation, not the mirror of reality.

The same words could be used to describe two *Nativities*, set in a landscape in which a mental idea of the setting and not its real condition is projected.

The great importance of Lippi in Florentine culture is measured by the considerable extent of his influence and by the fact that he was the root that gave impetus to Botticelli, the artist in whom Florence's artistic expression has been identified.

As for the numerous followers of Filippo Lippi, the most famous was Francesco Pesellino, present in the Gallery with one work — the predella with *Stories of the Miracle of the Greedy Man's Heart, the Martyrdom of Saints Cosmas and Damian and the Birth of Christ*, and with the *Annunciation*, executed to serve as a predella for Filippo Lippi's *Barbadori Altarpiece* — which is stylistically associated with this painter's early period. However, his previous education — inspired

ALESSIO BALDOVINETTI
(Florence, 1425-1499)

Madonna and Child with Saints

Tempera on wood
176x166
ca. 1454

This altarpiece was commissioned to Baldovinetti for the Medici villa of Cafaggiolo. Represented in the painting are, from left to right, Saint Anthony Abbot, Saint Julian, Saint Lawrence, Saint John the Baptist, and Saints Cosmas and Damian. Saint Peter the Martyr (right) and Saint Francis (left) are the kneeling figures.
Alessio Baldovinetti, like many other artists of his time, emerged from Beato Angelico's circle. Only apparently open to the innovations of Paolo Uccello and Domenico Veneziano, Baldovinetti actually grasped only some superficial hint of them, as for example in the vivid luminosity of his spaces, the atmospheric transparence discernible in the hyperbolic distances of his landscapes.

ALESSIO BALDOVINETTI
(Florence, 1425-1499)

Annunciation

Tempera on wood
167x137
1447

Faithfully adhering to the Florentine tradition, Alessio Baldovinetti made refined use of a clear, almost sharp line, together with a great curiosity for the tiniest details. In this work, note the slender elegance of the Madonna, whose traditional gesture of reverent surprise at the angel's announcement has been replaced by an almost mannered pose, worthy of some worldly ritual. The artist attempts a perspective view by setting the scene under a portico, thus creating a background plane with the tops of the trees that can be seen above the surrounding wall.

by Beato Angelico — clearly emerges, giving the stories of this predella a narrative rhythm that is more clearly defined in a space imbued with the sense of the profundity of reality.

An artist like Alessio Baldovinetti is also associated with Lippi's post-1450 period: how otherwise could the gracefulness of the gestures and movements of the two figures in the *Annunciation* be explained, the intricacy of the lines pervading them and the rhythm of the composition.

Over and above these similarities, however, Baldovinetti represents a clear challenge to the art of Filippo Lippi, and therefore keeps alive the essentially dialectic nature of the Florentine artistic environment.

The two paintings by Baldovinetti displayed in the Uffizi are radiant works. An extremely bright light whitens the colours and lightens the weight of the volumes. The use of Brunelleschian perspective for the construction of a splendid Renaissance colonnade in the *Annunciation*, or for the positioning of the figures in the depths of a *hortus conclusus* in the *Madonna and Child with Saints*, places Baldovinetti among the ranks of the great perspective painters like Domenico Veneziano (who was in fact his teacher) and Beato Angelico.

The transparency of the light and the mathematical certainty of the space are the sign of a perfect, beneficent world in which man and

BOTTICELLI (Sandro Filipepi)
(Florence, 1445-1510)

Madonna of the Rose Garden *

Tempera on wood, 124x64
1469-70

Compared to the version which Botticelli
painted of the same subject, now
conserved at the Louvre, in this work the
frontal pose of the Virgin and the way the
body is seated on the throne under a small
Renaissance portico reveal more striking
stylistic similarities with the artist's
youthful "Fortitude": the head slightly bent
in the usual attitude of reflective
meditation, and the typology of the radiant
face, framed by a delicate veil.

nature — due to a rational knowledge of space and reality — live together harmoniously. Note the splendid division of the ground in the *Annunciation*, half of it belonging to man and half to nature, the latter represented by the trees rising behind the wall.

Sienese painting of the fifteenth century is rather poorly represented in the Uffizi. Today only two paintings are displayed here, possibly a tribute to their avowedly Renaissance character: the *Madonna and Child with Two Saints and Two Angels* by Matteo di Giovanni, and the predella with the *Stories of Saint Benedict* by Neroccio di Bartolomeo Landi (which completed the large *Coronation of the Virgin* in the Chiesa dell'Archicenobio at Monteoliveto Maggiore, painted by Francesco di Giorgio in 1471 and now in the Pinacoteca of Siena). It is hoped that one day, alongside these, space will again be found for Vecchietta's altarpiece with the *Madonna and Child with Six Saints*, which portrays the kneeling figures of Saints Francis and Dominic. This painting would offer a glimpse of the early phase of Renaissance painting in Siena through the work of a genuinely Sienese artist, and therefore a better knowledge of the development of this school.

Matteo di Giovanni was born and educated in Umbria, although from an expressive point of view he was open to Sienese art, as is revealed by the tender, melancholic grace of the Madonna and Child in this painting at the Uffizi.

At the present time it must be said that fifteenth-century paintings in the Uffizi illustrate above all the history of Florentine art.

Next to Alessio Baldovinetti is the *predella* by Benozzo Gozzoli, really an artist belonging to an older generation. The siting of this painting is justified, however, by the fact that he was part of the Florentine artistic environment around 1458-60 when he returned to Florence to paint the chapel of Palazzo Medici-Riccardi. In the predella of the Uffizi, the artist reveals an extraordinary attachment to the teachings of Beato Angelico, of whom Benozzo Gozzoli was a direct pupil and one of the assistants who worked on the frescoes of the cells of San Marco: there, indeed, are the open backgrounds of bare, unadorned hills that reappear in the predella. The painting also reveals that, on a stylistic level, Gozzoli has learnt from the influence of Domenico Veneziano.

After 1460 Florentine painting and its social environment were dominated by some extremely important figures: Antonio del Pollaiolo, Botticelli, Verrocchio and Filippino Lippi.

From a creative and technical point of view, Antonio del Pollaiolo was certainly the most talented of these artists. He was a goldsmith, a sculptor, an engraver, an embroidery designer and a painter, and in each of these activities he occupied a role of prime importance, that of teacher (he ran a highly organized workshop) and innovator. Although in painting he often worked with his brother Piero, the two of them are clearly distinguishable, as can be seen from the extremely important paintings today at the Uffizi which are the result of joint workmanship: the *altarpiece* for the Cardinal of Portugal's chapel in San Miniato al Monte and the six cardinal and theological *Virtues* that formed the chairbacks for the Audience Hall of the Mercatanzia. Antonio alone was responsible for the *Portrait of Gian Galeazzo Maria Sforza* and the two small panels with *Hercules and Antaeus* and *Hercules and the Hydra* (from the Medici palace in Via Larga).

The two brothers are recognizable because they were inspired by two different visions, and therefore adopted distinctive stylistic techniques.

Antonio saw man, nature and the products of man as organisms in action, from which continuous vibrations were propagated; in order to define form, he made use of a fine but extremely firm outline.

Piero, on the other hand, was struck by the element of light and how it was capable of making forms appear in a very foreshortened fore-

Hercules and Antaeus:
detail before restoration.

ANTONIO DEL POLLAIOLO (Antonio Benci)
(Florence, 1431 - Rome, 1498)

Hercules and the Hydra *

*Tempera on wood, 17x12
ca. 1475*

This small panel, the companion-piece to "Hercules and
Antaeus", refers to three panels representing the Labours of
Hercules which Antonio del Pollaiolo painted for Cosimo or
Piero de' Medici around 1460, lost works we know about only
from later versions.
Here too is represented a ferocious fight between the hero,
his body tensed into an agile, muscular mass and the legendary
multi-headed monster. The outlines are very sharply defined,
and the movement of nerves and tendons observed down to
the last detail. Antonio del Pollaiolo worked at time when
thorough studies of anatomy were being made, and he
therefore renders the human body realistically in its moments
of greatest emotional excitement.
The dramatic force of the episode is expressed in the hero's
grimace of fatigue and horror, but also his certainty of victory.
Behind the proudly barbaric figure blue rivers meander
through a broad landscape of green and brown fields, the sky
above an enamel blue.

ANTONIO DEL POLLAIOLO (Antonio Benci)
(Florence, 1431 - Rome, 1498)

Hercules and Antaeus *

*Tempera on wood, 16x9
ca. 1478*

The subject was particularly popular with Pollaiolo, given that
this is the fourth or fifth version.
Hercules, the tutelary deity of Florence, the symbol of supreme
civil virtues, the typical Florentine hero, is represented here in
a fierce struggle which captures not only the movement of the
bodies, but also the nervous tension of every muscle and the
faces twisted into expressions of fatigue and horror.

PIERO DEL POLLAIOLO (Piero Benci)
(Florence, ca. 1443 - Rome, 1496)

Portrait of Gian Galeazzo Maria Sforza *

Tempera on wood, 65x42
1417 (?)

This small portrait may have been executed in Florence during a
visit by Sforza to the city. The identity of the person portrayed is
beyond any doubt since there exists a copy of the work bearing
Sforza's name.
Even the earliest documents attribute this portrait to Piero del
Pollaiolo. The painting, its rather dark colours unenlivened by any
landscape views, plays on the changing colour tones of the
materials and on the characteristic physiognomy of its striking
protagonist.

ANTONIO DEL POLLAIOLO (Antonio Benci)
(Florence, ca. 1431 - Rome, 1498)

Portrait of a Lady *

Tempera on wood, 55x34
ca. 1475

The profile of the lady, who is not of a classical beauty, is perfectly
defined by a sharp line that separates it from the delicate lapis-lazuli
blue background. The woman, with her colourful complexion and
fashionable hairstyle, has a distinctly human appearance.
The artist has paid particular attention to her clothes. The various
materials and textures of the precious dress have all been carefully
considered, from the imperceptible veil that adorns her hair to the
shining crimson velvet and lavish brocade.

PIERO DEL POLLAIOLO (Piero Benci)
(Florence, ca. 1443 - Rome, 1496)

Altarpiece with Three Saints *

Tempera on wood, 172x179
1467-68

The altarpiece with the same subject today displayed in the Cardinal of Portugal's Chapel is a
copy of this painting, of which it is thought that only the design was the result of the
combined efforts of Piero and his brother Antonio, whereas the actual execution is to be
ascribed entirely to Piero.
The traditional iconography, descended from Vasari, identifies the three characters as Saints
James, Vincent and Eustace.
The painting is part of a single decorative programme for the Chapel of the Cardinal of
Portugal, Jacopo di Lusitania, grandson of the king of Portugal, who died in Florence at the
age of twenty-five.

BOTTICELLI (Sandro Filipepi)
(Florence, 1445-1510)

Primavera (Spring) *

Tempera on wood, 203x314
1482-83

This painting, perhaps Botticelli's most popular and most exploited work, was, like the Birth of Venus, seen by Vasari in Cosimo I's villa of Castello. It was probably painted on the occasion of Lorenzo's wedding with Semiramide Appiani, which took place in May 1482.

The name with which the canvas is universally known also derives from Vasari, although it is more likely that the artist, open to the learned advice of Poliziano and Marsilio Ficino, actually intended to represent the Realm of Venus. If this was the case the work should be interpreted in the following way: on the right Zephyrus pursues Flora, who, being possessed, scatters flowers over the world; Venus, in the centre, represents Humanitas, for whom the humanists of the Medicean circle reserved high tributes; the dancing Graces follow, while Mercury, on the far left, disperses the clouds.

Various interpretations of the scene exist, of course, including one claiming that Botticelli attempted an allegorical characterization of the months of the year, making evident allowances for the fact that the ancients shrank from representing the winter months.

Leaving aside the suppositions there remains the profoundly humanistic nature of the painting, a reflection of contemporary cultural influences and an expression of many contemporary texts.

The precious setting, devoid of spatial depth, is perfectly consonant with the graceful bodies of the figures, all of them constructed on and defined by their outline and extremely weightless and ethereal, almost an echo of Gothic elegance.

Botticelli, Primavera: detail

ground. This effect was obtained both when the background was a distance (as in the *Assumption of the Virgin* in the church of Sant'Agostino in San Gimignano) as well as when it was a foreshortened distance as in the paintings of *Prudence*, *Justice* and *Faith*.

Both visions were inspired by early experience of the art of Domenico Veneziano and Alessio Baldovinetti, as is demonstrated by the *Altarpiece with Three Saints*, formerly in the Cardinal of Portugal's chapel: here too the size of the human figure is rendered not with a plastic effect but with the foreground, despite the fact that a bright, shadowless light illuminates a homogeneous carpet of colours.

Experience acquired through the practice (almost always prevalent) of the goldsmith's art and sculpture deeply transformed the painting of Antonio, who, discovering the form as an independent organism of space, came to distinguish himself markedly from his brother. This important discovery clearly determined the compositional innovations of the *Portrait of Gian Galeazzo Maria Sforza* and the two panels with the *Labours of Hercules*. Each of the two Labours of Hercules represents a group moving diagonally towards a progressive conquest of the foreground. The distant landscape and the transparent, crystalline sky serve to underline the extent of this conquest.

The portrait of Sforza was a complete innovation in Italian art, not only because it was a three-quarters profile, and not only because it was a bust-length portrait with the inclusion of the hands, but also because the person portrayed is represented in conversation with an invisible interlocutor — the observer — and this creates a sort of mystery. Antonio also cultivated the full-profile portrait, a technique which derived

JACOPO DEL SELLAIO
(Florence, 1442-1493)

The Banquet of Ahasuerus

Tempera on wood, 45x63
After 1490?

Jacopo del Sellaio was Botticelli's pupil, but was also open to the influence of Lippi and Ghirlandaio. He was a refined and accomplished narrator, especially in the decoration of chests, of which this Banquet of Ahasuerus is a part together with another two panels by the same artist: "The Triumph of Marduk" and "Queen Vasti's Banquet", whose subjects were taken from the Bible.
Venturi wrote that Jacopo del Sellaio was merely a luxury decorator, a gilder of figures and things who depicted his little stories with a hurried style but the result was always figurines lacking any precise or meditated structural study.
The small scenes are vivaciously narrated. The artist was indeed a decorator above all else and had a meticulous eye for detail. His architectural settings are accurately constructed, and there is a tense, vibrant line that confers dynamism to the entire composition.

FILIPPINO LIPPI (?)
(Prato, 1457 - Florence, 1504)

Portrait of a Young Man

Oil on wood, 53x35
15th C.

Considerable controversy surrounds the authorship of this painting. The
traditional attribution to Filippino Lippi has been questioned in this
century by those who see in the work the style of Lorenzo di Credi,
although the most recent studies on this artist have failed to arrive at any
concrete conclusion. The arguments in favour of this theory are based on
the suggestion of a soft, regular typology, characteristic of the latter artist;
the colour, however, applied with broad, pasty strokes, is certainly not
typical of Lorenzo di Credi's work, nor is the rich distribution of
chiaroscuro in which the presence of shadow prevails.

Portrait of a Young Man

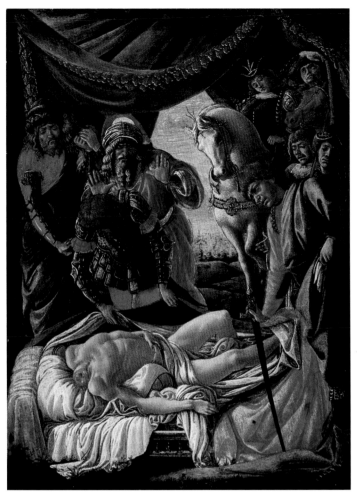

BOTTICELLI (Sandro Filipepi)
(Florence, 1445-1510)

The Discovery of the Body of Holophernes

Tempera on wood, 31x25
1470-72

The colours used in this work have livelier tones than
those used for the Judith. Here reds prevail, contrasting
with bright blues and whites, all colours that were
popular with the artist.
The armour of the dignitaries who have rushed to the
scene shine splendidly and the preciously braided velvets
of the Oriental tent in which the handsome decapitated
body of Holophernes lies is tinged with reflections of
light.
The glimpse of a distant landscape can be seen behind a
noble white steed wearing a rich harness.

BOTTICELLI (Sandro Filipepi)
(Florence, 1445-1510)

Coronation of the Virgin (San Marco Altarpiece) *

Tempera on wood, 378x258
ca.1488-90

This work, which was restored in 1989, shows God the
Father, above, crowning the Virgin between sixteen
angels; below, from left to right, are Saints John the
Evangelist, Augustine, Jerome and Eligius.

BOTTICELLI (Sandro Filipepi)
(Florence, 1445-1510)

The Return of Judith

Tempera on wood, 31x24
1470-72

Judith is seen returning from the enemy camp in the
uncertain light of dawn, the wind ruffling her thin
clothes. The sinuous line of her body betrays the
unsteadiness of her step; on her face a sense of
dreaminess, as if, after the cruel act that must have
required so much courage, a sense of emptiness had
taken over, a stasis, a nostalgic state of mind of great
uncertainty.
If Andrea del Castagno had confronted the problem of
human "decision" in his paintings, emphasizing it with
hard, heavy outlines, rugged, angular faces, and enduring,
unequivocal gestures, Botticelli suspends his Judith in a
hazy, emotional and uncertain atmosphere.

from medals and was preferred in the early Renaissance, in the splendid *Portrait of a Lady* set against a blue sky background.

In the second half of the fifteenth century interest in portrait painting on the part of the Florentine environment tended to grow. Botticelli himself, who painted portraits in a great variety of styles, reflected this interest. The *Portrait of a Young Man with a Medal* shows a figure viewed almost frontally in a more than half-bust length, his hands joined together in a symbolic gesture. Unlike the *Portrait of Galeazzo Maria Sforza*, which has a dark background, in Botticelli's work there is a landscape and a broad expanse of sky behind the figure.

With Botticelli we enter a period — the last four decades of the fifteenth century — which is of considerable interest for the political conflicts and cultural movements that were taking place in Florence, and for the fascinating artistic manifestations that contemporaneously were an expression of them. From a political point of view, this period witnessed a struggle for supremacy in the city which culminated in the Pazzi conspiracy and subsequently the progressive rise of Lorenzo dei Medici, son of Piero 'the Gouty', later called Lorenzo the Magnificent; and in the attempt at a reform of the Church and of the city of Florence, at first a religious reform and then a reform of society in general, on the part of the Dominican friar Girolamo Savonarola, which led to the expulsion of the Medici from Florence and the establishment of a democratic republic.

From a cultural point of view, this period saw the definitive creation of the Medici collections in the family palace in Via Larga. This drew attention to a different kind of relationship between society and art and therefore determined a new and in some respects already modern conception of the work of art itself. But the most important cultural development, and one that had a significant effect on the figurative arts, was the birth of Marsilio Ficino's neo-Platonism and the Accademia di Careggi, since in the last decades of the fifteenth century it also exerted a great influence of a 'poetic' nature.

Alessandro Botticello is rightly considered to be the greatest artistic exponent of late fifteenth-century cultural life in general and of Ficinian neo-Platonism in particular. He was also a favourite of the Medici family and therefore the artist most suited for expressing the complex and at times contradictory positions of this family, and especially of Lorenzo the Magnificent.

His close relations with the powerful Florentine family are confirmed not only by a series of extremely important works of his later years, such as the mythological allegories painted for Lorenzo di Pierfrancesco, head of the lesser branch of the family, but also by early works like the *Adoration of the Magi* of Santa Maria Novella, in which — with the pretext of the religious subject — the artist produced a subtle and at the same time explicit apotheosis of the Medici family.

Even small-sized paintings, like the two Stories of Judith, responded fully to the new conception of art determined by Medici collectionism. These two small works were intended for the pleasure of their owner; they were probably kept in a cupboard with other rare and precious objects rather than being hung on a wall. Stylistic refinement, subtle interpretation and perfect execution were the necessary requisites for this new function.

The pupil of Filippo Lippi, or possibly his assistant in the frescoes of Prato cathedral, and extremely similar to his teacher in temperament, Botticelli was already revealing a completely original temperament in the *Allegory of Fortitude* for the chair-back of the audience-hall of the Palazzo di Mercatanzia, painted to complete the series executed by Piero and Antonio del Pollaiolo.

Both the stylistic and expressive differences between Botticelli's Virtue and the other six painted by the Pollaiolo brothers, could almost

BOTTICELLI (Sandro Filipepi)
(Florence, 1445-1510)

Adoration of the Magi

*Tempera on wood, 111x134
1476-77*

The Adoration of the Magi was one of Botticelli's favourite subjects, one that he painted six times (one version being left unfinished). This one is full of important members of the Medici family and their circle, the question of their identity being what has fascinated art historians more than anything else.

The figures have been identified as Cosimo the Elder, the old man kneeling immediately in front of the Child, Piero 'the Gouty', kneeling in the centre foregound, Giovanni de' Medici kneeling in a similar position to his right, Giuliano de' Medici, standing behind him, Gasparre di Zanobi del Lama (who commissioned the work), pointing to himself, Botticelli himself on the far right, turned towards the onlooker, Lorenzo the Magnificent standing on the far left, with Agnolo Poliziano and Giovanni Pico della Mirandola next to him. According to some critics, Gasparre di Zanobi del Lama, who commissioned the work, is to be identified as King Gasparre, who is paying homage to the Child.

A regal host of courtiers witnesses the scene, which is built pyramidally towards the Virgin who is presenting her Child to the onlookers under a makeshift wooden roof.

BOTTICELLI (Sandro Filipepi)
(Florence, 1445-1510)

The Birth of Venus *

Tempera on wood, 172x278.5
1484-86

The subject probably derives from Ovid's "Metamorphoses" and "Fasti" — where the Hour (or Time) is described in the act of offering Venus her cloak — and therefore from all consequent humanistic literature.

Although some see the painting as a representation of Venus landing on the shores of Sicily, blown by Zephyrus and Cloris, or at Portovenere, the residence of Simonetta Vespucci, it is more likely that the painting has a neo-Platonic cultural significance, by which the scene would symbolize the birth of a new *humanitas* penetrated by Nature with its four elements, and a union of spirit and matter.

The image of Venus borne up by an enormous shell expresses an entirely spiritual beauty: her nudity is seen as simplicity, purity, sincerity. The sea, ruffled by eddies of wind and schematized into identical marks, is in fact symbolic, as is the shell on which Venus stands.

The plastic quality of the figures dissolves in the great breadth of the scene's linear arrangement, which cancels any realistic spatial depth.

Botticelli, The Birth of Venus: detail.

be seen as emblematic of the existence in Florence of two contrasting realities. In the Virtues executed by Antonio and Piero del Pollaiolo an intense vital force is unleashed, whose expression is the sum total of all the components of its style, from the composition and the design to the use of colour and light, and to the vanishing point which coincides with the meeting of the lines of vision of the Virtues with those of the spectators. Botticelli's *Fortitude*, in contrast, seems to withdraw from a contact with everyday, human reality in order to take refuge in a dream world of sweet enchantment. The rendering of movement, the arrangement of the drapery and the choice of the perspective point have the effect of drawing the figure back. The outlines are directed in an undulating linear rhythm that expands horizontally, thus breaking the tendency of the figure to loom into the foreground. The expression is reflective and serene. In this Virtue, the ethical ideals of Marsilio Ficino are already expressed remarkably ahead of time.

Botticelli's art was profoundly linked to a conception of reality, of the world and of man that was eminently philosophical in nature. This is revealed by the extreme stylistic coherence with which he interpreted the various themes entrusted to him: from dramatic subjects like the two youthful works of *The Return of Judith* and *The Discovery of the Body of Holophernes*, on display in the Gallery, and mythological scenes like *Primavera (Spring)*, *The Birth of Venus* and *Pallas and the Centaur*, to the great religious altarpieces like the *Madonna with Saints Cosmas and Damian* or the *San Barnaba Altarpiece*, and the altarpieces with the Virgin and Child like the *Madonna of the Rose Garden*.

Botticelli used a space that was perspectively determined by architectural structures; landscape, on the other hand, was an infinite expanse that faded into a distant horizon. In the infinite space moved a delicate, impalpable, continually undulating world of figures and things, a world that danced and expanded in space and was projected into a timeless dimension. For Botticelli neither reality, nor mathematical certainty, nor the peculiarities of the sensible world existed, only the abstract rhythm of line, which with its numerous variations penetrated the mind.

Colours are subjected to a mental transformation, which removes their specific qualities, yet, becoming diaphanous or bright, accompany the rhythmic modulation. Botticelli's ability to transfer painting into the abstract world of ideas is most clearly apparent in the mythological allegories painted for the Villa di Castello of the lesser branch of the Medici family. Three of these allegories are displayed in the Uffizi: the *Primavera*, the *Birth of Venus* and *Pallas and the Centaur*. They are conceived in a timeless dimension outside of history. They can be contemplated and relived philosophically and enjoyed through the intellect. Their sole aesthetic ideal is grace, the main spiritual virtue of beauty. It should come as no surprise that the *Primavera* was inspired by a literary work, Poliziano's *Stanzas*.

In this period, which extended into the eighth and ninth decade, Botticelli also painted a splendid series of works with religious themes, both for private and public use. For them he adopted new sizes of painting and new compositional designs. He used the large roundel for the *Madonna of the Magnificat* and the *Madonna of the Pomegranate*, and a small rectangular format, appropriate for collection, for the superb *Saint Augustine*, in which, with an ingenious touch, he took up the spatial and compositional ideal and meaning of Masaccio's *Trinity* in Santa Maria Novella, yet transformed its solemn certainties into the gentle passage of undulating rhythms that start with the delicate and perhaps momentary raising of a curtain.

In the sacred altarpieces, as well as favouring an architectural background, which becomes like a theatrical backdrop in the *San Barnaba Altarpiece*, he profoundly transformed the stylistic and interpretative

BOTTICELLI (Sandro Filipepi)
(Florence, 1445-1510)

Pallas and the Centaur

Tempera on canvas, 207x148
1480-85

Critics are divided over whether to interpret this painting as a political or moral allegory. In the former case, the work would refer to the diplomatic abilities of Lorenzo the Magnificent, who in 1480 persuaded the king of Naples to abandon the League of Pope Sixtus VI against Florence. Hence the Parthenopean city and its harbour in the background of the painting, the centaur symbolizing the city of Rome, and Pallas, holding a Florentine halberd, Florence. According to the latter theory, the moral allegory, this was linked to Ficino's idea that the double nature of the centaur, half-man and half-beast, would perhaps symbolize an invitation to Lorenzo di Pierfrancesco to allow himself to be guided by Lorenzo the Magnificent, whose emblem forms the decorative motif on Pallas's dress.

BOTTICELLI (Sandro Filipepi)
(Florence, 1445-1510)

Madonna of the Magnificat

Tempera on wood, diam. 118
1482-83

The composition of this roundel is somewhat unusual, framed as it is by a circular window.
The Madonna, sitting beneath a crown of stars and a golden nimbus with the Holy Spirit, is
writing the "Magnificat" in a book. The faces, however much altered by repaintings (the
Virgin's particularly) are all splendid; the colours are radiant, with the red of the clothes and
the gold of the hair and decorations prevailing. The figures, absorbed in their actions and
gilded by the reflections of an unnatural light, stand against a background in which part of a
rural landscape can be seen.
The work, exemplary for the harmony of the lines inside the round frame, is one of
Botticelli's most balanced and serene works.

BOTTICELLI (Sandro Filipepi)
(Florence, 1445-1510)

Madonna of the Pomegranate

Tempera on wood, diam. 143.5
ca. 1487

The composition almost seems to adapt to the structural form of the roundel, in those
enchanted angels with their terribly contemporary faces huddling around the lovely figure of
the Virgin. The latter holds a similarly handsome Child, with its light-golden curly hair, although
the colours here are more studied and a soft, golden, melancholy light pervades the entire
work. The effect of relative dullness in this roundel is due to the loss of all the gold parts
which Botticelli applied to embellish the painting.
This diminished resplendence further accentuates the sense of dreamy melancholy already
characterizing the faces of the Virgin and Child.

BOTTICELLI (Sandro Filipepi)
(Florence, 1445-1510)

San Barnaba Altarpiece

Tempera on wood, 268x280
1487-89

The painting was commissioned to Botticelli by the Consuls of the Guild of Doctors and
Apothecaries, patrons of the Church of San Barnaba, on whose high altar
it remained until 1700.
The composition is finely balanced in structure with a solemn symmetrical arrangement of
the forms. The Virgin sits in a raised position on an elaborate throne, flanked by four angels
holding up the curtain and six saints, three on each side.
The faces are typical of Botticelli. The colours, however, are darker than usual, with the
inclusion of some rather dull green tones which are not balanced fully by the pale clothes of
the splendid angels or by the marble of the throne.

Botticelli, Cestello Annunciation: detail of ▶
the predella.

BOTTICELLI (Sandro Filipepi)
(Florence, 1445-1510)

Cestello Annunciation *

*Tempera on wood, 150x156
1489-90*

Notwithstanding the decorative geometrical motifs of the
pavement, whose rectangles adhere to the rules of Renaissance
perspective, the linear movement of the Virgin is quite unusual
in the context of a cultural world regulated by the laws of
balance and harmony, as is the quivering Angel whose emotivity
is expressed in the elaborate broken folds of its robes.

BOTTICELLI (Sandro Filipepi)
(Florence, 1445-1510)

Calumny

Tempera on wood, 62x91
1495

The subject is sophisticated, as was appropriate for a sympathizer of contemporary neo-Platonic theories. The allegorical scene shows King Midas, enthroned, with ass's ears, the symbol of bad judgement. Midas, between Ignorance and Suspicion, is stretching a hand towards Malice, who in turn is leading Calumny. The latter, dressed up by Envy and Fraud, is dragging Innocence by the hair, a half-naked figure reduced to impotence; there follows the austere hooded figure of Remorse, who has turned to look at the beautiful figure of a naked woman symbolizing Truth.
The composition, with all its refined draftsmanship, typology, and subtle psychological insight typical of Botticelli, has provided abundant material for critics to launch themselves into a passionate search for the hidden meaning of the work. It is generally thought that it was executed by Botticelli in response to calumnies directed at the artist himself. All critics, however much their theories differ, agree in their dating of "Calumny" to the period of Botticelli's artistic maturity.

GHIRLANDAIO (Domenico Bigordi)
(Florence, 1449-1494)

Adoration of the Magi

Tempera on wood, diam. 172
1487

The subject is one of the most frequently interpreted in fifteenth-century Florentine painting.
The figures are arranged in a circle, spread out just enough to make noticeable the most
irrelevant details. The general atmosphere is one of the utmost tranquillity, with gracious
horses standing idly in the background and soldiers in their shining armour absorbed in the
event. A note of colour is provided by the exotic coloured boy dressed in a showy costume. In
the foreground are various figures with unmistakably Medicean features and Ghirlandaio
himself in the act of indicating someone, possibly the person who commissioned the painting.
In front of the kneeling Magi are the symbolic cube bearing the date of the work, the sack
and the flask, traditional symbols of the previous journey of the Magi.
In the background, between scenes of shepherds and mounted soldiers, is a faraway landscape
with an enclosed harbour.

tone of the altar painting. A vault-like line gently embraces the figures and pulls them towards worlds whose existence is left to pure imagination.

Feelings are also expressed in the lines created by movements and gestures more than by expressions. See, for example, the wonderful *Annunciation*, in which the angel's timorous announcement and the Virgin's surprise, anxiety and joy are expressed with linear rhythms.

It is quite clear, from what has been said, that before becoming a universal patrimony, Botticelli's art was associated with the refined circle of initiates to Florentine neo-Platonism.

Another artist, in contrast to Botticelli, satisfied the cultivated and at times demanding tastes of a Florentine society composed of merchant and banking families which by this time had become aristocracy. This was Domenico Ghirlandaio, the painter of the Vespucci, Sassetti and Tornabuoni families. His was a transparent painting, one that was well-suited to the meticulous depiction of those details of customs and surroundings which so delight a society when it turns in on itself and tends towards self-celebration.

The paintings by Ghirlandaio displayed at the Uffizi are a reflection of the artist's great success in producing religious works destined for private ownership (like the roundel with the *Adoration of the Magi*) and in the production of altarpieces, which are distinguished by their elegant, well-balanced composition, by the calm, noble expressions, by the bright, carefully chosen colours and by the image they conveyed of the richness, beauty and opulence of Florentine society. Ghirlandaio would have achieved all this with far greater difficulty had a Flemish painting of exceptional importance, the *Portinari Triptych* by Hugo van der Goes, not arrived in Florence in around 1478. This extremely large painting, which revealed to the Florentines the great achievements of fifteenth-century Flemish art, played a decisive role in causing the inversion of tendencies that took place in the city in the last two decades of the century. Its arrival, therefore, had consequences that were far more important and widely felt than the presence in Florence of Rogier van der Weyden's *Entombment*, a masterpiece that no one at the time seemed to take any notice of in this city.

In the 1470s Verrocchio took a third path, fusing various aspects of the complex Florentine tendencies into a conception of the monumental form, rich in light, chiaroscuro and sharpness of line.

Generally speaking, other Florentine artists of the time oriented their styles according to these three directions. Jacopo del Sellaio followed Botticelli, while Lorenzo di Credi was one of Verrocchio's leading pupils. Botticelli also had an extremely talented pupil in Filippino Lippi, the son of Filippo. The Uffizi has paintings of both the early and mature years of this artist. The former correspond to Botticelli's period between 1470 and 1490; the latter are associated with the same artist's later works.

Of the youthful works we cannot fail to mention the *Adoration of the Child* and the splendid *Signoria Altarpiece*, also known as the *Madonna degli Otto*. Although Filippino remained faithful to the teachings of his master, his artistic expression was absolutely original. He expressed himself with a variety of means, transforming Botticelli's integral linearism, which incorporated every form, into the re-evocation of a disquieting and melancholy world, in which Botticelli's linearity was combined with form and colour and enlivened with darting movements and flickering touches of light.

This colourful period of Florentine painting ended with the death of Lorenzo the Magnificent in 1492, an event which caused the explosion of numerous tensions and resistances against the power of the Medici family that had existed without the possibility of emerging and being expressed. The ferment found an exceptional exponent in the person of

GHIRLANDAIO (Domenico Bigordi)
(Florence, 1449-1494)

Madonna and Child with Angels and Saints

Tempera on wood, 190x200
1484

Domenico Ghirlandaio is a painter for whom art was not an exhausting research, but mere description and eye-witnessing, the inventor of a genre which only much later would be called the painting of historical subjects. The compositional scheme of this work is very similar to another Madonna and Child with Saints kept at the Uffizi but not displayed, and if anything is more static and balanced in the arrangement of the symmetrically kneeling figures of Saint Zenobius and Saint Just and in the semicircle of angels guarding the Virgin like a pearl in an enormous shell.

The archangels Gabriel and Raphael are standing calmly at the sides. In the background is a simple, elegant open arcade from which the light enters, and the tops of cypress trees rising above the surrounding wall.

HUGO VAN DER GOES
(Ghent, 1440 - Andergen, 1482)

Adoration of the Shepherds (Portinari Triptych)

Composite work, oil on wood
253x586 (overall)
1478

This large triptych is the most important work of the Flemish artist Hugo van der Goes, constituting the basis for a reconstruction of the artist's entire oeuvre. It was painted in Bruges and was commissioned to the artist by Tommaso Portinari, an agent of the Medicean bank who resided in the city with his family. The painting was intended for the high altar of Sant'Egidio, the church of the Arcispedale of Santa Maria Nuova founded in 1288 by the banker's ancestor Folco Portinari. Shipped from Bruges by sea, with the financial aid of the banker Niccolò di Giovanni Capponi, it arrived in Pisa by way of Sicily. The painting was then transported along the Arno and finally completed its tortuous journey at the Porta San Frediano in Florence on 28 May 1483. From here it was carried to its destination by sixteen strong porters under the surveillance of Meo di Tingo, an envoy of the Arcispedale. In 1567 the triptych was dismembered. When the work arrived in Florence, it immediately caused a sensation among the people and attracted a considerable following among contemporary artists. The triptych had an enormous impact, noticeably influencing the art of manuscript illustration in the late fifteenth and early sixteenth centuries as well as illustrious representatives of Umbrian painting like Luca Signorelli.

Exterior of the side panels

Oil on wood, 253x241 (each panel)

Soberly painted in monochrome, the panels are entirely occupied by the Archangel Gabriel and the Virgin of the Annunciation. The enormous figures are portrayed under a series of perspectively receding arches and in an extremely bare, linear setting, enriched only by the copious folds of the robes surrounding the figures.

HUGO VAN DER GOES
(Ghent, 1440 - Andergen, 1482)

Adoration of the Shepherds
(Portinari Triptych), left panel

Oil on wood, 253x241

Three members of the Portinari
family, Tommaso Portinari and his
two sons Antonio and Pigello, are
portrayed kneeling, their faces
pale, sculptural and almost ghost-
like. Above them stand Saint
Anthony Abbot and Saint
Thomas, two of the family's
patron saints, looking grave and
solemn, their majesty almost
compressed by the absence of a
surrounding space. In the
background, against a barren,
rocky landscape, Mary and
Joseph can be seen making their
way to Bethlehem, an episode
that prepares us for the holy
event of the central panel.

HUGO VAN DER GOES
(Ghent, 1440 - Andergen, 1482)

Adoration of the Shepherds (Portinari
Triptych), central panel

Oil on wood, 253x304

Dominated by the image of the Child,
radiantly lit in the centre of the scene with
the Madonna in Adoration, the central panel
reveals why the Portinari Triptych is
rightfully considered unique in the
panorama of fifteenth-century Flemish
painting.
In this scene Van der Goes constructs a
composition in which the surface of the
painting is conceived like a stage on which
the figures rise progressively the further
back they are positioned. There is a search
for an irregular, certainly unclassical beauty
in the faces which is evident in the group
of worshipping shepherds. For the first
time in Flemish painting we see the
peasant, popularesque element in their
shadowed features and in the "plebean"
countenance of Saint Joseph, standing back
respectfully from the central episode.
The group of shepherds has always been
one of the most admired elements of the
whole composition, one with almost a life
of its own. The shepherds reappear in the
background landscape, tiny astonished
figures in the presence of angels heralding
the birth of the Saviour.

BOTTICELLI (Sandro Filipepi)
(Florence, 1445-1510)

Portrait of a Young Man with a
Medal of Cosimo the Elder

Tempera on wood, 57.5x44

Various theories have been
advanced on the identity of the
man, who has been interpreted
either as a Medici, or as Pico

della Mirandola, or even as the author of the medal (possibly Niccolò di Forzore Spinelli). It is probable
however that it is a youthly self-portrait, or otherwise a portrait of the artist's brother, Antonio, a founder
and decorator of medals. The medal which the young man holds in his hand, a plaster cast, reproduces
precisely the one coined shortly after the death of Cosimo the Elder in 1464. Art scholars almost
immediately attributed the painting to Botticelli, though lengthy debates arose over the date, associated
with the various identifications that were advanced of the person portrayed.
We note here a type of face that is typical of Botticelli, a sensitive face with rugged, nervous features. It
constitutes a typical example of that extraordinary human repertoire that Botticelli expressed, and over
which he laid a veil of indeciphrable melancholy, assuming thus a wholly particular attitude towards reality.
Botticelli in fact interprets nature in a quite unnatural way, on the contrary he modifies it with the cultural
reality of his time. In the figures charged with psychological expression we can discern an artist
accustomed to thinking and meditating on the meaning of life.

LORENZO DI CREDI
(Florence, 1459? - 1537)

Venus

Oil on canvas, 151x69
ca. 1493-94

The canvas was found by chance at the
Medici villa of Cafaggiolo in 1869. It would
seem to be an unfinished work. A close
examination of the painting reveals the
transparency of the figure's extremely thin
skin, almost as if there had been only a
first, provisional application of paint. The
fair-haired, muscular young woman is
called Venus because of her clear affinity
with the classical prototype of the "Venere
Pudica".

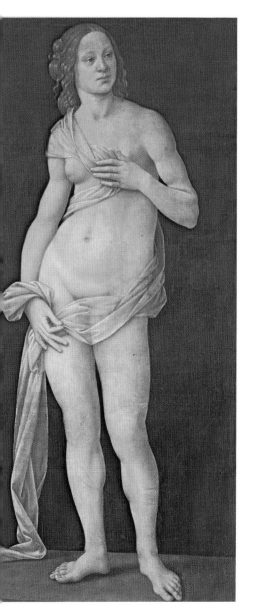

LORENZO DI CREDI
(Florence, 1459? - 1537)

Adoration of the Shepherds

Oil on wood, 224x196
ca. 1510

The painting shows meticulous draftsmanship and technical perfection, but is totally devoid of
any dramatic force, the artist having eclectically assimilated influences from other artists —
Perugino, Verrocchio and even Leonardo himself.
The absence of any emotional involvement may be due to the fact that at the end of his life
Lorenzo di Credi was a disciple of Savonarola. The figures in his paintings, as in this case, have
serious, meditative expressions, are charged with an inner gloom which the painter mitigates
only with that small amount of grace allowed in a church ceremony.
Only one angel, standing, seems to be engaged in reasoning with a companion on the
mysteries of the Birth. Saint Joseph, leaning on his staff, looks wistfully at the scene, and a
shepherd holding a lamb looks to be distracted by something else.

FILIPPINO LIPPI
(Prato, 1457 - Florence, 1504)

Saint Jerome

Oil on wood, 136x71
1490-1500

Vasari also mentioned that this work was commissioned by
the Badia Fiorentina. It shows Saint Jerome kneeling in front
of the Crucifix, with a wooded landscape in the background.
The composition is built up with numerous, broken planes
and the drama of the scene is enhanced by the rumpled
folds of the saint's robe. The sculpted, hollowed face reminds
us of the emotionally charged art of Andrea del Castagno.

FILIPPINO LIPPI
(Prato, 1457 - Florence, 1504)

Signoria Altarpiece ("Pala degli Otto")

Tempera on wood, 355x255
1486

The work is dated and represents the Madonna and Child
with angels and Saints John the Baptist, Victor, Bernard and
Zenobius.
Executed for the Lesser Council Hall in Palazzo Vecchio,
some critics have seen in this painting the hand of a young
Leonardo, although today it is accepted only that the artist
was inspired by one of Leonardo's drawings.
The whole composition is projected outwards, a movement
that is underlined by the various surfaces around the throne.
The clothes of the four saints are animated and rippled into
vibrant surfaces and the architectural elements are finely
sculpted and gilded in relief decoration.
The sharpness of his observation reveals to what extent
Lippi had studied the work of Leonardo, although his use of
bright colours — reds, blue and deep purple —
demonstrates that he followed his own line of personal
inspiration.

Filippino Lippi, Signoria Altarpiece
("Pala degli Otto"): detail.

FILIPPINO LIPPI
(Prato, 1457 - Florence, 1504)

Adoration of the Magi ∗

Oil on wood, 258x243
ca. 1496

One of the interesting things about this
composition, jammed full of figures, is
identifying the characters. Critics claim to
have identified Pier Francesco Medici the
Elder, as well as his two sons Lorenzo il
Popolano and Giovanni il Popolano (father
of the famous condottiere Giovanni dalle
Bande Nere), and Piero il Pugliese.
The work shows traces of the influence of
North European painting, which had come
to Florence with the Portinari Triptych by
Hugo van der Goes, while the figures
grouped excitedly around the central
nucleus are already sixteenth-century and
are derived directly from Leonardo da Vinci.
Filippino draws inspiration here from two
other well-known Adorations of an earlier
date, those of Sandro Botticelli and
Leonardo, both by portraying the crowd
that closes in around the divine group, and
by including the young man with a
characteristic tuft of hair on the right.

the Dominican friar Girolamo Savonarola, a brilliant preacher, an extraordinarily forceful writer, and an ardent advocate of the moral and spiritual reform of the Church and at the same time of Florentine society.

The Savonarolian period lasted from the beginning of the friar's preaching, which culminated in the expulsion of Piero dei Medici, the son of Lorenzo the Magnificent (1494), until the friar's execution in 1498. The vastness and importance of the explosive and intelligent action of this man represented a decisive turning-point in the course of Florentine history. At an artistic level, it marked the end of the early Renaissance and the beginning of a new age, an age that was to blossom in the following century, the Cinquecento.

This spiritual and cultural storm was deeply reflected in Botticelli and inspired his creativity: a painting like *Calumny* reveals that the artist's conception of style had not changed, but rather was used with a very different kind of moral commitment. The composition — although well-balanced — is characterized by violent linear rhythms that now have a clear direction, whereas before they floated freely within an abstract space. Later on, seized by an urge to express incumbent realities and no longer the vague lapsing into the realm of intellectual ecstasies, Botticelli would come to break his elaborate, refined and graceful linear schemes in favour of a more syncopated and dramatic composition.

This extreme phase — which resulted in great masterpieces like the *Mystic Nativity* of the London National Gallery and the *Crucifixion* of Glasgow — is unfortunately not represented in the Gallery.

The profound unease which Savonarola had instilled into the souls of men and the consciousness of the fragility of the human situation gave Filippino Lippi the idea for his *Allegory*. But the effects of the spiritual

FILIPPINO LIPPI
(Prato, 1457 -
Florence, 1504)

BEING
RESTORED

Adoration of the Child

*Oil on wood, 96x71
ca. 1483*

In this Adoration of the Child Lippi shows a grace in the definition of form that is already more vibrant and almost morbid compared to the linearism of Botticelli. The style is delicate and lyrical, still devoid of the Leonardesque chiaroscuro that Lippi would acquire later on. Already, however, the glimpse of a landscape on the left of the painting betrays an almost Flemish interest in nature and its irresistible appeal.

dilemma which Savonarola had preached to his contemporary world, with force and with the sacrifice of his own life, were also to become a fundamental component of the contrasting tendencies of the sixteenth century.

If Botticelli ruled supreme in Florence in the last decades of the fifteenth century (his only pupil would be Filippino Lippi), the new generations were educated in the workshop of Andrea del Verrocchio, an artist who in actual fact worked very little on painting. Both Lorenzo di Credi (as we have seen) and Leonardo da Vinci received their early training at his school. Two other contemporary painters came to his workshop from outside Florence, Pietro Perugino from Città della Pieve and Luca Signorelli from Cortona. Many artists felt the effects of Verrocchio's influence, among them Francesco Botticini; other painters who were involved in the stylistic turning-point at the close of the century, like Fra' Bartolomeo in the last decade, had to go through a certain apprenticeship at his workshop.

The hallmark of Verrocchio's style was based on a balanced relationship between design and chiaroscuro, in which the ideal of grace (cultivated in Florence, in painting, by Filippo Lippi in particular) found a complex and complete expression. The *Baptism of Christ*, from the Vallombrosan church of San Salvi, is almost an anthological collection of reasons for which Verrocchio's presence was one of the fulcrums in the development of Florentine artistic culture. It is a work that was certainly conceived by the master, and reveals, among other things, Verrocchio's considerable debt to his fellow citizen Antonio del Pollaiolo, six years his senior. Verrocchio's pupils, whose hands could already be identified, participated in its execution: Leonardo in the two angels and the landscape, clearer but at the same time mellow in tone, and Lorenzo di Credi in the figure of Christ. The result, in spite of the substantially static composition, is modern, soft and airy.

If this painting is used as a comparative model of Verrocchio's work (the artist's only one at the Uffizi), we are struck not only by how closely Francesco Botticini adhered to his master's example in *The Three Archangels*, but also by the faithfulness of Lorenzo di Credi throughout his artistic career, of which the *Annunciation* (where Leonardo's influence is already evident) is a late expression.

After leaving Verrocchio's workshop, Leonardo demonstrated the enormous breadth of his talent in his earliest works. If the *Annunciation* is a painting whose compositional structure and style reveal the influence of Verrocchio, in the *Adoration of the Magi*, which was begun and almost brought to completion between 1480 and 1481, he draws inspiration from Botticelli's much more expressive and restless compositions, even though he intended to transform their circling linear expressions into dramatic contrasts of light and shadow, into brief, fleeting apparitions of forms in movement.

From one painting to another Leonardo intuited the importance of movement as a dynamic force of the Universe. In the *Annunciation*, which was executed about a decade earlier, he used the light of evening, on the one hand to make the figure emerge, and on the other to emphasize the infinite distance of the horizon and of space; all this as nature seems to project itself into the mysterious silence of the night. The colour, immersing itself in the shadowy and luminous atmosphere, is alternately faded and enriched with pigment. In these two works, painted before his departure for Milan, Leonardo gave impetus to two new, equally important developments: with the *Annunciation*, to a new classicism, a harmony between man and nature that had never previously been attained; with the *Adoration of the Magi*, to the disruption of this harmony brought on by the anxiety of overwhelming situations and uncontainable forces.

VERROCCHIO (Andrea di Cione)
(Florence, 1435 - Venice, 1488)

LEONARDO DA VINCI
(Vinci, 1452 - Amboise, 1519)

Baptism of Christ *

Oil on wood, 180x152
1472x75

This is a fundamental work, though one tormented by historical vicissitudes. The rigidity of the dove and the archaic hands of God suggest that it may well have entered Verrocchio's workshop already prepared. Subsequently entrusted to some pupil, the painting was laid out in a traditional way, with two symmetrical margins at the sides and the figure of Christ in the middle. When Leonardo finally intervened he completely upset the symmetry of the composition by sawing off the left-hand margin, thus eliminating the centrality of Christ. He also did away with one of the rocky spurs and instead added a landscape of rivers and hills drenched in a dense, golden, vibrant light. Recent X-ray tests have confirmed the extent of Leonardo's participation. Whereas Vasari attributed only the figure of the angel to the Master, modern analysis has proved that he also worked on the landscape and the figure of Christ.

FRANCESCO BOTTICINI
(Florence, 1446 - 1498)

The Three Archangels

Tempera on wood, 153x154
ca. 1470

The elaborate, serpentine modelling of the drapery reveals that
the artist was under the influence of Verrocchio's style. But
although the figures are meticulously portrayed in all their details,
they have nothing of the impressive stature typical of Verrocchio.
In this painting the archangel Michael is so stiff in his shining
armour that he gives the impression of not moving at all, his left
foot appearing to be almost rooted to the ground. Raphael, leading
Tobit by the hand, has a disproportionate head and shoulders (too
narrow), while Gabriel has struck an affected pose that is
supposed to render him more gracious — all elements which are
absent in Verrocchio's decisive and straightforward style.

LORENZO DI CREDI
(Florence, 1459? - 1537)

Annunciation

Oil on wood, 88x71
ca. 1480-85

This small work is entirely based on the precise division of spaces
and surfaces and is valuable evidence of interior decoration
during this period (note the elegance of the carved wood which
was widely used in those years).
It almost seems as if the central theme is not so much the event
of the Annunciation as the room itself, which is entered by way of
the small step of the simulated predella, and which leads out
through a colonnade into an enchanting, orderly garden.

LEONARDO DA VINCI
(Florence, 1452 - Amboise, 1519)

Annunciation

Oil on wood, 98x217
1472-75

This Annunciation was traditionally attributed to Ghirlandaio and subsequently to Verrocchio. The prevailing view today is that the painting is an early work by Leonardo, this being suggested by the complex nature of the work which introduces many new elements. The composition, for example, is quite unsymmetrical. The angel bowing down in front of the Madonna is constructed along bisecting diagonal lines; in this way Leonardo avoids any temptation to arrange the two figures as complementary structural forms. A coastal city, its harbour full of boats, can be seen in a faraway hazy distance, a feature which, like the sumptuous drapery of the garments, derives from Flemish painting. The extraordinary flowering of the grass lawn, which has been called a herbarium, is depicted with such an eye for detail that it recalls the speculative, scientific vocation of Leonardo, a man of great realism.

LEONARDO DA VINCI
(Florence, 1452 - Amboise, 1519)

Adoration of the Magi

Tempera on wood, mixed with oil with parts of red and greenish lacquer, 243x246
1481-82

The painting was commissioned by the monks of San Donato a Scopeto and was left unfinished probably due to an incompatibility of intentions. The monks had asked Leonardo for a celebratory work destined for the public and therefore suited to performing a social as well as religious function, a traditional edifying work that could be appreciated by all. Leonardo composed the subject in an unconventional way, replacing the customary joyful atmosphere with a general air of consternation and dramatic tension. In the background he practised various artistic techniques: a study of perspective in the ruins, a research into the representation of movement in the group of mounted horsemen, and a study of naturalistic elements in the trees.

It seemed, therefore, that Leonardo left the painting unfinished and considered it finished once he had exhausted and resolved various questions of pictorial method and inner clarification. The work is in fact little more than a sketch, executed in yellowish and bistre tones, which actually heightens the emotional character of the crowd surrounding the Madonna, amazed above all by an event that appears enigmatic.

LUCA SIGNORELLI
(Cortona, ca. 1445 - 1523)

Crucifix with Mary Magdalen *

Oil on canvas, 247x165
1502-1505

This is a late work, one of those in which
the artist's academic training more
frequently makes its appearance.
Nevertheless, the painting has some fine
touches in spite of various elements of
discontinuity. The composition is based on
elements of theatricality, ennobled by a
simple, popularesque scheme. Grandiose
figures dominate the foreground: the
leaden body of Christ, barely covered by an
exotic, sophisticated loincloth, and the
splendid mass of colour that is Mary
Magdalen, the reds and blues of her clothes
set off by the cascading blonde hair that
spreads like a delicate filigree over her
shoulders.
On the right are the events that come after
the Crucifixion: note the Descent from the
Cross and the Transportation of the body
down the side of the hill.

LUCA SIGNORELLI
(Cortona, ca. 1445 - 1523)

Three predella panels

Oil on wood, 32,5x204.5
1510

The predella, on which the Last Supper, the Agony in the Garden and the Flagellation are depicted, completed the painting of the Trinity, the Virgin and Two Saints, and was commissioned to Luca Signorelli by the Confraternita dei Pellegrini of Cortona.
The composition is animated by the feeling of intense dramatic tension, both in the scene of the Flagellation, in which the artist has occasion to mould the athletic bodies of the two gaolers, as well as in the scene of the Agony in the Garden, which shows a feverish movement of armed soldiers in the background.
The third scene, the Last Supper, has a calmer quality, an effect produced by the large table around which all the other planes of the composition are constructed.

It was perhaps the profound contrast between this being ahead of his times and the Florentine environment, in which distinctly conservative forces prevailed (think of Ghirlandaio's workshop), that prompted Leonardo to leave for Milan.

Verrocchio's workshop established its reputation in the 1480s, during which time it drew two non-Florentine artists into its sphere of influence, both endowed with strong and distinctive personalities: Pietro Perugino and Luca Signorelli. The *Crucifixion*, painted by the two artists jointly, as a fairly widely accepted critical tradition would have it, or perhaps better, by Perugino alone, shows the artist's debt towards Verrocchio's teaching.

Signorelli, for his part, is represented at the Uffizi by some fairly late works: the roundel with the *Holy Family*, originally from the Palazzo di Parte Guelfa, the work with a somewhat complex structure, dominated by a roundel, representing the *Madonna and Child*, painted for Lorenzo di Pierfrancesco dei Medici (both works datable to the last decade of the fifteenth century), the *Crucifix with Mary Magdalen*, which already belongs to the first years of the sixteenth century, and still later the altar-

LUCA SIGNORELLI
(Cortona, ca. 1445 - 1523)

The Trinity, the Virgin and Two Saints

Tempera on wood, 272x180
1510

The painting was commissioned to Luca Signorelli by the Confraternita della Trinita dei Pellegrini of Cortona and shows a compact, tightly constructed composition. The Virgin and Child represent the central axis around which the Archangels Michael and Gabriel and Saints Augustine and Athanasius are grouped.
More rhetorical and at the same time archaizing is the glory of cherubim surrounding the symbolic apparition of the crucified Christ and God the Almighty.

piece of *The Trinity, the Virgin and Two Saints* with the *predella*. With the exception of the latter, which was in fact painted for Cortona and in which the contribution of assistants had a significant role, these paintings are of a very high level, revealing both the qualities and limitations of this artist. Signorelli's limitations consisted in his inability to modernize and in the fact that technique prevailed over the creative process. After the very first years of the sixteenth century he failed to adapt to the great innovations introduced by the masters of the second Renaissance: Leonardo, Michelangelo and Raphael. He remained irremediably attached to the old school, despite the fact that for thirty years he had painted works which even in Florence represented an absolute novelty and were remarkably popular because they satisfied that secure taste for plastic art that would shortly celebrate its triumph with Michelangelo. However, that there was a relationship between these two artists is demonstrated by the fact that Michelangelo certainly drew the idea for the figures in the background of the *Tondo Doni* from Signorelli's *Madonna and Child* for Lorenzo di Pierfrancesco dei Medici. Michelangelo's interest was probably aroused also by the roundel of the *Holy Family* for the Parte Guelfa, in which Signorelli had created a solemn convergence of imposing volumes. Even at the beginning of the first decade of the sixteenth century, the *Crucifixion with Mary Magdalen* was an image of enormous power.

No less original, even if completely different, was the personality of Pietro Perugino. His activity in Florence, which was carried out above all in the last decade of the fifteenth century, had a very important role in the birth of sixteenth-century Florentine classicism. Fra' Bartolomeo della Porta and Mariotto Albertinelli, who were the founders of this current, were inspired by him.

The first religious work Perugino executed in Florence was the *Agony in the Garden* for the church of San Giusto dei Gesuati (ca. 1492), an already classical painting worthy of Raphael. The figure of Christ, rising from below through a harmonious relationship of colour planes that blend the figures into the landscape, is set against a brightly-lit, distant sky. The composition thus takes on a pyramidal form. In his later works Perugino would establish some of the canons of early sixteenth-century Italian classicism.

One of the first unmistakable stylistic developments of the new century was in the use of colour. Following the example of Leonardo and Perugino, artists now used richer, softer, thicker paint mixtures. They sought a rapport with space that was no longer defined by perspective and mathematics, but was atmospheric. This yearning for new space and new distances, which at about the same time spurred Christopher Columbus to sail his caravels across the Ocean in search of new horizons, was present in the figurative arts and was manifested in the overcoming of the limits of Brunelleschi's perspective grid. A splendid example of this new union with nature, rendered with intense, vivid colours and a majestic pyramidal composition, is the *Immaculate Conception* by Piero di Cosimo (dating to just after the turn of the century). In this painting, as in the youthful works of Leonardo, to whom Piero di Cosimo was closely linked, there is another influence — the North European one — which led to the rediscovery of nature and light.

In *Perseus Frees Andromeda*, which according to Vasari was painted by Piero di Cosimo for Filippo Strozzi, the rediscovery of space, linked to nature and therefore atmospheric, was taken to such an advanced stage that it was transformed in a purely sixteenth-century sense. The broad landscape allowed a more complex and organized composition, but one that was at the same time fluid, united and harmonious. For this reason the painting would be better placed in the Tribune, where it was originally displayed.

Agony in the Garden: detail before restoration.

PERUGINO (Pietro Vannucci)
(Città della Pieve, ca. 1448 - Fontignano, 1523)

Agony in the Garden *

Oil on wood, 166x171
ca. 1492

The whole composition is based on rigorous principles of formal balance. The artist sets the
scene in a broad landscape that fades into the distance; the slopes of the hills act as scenic
wings and create a sheltered space in which Christ is portrayed praying above his sleeping
disciples. The figures balance each other symmetrically, with measured gestures and matching
postures.

Piero di Cosimo, Perseus Frees Andromeda: detail.

The North European influence which can be discerned in the painting of Perugino cannot be entirely explained by the presence of Hugo van der Goes' *Portinari Triptych*; it presupposes the knowledge of another Flemish painter — Hans Memling — who was active in Bruges. The link between him and the Florentine artistic environment was made by the great families of Florentine merchants and bankers who had trade links with the Flemish city: the Tani, Baroncelli and Portinari families. The celebrated *Last Judgement*, now in the Marienkirche in Danzig, was painted for Angelo Tani in 1470-73 and was intended for a church in Florence. Benedetto Portinari commissioned the diptych with his own portrait and *Saint Benedict* in prayer, now hanging in the Uffizi. Memling painted the *Ascent to Calvary* of Turin as well as the two portraits of the Metropolitan Museum for Tommaso Portinari and his wife Maria Baroncelli, while a painter associated with him, although very distinctive, the so-called Master of the Baroncelli Portraits, executed the Uffizi *Portraits of Pierantonio Baroncelli and his wife Maria Bonciani*.

Memling's other paintings, which arrived at the Uffizi later on and now enrich the gallery's collections, are important expressions of both the qualities of this painter and the influence he had on Italian art. A painting like the *Portrait of a Man* was the model which Pietro Perugino in central Italy and Giovanni Bellini in Venice used to produce works in which the figure portrayed was in some way linked to the landscape. The *Portrait of Benedetto Portinari* had the same effect as regards the three-quarter profile and half-figure portrait.

The small painting representing the *Madonna and Child Enthroned with Two Angels* portrays the figures grouped beneath a baldachin whose backdrop opens onto two views of wooded landscapes, a castle and a country house, views characterized by passages from penumbra to light. It is a painting that could well have been familiar to Fra' Bartolomeo

PIERO DI COSIMO (Piero di Lorenzo) Florence?, 1461/62 - 1521)

Perseus Frees Andromeda

Oil on wood, 70x123
ca. 1515

None of Piero di Cosimo's works are signed or dated, making a reconstruction of his stylistic development extremely tentative The dating of this Andromeda Frees Perseus is therefore unclear, although critics are generally agreed that it is a work of the artist's maturity since it contains stylistic elements reflecting the transition to sixteenth-century art: the presence of Leonardesque "sfumato", the Raphaelesque typology of the figures and the proto-Mannerist character of the overall structure.

PIERO DI COSIMO (Piero di Lorenzo)
(Florence?, 1461/62 - 1521)

Immaculate Conception with Six Saints

Oil on wood, 206x172
ca. 1505

Initially close to Filippino Lippi and
Leonardo, the artist dedicated himself
particularly to easel painting and interior
decorations. He was fascinated by the
Portinari Triptych and shows in his work
that he was influenced both by the taste
for detail typical of Flemish painting and
by fifteenth-century perspective. Since
both currents aimed at objective truth,
Piero di Cosimo found an element of
cohesion in the rendering of a luminous
atmosphere.
Note the symmetrical arrangement of the
figures and the landscape, the latter formed
by two steep rocky hills on which the
episodes of the Birth of Christ, the
Annunciation of the Shepherds and the
Flight into Egypt are taking place at the
same time as the scene in the foreground.

HANS MEMLING
(Seligenstadt, ca. 1435 - Bruges, 1494)

Madonna and Child Enthroned with Two Angels

Oil on wood, 57x42
ca. 1480

One of the finest examples of this iconography that the artist left
us, this painting forms part of a group of works with the subject of
Mary characterized by the presence of an arched frame.
Memling was discovered by the German romantics, who were
enchanted by the delicate poetry of his works. They even saw him
as a northern counterpart of Beato Angelico, a spirit pervaded with
ecstatic religiosity.
The Madonna — this of the Virgin between two angels is a
recurrent theme in his art — is portrayed with a balanced, placid,
gentle demeanour. The landscape is perfect in its delicacy, and the
character of the work is produced by the sense of elegiac peace,
by an extraordinary compositional balance, and by the almost
timeless and enchanted atmosphere.

Hans Memling, Madonna and Child Enthroned with Two Angels: detail.

HANS MEMLING
(Seligenstadt, ca. 1435 - Bruges, 1494)

Portrait of a Man

Oil on wood, 35x25
ca. 1490

As a portraitist, Memling was highly esteemed by the well-to-do
families of Bruges. He knew how to arrange his sitters, ennobling
their demeanour, idealizing their features and softening their
expression. This small oil painting forms part of a series of delightful
portraits kept at the Uffizi and, until recently, not studied sufficiently.

Andrea Mantegna, Circumcision: detail.

and Mariotto Albertinelli, who drew inspiration from it both stylistically and thematically. A lucid and yet at the same time soft painting (in whose realization on the part of the Flemish artist an Italian, and more precisely a Leonardesque influence cannot be excluded), it had qualities aimed at exploiting the new fullness of volumes which Florentine artists of the new generation felt as indispensable to their world.

The great chapter of the Renaissance in northern Italy starts with Andrea Mantegna, a chapter which in the Uffizi, as far as the fifteenth century is concerned, is poorly represented. This is understandable when one considers the circumstances in which the Gallery was created, linked as it was to the post-sixteenth-century phase of the Medici collections, to the Lorraine period and to the collection of art works deriving from the suppression of the Florentine churches.

The presence of three masterpieces by Mantegna — the *Portrait of Carlo dei Medici*, the *Triptych* with the Adoration of the Magi and the *Madonna and Child* — is attributable both to the artist's stay in Florence in 1466, and to contacts made later, and above all to the numerous links that existed between the Gonzaga family and Florence. The three paintings belong to Mantegna's Mantuan period, a period which saw the artist engaged with all his energies in creating a new world in which Humanism became fully a part of the patrimony of both nature and civilization (i.e. of all human manifestations). Nature became rock or crystal; fields when they existed were of jade; buildings were built of precious coloured marbles, eternal symbols of profound meanings understandable only to the humanist, to the man who had studied and who knew the secrets of man himself and history. Man was the centre of the universe and his power was absolute; such was the significance of a portrait like that of Carlo dei Medici, carved into agate and sardonyx. But *humanitas* was expressed fully only when there was 'religion': then the figures were sublimated by a Virgilian *pietas*: whence derives that softness pervading the faces of the sacred figures portrayed in the three evangelical stories of the triptych and in the *Madonna and Child*.

To conclude our survey of fifteenth-century art in central Italy there

ANDREA MANTEGNA
(Isola di Carturo, 1431 - Mantua, 1506)

Triptych

Tempera on wood, 86x161.5 (overall)
1460-70

Circumcision (right panel)

Tempera on wood, 86x42.5
1464-70

Critics have suggested that this triptych,
whose dating is a difficult and
controversial issue, may correspond to
some of the "stories" seen by Vasari in the
Cappella del Castello in Mantua, and
surmise therefore that this is where it
came from. The three panels, in the
possession of the Medici family from 1587,
and portraying (from right to left) the
Circumcision, the Adoration of the Magi
and the Ascension, vary in both style and
dimension. However, one characteristic
common to them all is the meticulous,
crystalline pictorial style typical of the
artist's late Paduan period, and in any case
not datable to much later than the
beginning of his subsequent stay in
Mantua.
The episode takes place in a room
decorated with polychrome marbles,
friezes and intarsias, an elegant and ornate
setting which could almost be a Roman
temple depicted in response to a
passionate taste for classical antiquity. A
religious subject treated, as was the artist's
custom, more as a pretext for portraying
antiquity than for the expression of
genuine Christian feeling.

ANDREA MANTEGNA
(Isola di Carturo, 1431 - Mantua, 1506)

Triptych

Tempera on wood, 86x161.5 (overall)
1460-70

Ascension (left panel)

Tempera on wood, 86X42.5
ca. 1460

Of the three paintings the Ascension is
perhaps the one in which the austerity and
mystical dimension inherent in scenes of a
religious subject most clearly come to the
fore.
The sculptural figures of the Madonna and
Apostles in the foreground are given a
distinct characterization, and yet at the
same time are portrayed in attitudes of
bewildered and ecstatic adoration. The
monumental figure of Christ triumphant
stands against a leaden sky enlivened by the
fiery red heads of the angels encircling the
Saviour. These coloured fragments of
paradise also crown the grotto and
surround the Madonna in the scene of the
Adoration of the Magi.

Adoration of the Magi (central panel)

Tempera on wood, 76x76.5
1462-63

The main event has been shifted away from
the centre and is represented on the right
of the scene, leaving plenty of space for the
surrounding landscape and the procession
of the Magi. A panoply of human types,
from fine-looking youths to stern, imposing
old men. As in the other two works, the
composition is sustained by a miniaturism
of Flemish inspiration and by the unusual
splendour of the extremely varied range of
colours.

remains only to present the most important works executed in Florence in the last decade of the century by Pietro Perugino. In addition, alongside the paintings by Luca Signorelli (already recorded) and Pietro Perugino, there is in the Gallery a group of artists from the Marches and neighbouring Romagna, including Bologna, which is part of Emilia, but which in those years gravitated culturally towards central Italy.

Perugino's altarpiece representing the *Madonna and Child with Saints John the Baptist and Sebastian*, from the church of San Domenico near Fiesole, when it was completed and displayed to the public it was a significant expression of the innovations which the artist had brought to Florentine art. For the first time, in fact, Leonardo's *sfumato* had been combined with pale colours and well-defined tints which clearly revealed its derivation from Piero della Francesca, an artist who Perugino, whose native town was Città della Pieve, undoubtedly knew well.

The draughtsmanship, the composition, the gestures, the architecture, everything is reduced to an extreme simplicity without it losing the harmony which is conveyed through the even shading of the modelled forms. The figures dominate the scene against the background of a sober, monumental structure formed of arches and vaults, maintaining the grace of their movements intact. At this point the distinction between Perugino and the very young Raphael is almost non-existent; and without the example of the painter from Città della Pieve, Fra' Bartolomeo together with Mariotto Albertinelli would never have executed that *Last Judgement* in fresco in the hospital of Santa Maria Nuova, a work which although painted in the very last years of the Quattrocento ushered in the new classicism of the sixteenth century.

Perugino dedicated much of his energy in Florence to portraiture, breathing new life into this art form from both the expressive and the compositional and structural point of view. In the *Portrait of Francesco delle Opere* the person portrayed is immersed in the landscape in an atmospheric, compositional and psychological communion. With reference to Hans Memling we have already mentioned the importance of the influence of Flemish painting in this regard. More traditional, on the other hand, is the scheme for the *Portrait of a Young Man*, in which the face is turned towards us with a soft, mysterious expression charged with meaning. A soft colouring, at once drenched in light and yet immersed in shadow, gives the figure movement and pulls it further into the foreground.

Perugino also painted two profile portraits, adopting a scheme that had been popular throughout the fifteenth century: these were portraits of two famous Vallombrosan monks, *Don Biagio Milanesi* and *Don Baldassare*. The profile portrait probably reflected an interest in reviving the classical model of the medal, which in the sixteenth century would be favoured in sculptutre.

One of the artists from the Marches was Girolamo Genga, a pupil and assistant of Luca Signorelli. Genga transformed Signorelli's art in a sixteenth-century sense, as can be seen in the *Martyrdom of Saint Sebastian* (a work of the artist's youth), first softening his master's hard, aggressive plasticism with a more shaded chiaroscuro, then incorporating North European influences that would lead him towards anti-classical tendencies.

The Marches are an Adriatic region, and as such enjoyed close relations with Romagna. Two artists from Romagna worked there: Melozzo da Forlì and Marco Palmezzano, also from Forlì. While the former is represented here with a fragmentary *Annunciation*, which the Gallery purchased on the antiques market, Palmezzano painted a splendid *Crucifixion* for the sacristy of the church of Monteoliveto outside Porta San Frediano in Florence, now also at the Uffizi. This painting showed clear traces of the influence of Giovanni Bellini's art after 1480.

PERUGINO (Pietro Vannucci)
(Città della Pieve, ca 1448 - Fontignano, 1523)

Madonna and Child with Saints *

Tempera on wood, 178x164
1493

Pietro Vannucci, called Perugino, was trained in two great traditions, that of Piero della Francesca — whom he knew indirectly from the artist's numerous works in Umbria, the Marches and Tuscany — and that of Verrocchio, whose pupil he was in Florence between 1470 and 1472.
In this canvas, the representation is built up according to an extremely rigorous compositional structure. Balance is the dominant note. This is suggested by the arrangement of the two saints in relation to the Virgin, and underlined by the centrality of the simple decorated parallelepipedon, the loggia supported by bare pilasters and the perfect cross vault. A vast landscape in the background, which lets in the light, clearly reveals the influence of Piero della Francesca. The painting is signed and dated on the block.

PERUGINO (Pietro Vannucci)
(Città della Pieve, ca 1448 - Fontignano, 1523)

Portrait of Francesco delle Opere

Oil on wood, 52x44
1494

According to an annotation on the back of the painting this work,
rightly celebrated, is a portrait of Francesco delle Opere, the
Florentine artisan who was the brother of the gem-engraver
Giovanni delle Corniole. The man, who has a serene and dignified
expression, is portrayed as a bust and is harmoniously balanced with
the sweeping landscape behind him, possibly a view of Lake
Trasimeno.

PERUGINO (Pietro Vannucci)
(Città della Pieve, ca 1448 - Fontignano, 1523)

Pietà *

Oil on wood, 168x176
1494-95

This painting shows Christ lying across the Virgin's knees and held
up by Mary Magdalen and a saint, thought by some to be John the
Evangelist, by others Saint Joseph. Immediately behind them, at the
sides, stand two saints of unknown identity. The figures, their faces
suffused with the gentle melancholy characteristic of Perugino's
art, are grouped within a perspectively defined arcade that opens
onto a brightly-lit landscape.

LUCA SIGNORELLI
(Cortona, ca. 1445 - 1523)

Holy Family

*Oil on wood, diam. 124
1490-91*

Another roundel representing a religious subject of long-standing tradition, in which Signorelli appears to react provocatively to the contemporary achievements of Sandro Botticelli. The figures seem to have been squeezed unnaturally into the form of the roundel. The Madonna especially tends to force the limits of the roundel with the lower part of her body, emphasized by the ample folds of the drapery. The Child, almost hemmed in by the two larger figures, is the ideal fulcrum around which the entire composition revolves.

Unlike Botticelli, however, who dematerialized his figures in a kind of fluttering lyricism, Signorelli exalts their plasticity. The space taken up by the landscape, which frames the group, is extremely scanty, indeed almost non-existent. The figures alone dominate the composition, in a plastic exaltation which is a foretaste of Michelangelo's heroic vision.

LUCA SIGNORELLI
(Cortona, ca. 1445 - 1523)

Madonna and Child with Allegorical
Figures

Oil on wood, 170x117.5
diameter of inner roundel 117.5
1490

The already demanding structure of the composition is further complicated, in the upper part, by the false reliefs of the Prophets, executed in grisaille and inserted in the roundels flanking the figure of Christ, below which, in the traditional scroll, we read "ECCE AGNUS DEI".
The figure of the Madonna is inserted into the roundel in a singularly anomalous fashion, constructed on various planes and subjected to numerous torsions of the body.
In the foreground we note a naturalistic abandon, reminiscent of Leonardo, in the cluster of flowers which encloses the group.
Signorelli uses the space behind the Madonna to express classical themes popular with the culture of his time. Sturdy young shepherds play flutes in a bucolic atmosphere against the background of a rocky landscape dotted with ruins, which evoke the opulence of a fabulous intellectually reinterpreted civilization.

LORENZO DI ALESSANDRO DI SANSEVERINO
(Sanseverino Marche, doc. 1468-1503)

Pietà

Tempera on wood, 62x158
ca. 1491

Lorenzo di Alessandro di Sanseverino is certainly one of the leading exponents of the art of the Marches, a region whose art we are familiar with in a rather summary way and whose artists have lacked adequate critical appraisal.
This "Pietà" is a lucid work, but one in which the tension characterizing much of Lorenzo's art is barely able to emerge, frozen as it is by an excessive, rather over-sweet sentimentalism and the intensely contorted line.

Luca Signorelli, Madonna and Child with Allegorical Figures: detail.

At the beginning of the sixteenth century Florence, yearning for renewed energy, opened to the painting of northern Italy. Lorenzo Costa, whose *Saint Sebastian* of the Uffizi has divided the critics, was an artist from Ferrara, who worked a great deal in Bologna. His painting reveals that at this time the city was a meeting-place of Venetian and central Italian influences (particularly Perugino).

Even more closely associated with the artist of Città della Pieve was Francesco Francia, the leading name in Bolognese painting in the decades that straddled the turn of the century, as the severe, classical *Portrait of Evangelista Scappi* demonstrates — so obviously in fact that it requires no further explanation.

The three paintings (the *Portrait of a Young Man*, the *Sacred Allegory* and the *Lamentation over the Dead Christ*) by the great father figure of Venetian painting in the fifteenth century, Giovanni Bellini,

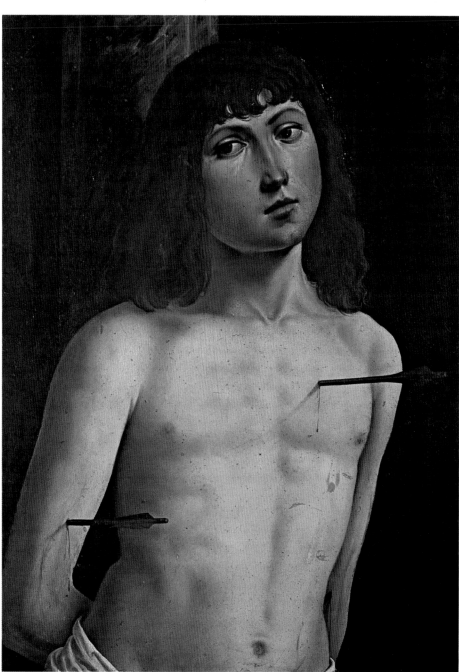

LORENZO COSTA
(Ferrara, ca 1460 - 1535)

Saint Sebastian

Tempera on wood, 55x49
1490-91

This is a highly controversial painting.
Some critics regard it as a work of great
beauty; others play down its importance,
claiming that the saint, although displaying
an undeniable beauty of form, has no
particular facial expression, being nothing
more than a simple reproduction of the
youth who served as the artist's model.

entered the Gallery in the second half and at the end of the 18th century, the reason evidently being the desire to fill in the Gallery's most conspicuous artistic lacunae. Today these invaluable acquisitions give us, without our having to leave Florence, a fairly comprehensive understanding of the basic aspects of the art of this remarkable painter.

The painting of northern Italy, on the other hand, is for the most part represented by 20th-century acquisitions, which provide only brief glimpses of a regional tradition. For this reason it would be useful to place them in their historical context, without taking away the anthological character which by now they have assumed in the Gallery.

The *Saint Dominic* by Cosmè Tura and the *Saint Louis of Toulouse* by Bartolommeo Vivarini remind us that the birth of the Renaissance in northern Italy was marked by Donatello's arrival and long stay in Padua between about 1444 and 1450. However, the arrival of a sculptor would never have provoked such far-reaching and definitive consequences in painting had there not existed in Padua the workshop of Squarcione, where young artists from the surrounding area gathered, attracted by the presence of classical archeological finds, epigraphs and sculptures. The young artists of Squarcione's workshop were therefore already predisposed to studying sculpture.

Around the middle of the century an exceptional group of artists assembled in Padua: Andrea Mantegna, who was the first and who shortly afterwards assumed the role of master, Cosmè Tura, who was to become the founder of Ferrarese painting, Vincenzo Foppa, the creator of the Lombard Renaissance, and the great painters of Romagna and the Marches — Bono da Ferrara, Ansuino da Forlì and Girolamo di Giovanni da Camerino. Through the early activity of Mantegna, the painter of the Venetian lagoon, the Muranese Bartolommeo Vivarini and the future founder of Venetian painting, Giovanni Bellini, started their artistic activity in the Paduan environment.

Tura's *Saint Dominic*, however much a late work, is a moving expression of the climate of enthusiasm and heroic creative tension aroused in Padua by Donatello's bronze figures for the high altar of the Basilica of Sant'Antonio. However, Donatello's model was profoundly personalized and transfigured. The image of power and vitality expressed by Donatello's sculptures is replaced by that of an inner torment that enflames and at the same time freezes the pictorial material. A tormented use of light seems to carve into the colours and forms with little blows of the chisel. The saint's head is bowed and turned in on itself, oblivious of the surrounding reality.

The Muranese artist Bartolommeo Vivarini is linked instead to the meeting and fusion of Donatello's influence with the art of Mantegna. His adhesion to the plastic, dynamic and spatial ideals of the Renaissance is evident, as is revealed by the *Saint Louis of Toulouse*, which must certainly have formed one of the upper panels of a polyptych.

The birth and subsequent development of Giovanni Bellini's pictorial activity in the second half of the fifteenth century was one of the most important events in the history of both Italian and European art. His distinctive personality and talent were at the root of Venetian painting of the Renaissance, in other words one of the solid cornerstones and points of reference for European painters up to the historical avant-gardes.

Observing the three works by Giovanni Bellini displayed in the Uffizi, it seems almost impossible that Mantegna's harsh plasticism lay at the root of his artistic training, since the paintings are the expression of a totally different philosophical vision and artistic style. And yet the splendid *Lamentation over the Dead Christ* retains the distant memory of Donatello's dramatic compositions and Mantegna's severe style. Here the meaning is quite different. A warm, soft light envelops the group soothingly. The gestures have become solemn, the expressions com-

GIAMBELLINO (Giovanni Bellini)
(Venice, 1425-30 - 1516)

Lamentation over the Dead Christ

Tempera on wood, 74x118
ca. 1500

Son of Jacopo and brother of Gentile, Giovanni began his artistic career in his father's
workshop. Although consistently attributed to Giambellino, the unusual technique has raised
some doubts over the painting's authorship. Some critics have interpreted it a preparation
that was never painted, but the formal perfection suggests that it is a finished work, an image
of intense religious feeling which Bellini deliberately rendered with a chaste chiaroscuro.
The composition is of a complex simplicity with the figures solemnly arranged around the
body of the dead Christ.
As in the Brera Pietà, the expressions on the faces of the onlooking figures convey a sense of
grievous dismay for the Mystery that has been consumed, the mystery of nature, birth and
death.

posed: a certainty has been re-established which surpasses all grief. This work, thought to have been painted in 1500, came at the end of man's age of discovery and at the beginning of another age that sought to sublimate man in God's image (and for some years — between 1500 and 1515 — miraculously succeeded).

The sublimation of man capable of shaping nature is represented in Bellini's *Sacred Allegory*. The centre of the composition is occupied by a vast stage surrounded by a balustrade. The pavement is constructed along lines of perspective which converge towards a vanishing point in the hills and valleys beyond. Nature thus becomes an integral part of the work and of the presence of man. Numerous influences were required for Giovanni Bellini to execute this small painting, from Piero della Francesca's "synthesis of form and colour" to the soft, luminous painting of Northern Europe and the solemn forms of Antonello da Messina's Italian classicism. In this work design does not exist as an independent means of style and expression, but serves only as a verification of space. Everything is created with the brush, which composes the colours directly on the palette and then transposes them in the painting. At the level of style, technique and content, this *Sacred Allegory* is the foundation of the Venetian school and can stand alongside Giorgione's *Tempest*, which was executed no more than five or six years later.

Without a painting like this we would scarcely have arrived at the Bacchanals of Titian, and those of Poussin, and so on throughout the entire course of modern painting.

The *Portrait of a Young Man* also reveals the high point of Bellini's achievement. Here the plastic quality of the form is rendered with colour in a fully experienced accord between man and nature — the fullness and fluffiness of the clouds, and the puffy face and thick red hair

GIAMBELLINO (Giovanni Bellini)
(Venice, 1425-30 - 1516)

Sacred Allegory

Oil on wood, 73x119
1490-1500

This work by Bellini is undoubtedly one of the most fascinating and enigmatic paintings of the Italian Quattrocento, not so much because of its formal perfection, but for the still unknown significance of the allegory represented. Saint Paul is depicted beyond the balustrade of the brightly-lit terrace, while Saint Job and Saint Sebastian are shown worshipping the Child. A young woman wearing a crown is praying in front of the Virgin, while another woman wearing a dark cloak seems to be watching, or looking after, the children playing. A mysterious bend of a river, or a coastal inlet, suggests even more intensely a metaphysical or religious meaning, which is further emphasized by the figures of the shepherd and centaur in the background.

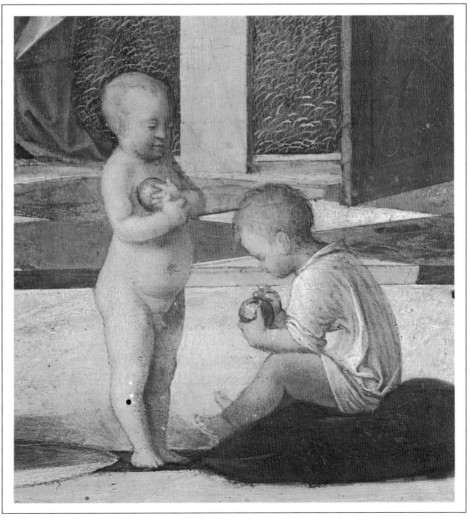

Giovanni Bellini, Sacred Allegory: detail.

IOANNES BELLINVS

GIAMBELLINO (Giovanni Bellini)
(Venice, 1425-30 - 1516)

Portrait of a Young Man

Oil on wood, 31x26
1500

This work, along with the Portrait of a Young Man conserved in the Galleria Capitolina, is recorded in the Inventories of 1753 as a self-portrait, and as such it continues to be regarded, even though this supposition lacks any scientific foundation. The portrait is highly distinctive, the face having a mellow, moulded quality accentuated by its halo of soft curls and the round clouds which fill the sky in the background.

of the young man.

Giovanni Bellini's greatness was also measured by the influence he had on the Venetian artistic environment, for he inspired one of the most important artistic explosions of all time. We need only recall those masters that are today represented at the Uffizi, like Carpaccio and Cima da Conegliano.

A new civilization was founded, based on the love of nature in itself, as a reference point for man and as a reflection of God's perfection; and together with nature, man and his magnificent works were loved with the same intensity. Even fragmentary paintings like Carpaccio's *Halberdiers* show a vast range of interests towards society and its customs, and towards the aspects which form and accompany its social life. All this variety, as the artists themselves would theorize in the sixteenth century, would find expression in colour and painting.

The arrival of Giorgione from his home in Castelfranco Veneto gave Venice the possibility of creating a style that was more advanced in the expression of even the formal qualities of reality. He was responsible for elaborating an artistic style that was no different from the one Leonardo had developed in Florence twenty years earlier. Vasari, indeed, has no hesitation in placing Giorgione immediately next to Leonardo among the founders of the third age — the age of perfection.

CIMA DA CONEGLIANO (Giovan Battista Cima)
(Conegliano, ca. 1460 - 1517-18)

Madonna and Child

Tempera on wood, 66x57
ca. 1504

There is no really reliable information concerning the formation and early activity of this painter, who was to a large extent responsible for the spread of the artistic culture of Venice throughout Venetian territory. This painting, probably a late work, is characterized by its serenity and balance and its extraordinary formal and expressive composure.

LORENZO COSTA
(Ferrara, ca. 1460 - 1535)

Portrait of Giovanni Bentivoglio

*Tempera on wood, 55x49
ca. 1492*

This signed work is one of the most well-known of Lorenzo Costa's artistic production. In the portrait of Bentivoglio there is obviously a sound knowledge of Antonello da Messina's style, but what really dominates is the solidity and sculptural relief of the form, which Costa draws from Venetian painting. This is visible in the sturdy build of the whole figure, the imposing neck, and the well-placed head. Costa, who moved to Bologna from his native Ferrara in 1482, was one of the most interesting and modern exponents of Northern painting in this period.

For the sixteenth century form was above all volume, not the drawing which defines a surface, nor made exclusively linear as in the fifteenth century. Giorgione's problem was to give volume to both the figures and the landscape. This is evident in the paintings of the Uffizi (which are works of the artist's youth): *Moses Undergoes Trial By Fire* and *The Judgement of Solomon*. Here both nature and man acquire their own solidity due to the presence of a clearly defined chiaroscuro, however much the latter may be defined in the *impasto* of the colour and therefore fused with the material in such a way as to give a sense of throbbing continuity to their rapport. The use of chiaroscuro and *sfumato* suggests that a connection may have existed between Leonardo and Giorgione, a link made culturally possible by the presence of the Tuscan master in Lombardy and also in Venice.

The vertical format of these two paintings is also modern. It would be preferred in the sixteenth century because it responded better to new ways of composing the pictorial image and representing space.

Space was no longer represented through a fixed focus perspective but by a moving lens which was the human eye, an eye able to choose a position which best enabled it to appreciate the vastness of the landscape and the central position of man.

The painting *Warrior with Equerry* belongs instead to the late period of Giorgione, who was certainly responsible for its conception. The attribution of its execution to Cavazzola does nothing to diminish the importance of the work. It is in fact an example of that painting with a half-length figure against a plain background which Vasari celebrated as extremely modern. Although almost certainly a portrait, the painting was interpreted and composed in the manner of a genre figure, and is thus a foretaste of a particular type of art characteristic of the seventeenth century. The foreshortening gives the figures a monumental stature, the atmosphere and tone of which are harmoniously rendered by a series of contrasts between large areas of darkness and shimmering touches of light.

GIORGIONE (Zorzon da Castelfranco)
(attributed to)
(Castelfranco Veneto, ca. 1477 - Venice 1510)

Portrait of a Man in Armour with Equerry *

The problem of this painting's attribution has also been particularly troublesome: the names of Michele da Verona, Caroto and Cavazzola have all been advanced. The most recent studies attribute it to Giorgione, or as an old copy from a lost original by Giorgione. For a long time erroneously identified as a portrait of Gattamelata, the painting undoubtedly appears to be of Giorgionesque origin, particularly owing to the general tone of calm melancholy that is expressed by the face of the warrior, despite a subject that should instead suggest force and virility. It is a painting of good quality, as can be seen from the original form of the composition, from the strange posture of the two figures, from the use the artist makes of the light, glimmering on the polished armour, yet at the same time a vigorous constructor of facial planes. However, undoubtedly what most strikes one particularly in this painting of uncertain authorship is the solemn expression of the handsome captain with his archangel's face, who, as he emphatically clasps the hilt of his sword, seems intent on more elevated concerns. The succession of planes of light and shadow almost annuls the depth of the painting, despite the fact that the scene is complex and complicated by the different positions of the various pieces of armour in the foreground.

GIORGIONE (Zorzon da Castelfranco)
(Castelfranco Veneto, ca. 1477 - Venice, 1510)

Moses Undergoes Trial by Fire *
The Judgement of Solomon *

Oil on wood, 89x72 (each panel)
ca. 1502-03

Little is known about the life and works of this great painter, who died at an early age in Venice. We know
for certain that he studied with Giovanni Bellini, though Bellini was certainly not the only source of his
artistic education since he was described by the writers of his time as a cultured person, with interests
that ranged from painting to poetry; he was therefore a true gentleman-painter.
Giorgione's deeply meditative approach was reflected in the biblical, literary and cultural themes he
depicted, even though the mysterious meanings of many of his works escaped his contemporaries, even

Vasari. However, despite the fact that his paintings were frequently impossible to decipher, their extremely high quality was widely appreciated.

Giorgione signalled a turning-point in Venetian art, a change reflected in the new importance given to the landscape, which was represented with delicate changes of light and colour.

In "Moses Undergoes Trial by Fire", a rare subject, the newborn Moses is subjected to a test of fire for having trampled on the Pharaoh's crown. The theme is a subtle one and the general conception is complex, as is the background landscape to which much space is devoted. In spite of the divergent opinions over the attribution of the painting to Giorgione, we can safely say that the general layout was by the master. The broad landscape in the upper part of the composition is particularly impressive, with the scenic wing formed by the trees, the blue river and the gently undulating hills receding into the distance.

The critical history of "The Judgement of Solomon" is closely linked to "Moses Undergoes Trial by Fire", of which it forms the companion-piece, although art historians have tended to appreciate it less. The poetic and contemplative quality of the Moses is here too, but the pictorial quality is different, especially in the drapery of the figures, an element which has given rise to oscillating and controversial attributions.

NORTH EUROPEAN PAINTING

Maria Grazia Ciardi Dupré dal Poggetto

Vasari narrates that when Michelangelo entered the workshop of Domenico Ghirlandaio as an apprentice he was greatly attracted by an engraving by the German artist Martin Schongauer representing the *Temptations of Saint Anthony Abbot*. Indeed, the first relations and exchanges between Germany and central and northern Italy date from the last decade of the fifteenth century.

The protagonist of the first journey to Italy was Albrecht Dürer of Nuremberg, who subsequently became the founder of the German Renaissance.

The five paintings by Dürer at the Uffizi are important examples of this painter's art, both because they represent the various phases of his artistic activity and because of the variety of themes depicted. The *Portrait of the Artist's Father* (signed and dated 1490) is the first known painting by the artist which reveals his knowledge of Flemish painting through the filter of the German tradition (particularly the engravings of Schongauer and the Meister des Hausbuches). It also already shows great qualities, the moulded quality of the form, the draughtsmanship, and the penetrating realism.

The *Adoration of the Magi*, dated 1504 and monogrammed, belongs to a mature phase, in which the artist shows that he has assimilated the teachings of the Italian Renaissance which he had known during his first journey to Italy in 1494-95. We might call it the first religious composition of the German Renaissance. In fact, Italian influences — particularly Venetian — have given the composition a more complex structure. It is centralized and yet organized in depth, even if the Virgin is placed on a horizontal axis, in a classical profile pose. The perspective organization of the space and the colours built up in broad zones are also Italian. All these elements are moulded with an intense vital force, which transforms the Flemish micrography into an incessant volumetric definition. The combination of these apparently contrasting effects was made possible by the artist's exceptional experience which ranged from ink drawing and tinted paper to woodcuts and copperplate engraving.

Another example of it is the *Calvary* displayed in the Gallery, and executed in pen and brush with highlights in white lead on dark green-tinted paper, dated 1505. The painting forms part of the *Green Passion*, the

Portrait of the Artist's Father: detail before restoration.

ALBRECHT DÜRER
(Nuremberg, 1471 - 1528)

Portrait of the Artist's Father *

Oil on wood
47.5x39.5
1490

The figure of Albrecht Dürer dominated that period in Germany straddling the fifteenth and sixteenth centuries which many consider the equivalent of the Italian Renaissance.
This portrait of the artist's father, the goldsmith Albrecht, is an early work, executed when the painter was only nineteen. Even at this tender age, Dürer flaunts his own personal style, even though it still shows a certain stiffness in the studied workmanship.
Following the example of the Flemish school the artist meticulously renders every detail of the face, though in the manner of Van Eyck does not overlook the importance of large forms and simple volumes. Already in this early work the artist goes beyond Flemish portraiture, which was intended as a document, and presents us instead with the image of a Renaissance figure charged with human and psychological expression that speaks of life, history and aspirations.

other eleven sheets of which are at the Albertina. This drawing represents the great synthesis of North European narrative experiences with the crystallographic, volumetric and perspective definition of the Italian Renaissance.

The two heads painted in tempera on canvas representing *The Apostles Philip and James* belong to Dürer's late period. They attest splendidly to the artist's assimilation of the Italian Renaissance, which was consolidated during his second stay in Italy between 1505 and 1507. As previously he took up residence in Venice, but here, especially through drawings, he also became familiar with Tuscan art and in particular Leonardo. In 1506 he probably met Michelangelo during a visit to Bologna. However, the two heads of the Uffizi — ample, solemn and contemplative — reveal above all his close adhesion to the classicism of Giovanni Bellini's late period. The great German master had finally conquered not only the formal qualities but also the ethical values of classical art.

But anyone interested in fully appreciating Dürer's remarkable achievement in mastering the canons of classical beauty, through the Italians, in an attempt to give Germany a modern artistic foundation, should observe the splendid replicas (unautographed, but possibly by Hans Baldung Grien) of the *Adam* and *Eve* of 1507 (the originals are at

ALBRECHT DÜRER
(Nuremberg, 1471 - 1528)

Adoration of the Magi

Oil on wood
99x113.5
1504

In this work the angularity and the accentuated, Gothic-inspired elongation of forms typical of earlier works disappear, and instead Dürer's contemplative spirit suggested by Italian art comes to the fore, permeating the whole scene with a gentle, moving beauty.
The extremely celebrated painting is highly representative of Dürer's art since it blends perfectly the various aspects of his artistic character: a predilection for the perfect execution of the image, a nimble, incisive and vibrant line, and the study of problems connected with perspective.

ALBRECHT DÜRER
(Nuremberg, 1471 - 1528)

Calvary

Pen and brush with highlights in white
lead on green-tinted paper
58x40
1505

Although this Calvary does not reach the
sweeping heights which distinguish the
artist's greatest works, it is nonetheless a
splendid composition notable for the
almost dizzying effect of perspective
produced by the feverish crowd of tiny
figures arranged in a number of different
planes. The line is vibrant and serpentine,
and the figures and landscape are rendered
with a vigour that would be difficult not to
attribute to Albrecht Dürer.
The Calvary, together with another eleven
drawings conserved at the Albertina in
Vienna, comprise the "Green Passion".

ALBRECHT DÜRER
(Nuremberg, 1471 - 1528)

Madonna and Child with a Pear

Oil on wood
43x31
1526

This is one of Dürer's later works, and can therefore be placed at the end of the period in
which the artist journeyed tirelessly from one end of Europe to the other in the incessant
search for new stimuli and new knowledge. An obvious reflection of it is the remarkable
change that is visible in the treatment of the forms, which in this painting are round and fully
sixteenth century and arranged in the space of the composition with absolute confidence,
and the complex play of complementary curves created by the movement of the arms and
hands of the Child.

HANS BALDUNG GRIEN
(Schwäbisch Gmünd, 1484-5 - Strasbourg, 1545)

Adam and Eve

Oil on wood
212x85 (each panel)

Hans Baldung Grien was probably the greatest and most talented of Dürer's pupils, his works being expressions of both an artistic and spiritual intensity. He exulted particularly in his interest for the female nude, a subject which he treated several times and portrayed in a dramatic confrontation with death and therefore with the frailty of the body, thus offering up a macabre interpretation of the classical theme of *vanitas*.
The two figures are given solidity and cultured, gracious expressions emerge from their faces, thus revealing the painter's interest for Italian Renaissance art. Baldung Grien was in fact a man of high culture; born into an educated family, he became the most authoritative exponent of the humanistic circle in Strasbourg, belonged to the cultural aristocracy and throughout his life had contacts with intellectuals and thinkers.

ALBRECHT DÜRER
(Nuremberg, 1471 - 1528)

The Apostles Philip and James

Tempera on canvas
45x38; 46x37
1516

Dürer's monogram and the date are visible in the upper part of the two canvases, which are part of a series of twelve heads of apostles which the artist planned, though never completed. The two heads are constructed with an incisive and meticulous line, a reflection of Dürer's troubled search for moral austerity. We may recall that this was a particularly delicate time in German history, shortly before the emergence of Martin Luther and the Reformation.
The two saints inspire a diffused sense of solemn veneration, in the passionate, severe eyes, the embittered curve of the mouths, and the overabundant beards, depicted as heavy, noble masses of coiling hair.

Hans Baldung Grien, Eve: detail.

the Prado in Madrid).

Lastly, the *Madonna and Child with a Pear* (signed and dated 1526) is a product of Dürer's late period, when the artist returned to Flemish painting in the light of the new formal and cultural innovations so passionately expounded by the Italian Renaissance.

The Uffizi possesses other paintings of considerable quality by another great German painter, Lukas Cranach the Elder. Unfortunately all the works belong to the artist's late period, when the activity of the workshop had begun to prevail. If the portraits of *Martin Luther and his Wife Catherine Bore*, are 'routine' works, the products of particular historical circumstances, the *Adam* and *Eve* are autographed as a whole and reveal the extent to which the artist differed from Dürer. These two nude figures do not represent the passionate search for a classical standard, but express an ideal of softness and grace, in which curved lines, dancing movements and the sense of a fleeting, transient presence prevail. Even the portraits reveal a penetrating, unprejudiced, antiheroic and antiplastic attitude. The divergence from the portraits of Dürer could not be more macroscopic. We get an idea of it only by comparing them with Dürer's serious and intense portrait of his father, even if it is the artist's first work.

Returning again to Cranach, the ironic and affectionate vein with which he seems amiably but at the same time clearly to take a distance from the great artist of Nuremberg, comes through in the two portraits of the Electors of Saxony, *Frederick III the Wise* and *Johann I*. These

LUKAS CRANACH THE ELDER
(Kronach, 1472 - Weimar, 1553)

Portrait of Martin Luther

Oil on wood
36.5x23
1529

Lukas Cranach appeared in Wittenberg in 1505 as the court artist
of Frederick the Wise. Wittenberg, a university town which
became the greatest and most authoritative centre for the
preparation of the Reformation, favoured Cranach's contacts and
relations with men of culture, like Martin Luther and Philipp
Melanchthon.
Because the artist too adhered to the Reformation it was only
natural that he executed many portraits of Luther.
In all Cranach's versions of the famous reformer, the image
conveyed is physically faithful, and makes no attempt to conceal
the harsh coarseness of Luther's peasant-like head and a certain
petit-bourgeois expression.

LUKAS CRANACH THE ELDER
(Kronach, 1472 - Weimar, 1553)

Portrait of Catherine Bore

Oil on wood
37x23
1529

The two portraits of Luther and his wife are recorded still
attached together in 1724. Cranach produced many versions both
of the double portrait of the couple as well as of the figure of
Luther alone, popularizing a type of painting which became
established towards the middle of the 1520s and was destined to
survive to our own day.

LUKAS CRANACH THE ELDER
(Workshop of)
(Kronach, 1472 - Weimar, 1553)

Portrait of Frederick III the Wise, Elector of Saxony

Portrait of Johann I, Elector of Saxony

Oil on wood
20x15 (each panel)
1533

The figures occupy only the upper part of the two small portraits, the lower part being taken up by long inscriptions. The paintings portray the two Electors in solemn dress in keeping with their status. In these two small works we see again the German artist's marked predilection for an almost popular realism, which is achieved by means of a crisp, forceful outline and attention to detail. In Cranach the search for Italian Renaissance beauty is absent; the faces of the sovereigns, both in countenance and expression, are taken to the limit of caricature.

LUKAS CRANACH THE ELDER
(Kronach, 1472 - Weimar, 1553)

Adam and Eve   BEING RESTORED

Oil on wood
172x63; 167x61
1528

To the rigorous, perfectly Renaissance Dürer, troubled by the question of the proportions of the human body, Cranach, in his nudes, responds by freeing himself from every rule and from any observation of anatomical accuracy. His figures are elongated out of all proportion, seem boneless, and are shown in affected, theatrical poses. The naked bodies, ivory-coloured against a dark background, emanate a totally cold, intellectual eroticism. The effect is accentuated in this work, for example, by the malicious gesture with which Eve holds out the apple, with her other hand bent unnaturally to hold the frond which covers her loins, but above all by the sly expression on her slightly cruel face.

LUKAS CRANACH THE ELDER
(Workshop of)
(Kronach, 1472 - Weimar, 1553)

Portrait of a Young Woman

Oil on wood
42x49
ca. 1530

Cranach's productive workshop closely
follows the master's example in presenting
us with this bizarre and highly
characterized portrait of a lady, achieved
with a sinuous and undulating line.
The punctilious attention to detail
expressed in the tiny decorations of the
dress, the tight curly hair and the
effervescent hat tells us that this is a fine
example of German artistic workmanship.

GEORG LEMBERGER
(Landshut, ca. 1490-95 - Magdeburg?, ca.
1540)

Saint George Freeing the Princess

Oil on wood
19x18
1520

This small composition represents a theme
popular in North European painting and
gives us an interpretation of the legend
which is particularly charged with fantastic
effects. The strangely elongated trees appear
to sprout up one on top of the other,
waving their ghostly fronds as if in a dream-
like vision. The three small archaic figures
are somehow lost in the painting, which
seems to aim more at conveying the
unknown, mysterious forces of nature. The
fully-armoured knight with his plumed
helmet and the fragile kneeling princess
thus become merely the pretext for the
representation of a far loftier and subtle
magic.

paintings are replicas, executed with great skill in the workshop, which
preserve intact the extraordinary originality of the prototype. That
Cranach was endowed with keen powers of observation is demonstrated in the bashful, melancholic portrait of *Melancthon*, important for
being the replica of a lost original.

The Gallery possesses a masterpiece of the Cranach workshop in the
small painting of *Saint George Freeing the Princess*, previously attributed to the master but today more usually associated with the activity
of his pupil Lemberger. It reveals the most original aspects of the
Cranach school. The real protagonist of the painting is the landscape,
which through symbiosis with the monstrous dragon which lives in it
assumes a magical aspect, almost as if the trees themselves were about
to be transformed into living beings. It is tempting to think that there is

here, transposed in artistic terms, a none too veiled undermining of absolute certainties and man's control over nature, principles at the heart of the Italian Renaissance.

Cranach is considered to be the founder of the Danubian school. In fact if we compare his *Saint George Freeing the Princess* with the eight panels representing the *Stories of Saints Peter and Paul* by Hans Kulmbach, another painter who gravitated around this artistic circle, the similarities between them are clearly noticeable.

The other works displayed in this room are a fragmentary and limited representation of other German painters or schools. By Hans Burgkmair of Augsburg, the Gallery has only a *Male Portrait*, too little to reveal all the qualities of this artist, but enough to show his profound interest in Italian, and particularly Venetian art.

The Gallery has recently increased its already large group of German painters with the acquisition of two masterpieces by the leading exponent of the Danubian school, Albrecht Altdorfer. The two paintings *Saint Florian Taking Leaving of the Monastery* and *The Martyrdom of Saint Florian* probably come from a polyptych with folding wings from the Church of Saint Florian in Linz. They date from around 1520. The two scenes are characteristically sixteenth-century: the pictorial and compositional harmony between the figures and the natural surroundings is perfectly rendered, while the figures are arranged in such a way as to create a sense of depth yet are linked by a unifying atmosphere. The landscape is vast and far-reaching, in places dense, in others light, depending on the varied distribution of light and shadow. Altdorfer clearly breaks away from the ironical formulas of Cranach's art by virtue of the deep moral commitment with which he explores the actions of both men and nature.

Hans Holbein the Younger also belongs to the Germanic area. Despite being favoured by his long residence in Basel, he assumes a singularly intermediary position between the Rhine area, France and Italy. This is particularly evident in his religious works, but also in his portraits, like the one of *Sir Richard Southwell*, a painting which dates from his English activity and entered the grand-ducal collections at an early date. It is a splendidly executed work, expressing a synthesis between the monumentality of French origin (in the style of Fouquet, let's say) and the sure arrangement in space of Italian origin. The calm certainty which emanates from this portrait reflects the classical outlook which had established itself in Italy in the first half of the sixteenth century, despite the fact that political and religious developments were far from reassuring. But one of the characteristics of this century was the presence of strong even if apparent contradictions, a sign of the profound crisis affecting the social, religious and political world in Europe.

Let us now consider developments in Flanders and Holland in the second half of the fifteenth century. On the one hand the two regions were closely linked; in fact, many Flemish artists were of Dutch birth (starting with Gerard David). On the other hand two different artistic orientations were forming, a phenomenon due particularly to new tendencies developing among the Dutch, tendencies which induced them to break away from their Flemish matrix.

The forerunner of this tendency was the artist known as the Master of the Virgo inter Virgines, active in Delft in the last three decades of the fifteenth century, whose masterpiece, a small panel with the *Crucifixion*, is at the Uffizi. This painting expresses values which belong to the Dutch tradition, founded by the sculptor Nikolaus Gerhaerdt of Leyden. Here too an intense pathos is expressed by the figures, whose twisted poses form highly accentuated curves and vibrantly whirling drapery, according to the old but still vital tradition established by Klaus Sluter. This intense, overwhelming sentimentalism is however set within a

MASTER OF THE VIRGO INTER VIRGINES
(active in Delft, ca. 1470-1500)

Crucifixion

Oil on wood
57x47
15th C.

This Master of the Virgo inter Virgines, whose name derives from a painting now at the Rijksmuseum in Amsterdam, had one of the three most active workshops in Holland at the end of the fifteenth century.
The artist certainly possessed an exceptional expressive talent, which is plainly revealed by the intense dramatic force of the scene represented, by the serpentine and tormented line with which the figures are delineated, by the agitated poses and by the agonizing figure of the tortured Christ. Even the range of colours is emotionally charged, the reds, blacks and whites a deliberate clashing accompaniment to the awesome tragedy of Christ's death.
Figures like the swooning Virgin, who has collapsed upon herself, and Mary Magdalen, have nothing rationally calculated about them; they serve rather to emphasize a dramatic intensity and almost savage, inhuman anguish, reflecting an anticonventional and certainly highly individual temperament.

ALBRECHT ALTDORFER
(1480? - Regensburg, 1538)

Saint Florian Taking Leave of the
Monastery
The Martyrdom of Saint Florian *

Oil on wood
81.4x67; 76.4x67.2
Before 1530

Albrecht Altdorfer was a painter who tended to specialize in landscape and architecture to such an extent that these elements, from being simple background decorations, often became the central theme of his paintings. The dramatic and enchanted images that were the hallmark of his style caused him to be considered one of the precursors of Romanticism.

Altdorfer's fantastic, visionary art represented the other side of sixteenth century culture. In his paintings he borrows the extremely vivid colours from dreams, the narration becomes impassioned, and the space-time elements narrow and expand irrationally.

Particularly noteworthy is the crystalline clearness of the colours, especially the whites, which contribute to giving the story and the whole scene a somewhat unreal atmosphere.

MASTER OF HOOGSTRAETEN
(active between ca. 1490 and 1530)

Madonna and Child with Saints Catherine
and Barbara

Oil on canvas
84x70
15th C.

Art historians have otherwise attributed the painting to Hugo van der Goes and Civetta, and certainly elements of Van der Goes are readily discernible in the pointed, fluttering angels, the smooth, compact face of the Virgin, the fascinating landscape conceived as a theatrical wing, and the pose of the Madonna. The latter, besides having a typology typical of Van der Goes, sits on a throne pushed into the foreground with extraordinary dramatic effect.

Master of Hoogstraeten, Madonna and Child with Saints Catherine and Barbara: detail.

vast, silent landscape, and in the light of one of those clear, transparent days so typical of northern climes. On the surface, therefore, certain principles of lighting are crystallized which less than two centuries later would be those of Vermeer. The same intensely vibrant luminosity links the *Sacra Conversazione* by the Master of Hoogstraeten to this tendency, breaking it away from the Flemish cultural matrix to which it otherwise belongs.

The representative of the most authentic Flemish tradition was Gerard David, who was active in Bruges throughout his life. As often happens at the end of a century David seems able to go back through the artistic developments of a century of Flemish painting until he reclaims its roots — in this case the Van Eycks, Petrus Christus and Rogier van der Weyden. "In the soft blending of colour and in the monumental simplicity of the composition, a silent and composed pathos animates the

GERARD DAVID
(Oudewater, 1460 - Bruges, 1523)

Deposition

Oil on wood
20x14
1520

Initially catalogued as the work of Luca d'Olanda, it reproduces a detail of the painting by David now in the Frick Collection in New York. It shows a quite characteristic compositional arrangement of the scene, almost as if the artist had enlarged part of a much larger painting. David devotes hardly any space to the landscape. It is the men and women, grouped around Christ's dead body, who with stunned and solemn expressions underline the dramatic mystery which has been consumated.

Adoration of the Magi of the Uffizi, a late work datable to around 1515. In a work like this Gerard David brings the old Flemish tradition to more wide-ranging expressions pervaded by a tranquil and dreamlike simplicity" (Salvini).

Later, North European artists, especially those active in the wealthiest and most important city of the Low Countries, Antwerp, assimilated various fundamental principles established by Italian art and humanism, like the supremacy of the human figure. Joos van Cleve and Bernart van Orley (the latter active in Brussels) contributed to this tendency and are represented in the Gallery, the former with the *diptych with portraits*, signed with a key and dated 1520, and the latter with another *diptych with portraits*, probably those of a married couple.

But towards the middle of the century Italian painting was to triumph throughout Europe. An expression of this at the Uffizi is the *Portrait of a Young Man* by Georg Pencz, dated 1544, in which we see not only the Italian pictorial style but also its fashion.

GEORG PENCZ
(Nuremberg, ca. 1506 - Leipzig, 1550)

Portrait of a Seated Youth

Oil on wood
91x70
1544

Pencz was above all a portrait painter, although he is remembered mostly for the tiny engravings which still place him among the ranks of the so-called German "small masters". In this work Pencz presents a vigorous image of a young man, a painting full of plastic force and psychological tension, and one that reveals the importance which portrait-painting had in that period of German art which we could call late Renaissance.

ÆATATIS SVE
XVIII
P
1544

JOOS VAN CLEVE
(Antwerp, ca. 1485 - 1540-41)

Portrait of a Man
Portrait of a Woman

Oil on wood
57x42 (each panel)
1520 and 1527 respectively

Known for a long time as the Master of the Death of the
Virgin, from one of the first important works he executed,
Joos van Cleve is mentioned for the first time in 1511
when he became a member of the corporation of Antwerp
painters.
A talented and highly esteemed portraitist, he was chosen
to paint the portraits of Francis I of France, his wife
Eleonora of Austria, the Emperor Maximilian and the young
Henry VIII.
The diptych of the Uffizi, which represents the portrait of
an unknown man and woman, was once thought to be a
self-portrait of Quentin Metsys and his wife. Later its
author was identified as the Master of the Death of the
Virgin, Joos van Cleve.

HANS MEMLING
(Seligenstadt, ca. 1435 - Bruges, 1494)

"Mater Dolorosa"

Oil on wood
55x33
15th C.

The most widely accepted tendency at present is to
attribute the work to Hans Memling, and this painting of
the Uffizi would constitute the best of the many later
versions conserved in other museums. For a long time,
however, it was attributed to Dürer and to Joos van Cleve.
It probably formed part of a diptych portraying the Mater
Dolorosa on one panel and Christ crowned with thorns on
the other.

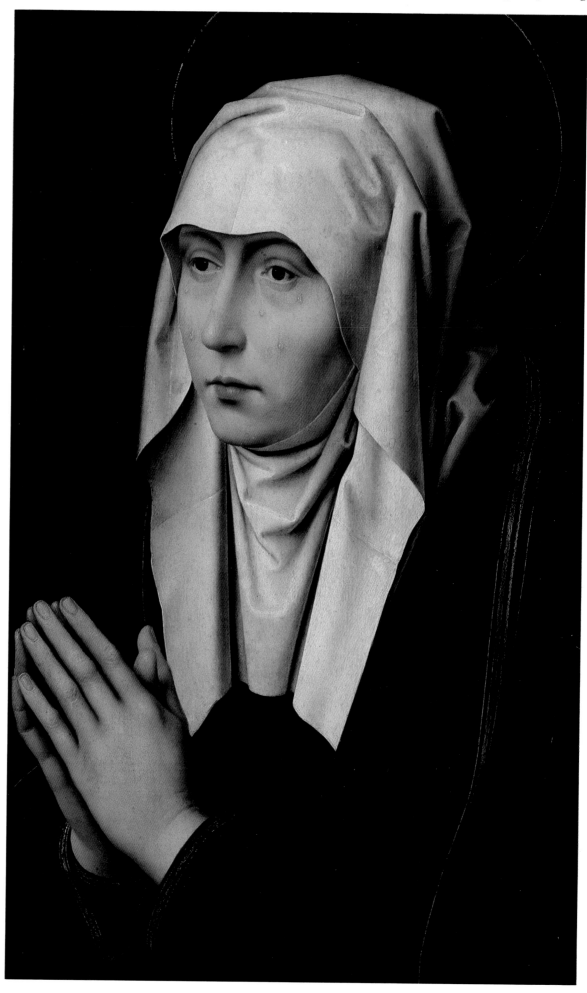

THE TRIBUNE

Maria Grazia Ciardi Dupré dal Poggetto

The Tribune was built for Grand-duke Francesco I de' Medici by Bernardo Buontalenti and completed in 1589. It was furnished in such a way as to accommodate both sculptures and paintings of large and small dimensions. It was also intended as an anthology of the treasures of the Medici collections and a reflection of late sixteenth-century culture and artistic tastes at the end of the Renaissance. Over the centuries the treasures of the Tribune have been displayed in a variety of ways. The present arrangement represents a compromise between various aspects of the original layout and a choice of paintings, a somewhat questionable initiative as some of them have never before been displayed here. The choice is not entirely arbitrary, however, since it retains a reflection of the original aims. There is no doubt in fact that the Tribune today presents a panorama of mature sixteenth-century art as it developed in Tuscany and Rome. The original arrangement of the paintings exhibited was

G. Galli: 19th-century view of the Tribune.

175

more clear-cut, since early Florentine classicism was represented, in a logical development of artistic styles, by the works of Leonardo (the Young Saint John), Giorgione (Saint John) (Giorgione was included as a tribute to what Vasari called his Leonardesque training), Fra Bartolomeo, Granacci, Puligo and Andrea del Sarto, the latter present with eight paintings, clear evidence of the fact that he was identified as the true protagonist of the early sixteenth century in Tuscany. The great achievements of Roman classicism were represented with seven splendid works by Raphael and three by Giulio Romano. The leading exponents of the first generation of Mannerism, i.e. Pontormo and Beccafumi, were also present. There was also the symbolic but highly significant presence of North European painting, which enjoyed great popularity at the end of the sixteenth century. The direct expressions of the second and third generations were limited to four paintings by Alessandro Allori, two by Buontalenti and one by Vasari.

Today the Tribune is dominated by Florentine painters of the second half of the sixteenth century, starting with the generation of Salviati and Vasari. There is also a collection of portraits, particularly of the Medici family, to commemorate the founders of the Gallery and Florence's fame in Europe. The portraits include *Cosimo the Elder* by Pontormo, *Lorenzo the Magnificent* by Vasari, *Cosimo I* and his wife *Eleonora of Toledo* with Cosimo I's children, *Bia, Maria, Giovanni* and *Francesco* (the future Grand-duke Francesco I), the masterpieces of Agnolo Bronzino, and the portrait of *Bianca Cappello* by Alessandro Allori. In addition to the Medici portraits, there are also those of *Bartolomeo* and *Lucrezia Panciatichi* and an *Unknown Young Man Dressed in Black*, which are to be regarded as pieces of anthology in the portrait-painting of all time.

As is known, the art of portrait-painting flourished in the sixteenth century for complex and in certain cases contrasting reasons. The consolidation, or, as in the case of Florence, the formation of a dynasty with absolute power led to the need for a court portraiture and an official portraiture. At the same time the changed political and social conditions confined many people to the private sphere of the home and the family, leading to the birth and spread of a portraiture 'of remembrance', for which a small format was usually preferred. But whether destined for public or private use, the purpose of the portrait was always to display to best effect the social standing of the person portrayed. This is quite obvious in the two splendid portraits of Bartolomeo Panciatichi and his wife Lucrezia Pucci. In these portraits, which can be dated between 1540 and 1550, Bronzino succeeded in directing his message at eternity, employing the stylistic methods he found most congenial, a firm and clearly defined line, dense colours, clear, uncontaminated tints and a crystalline and indefinite light.

As regards the other paintings in the Tribune, the *Saint John the Baptist in the Desert*, executed by Raphael with the assistance of Giulio Romano, and the *Madonna and Child* by Giulio Romano, are expressions of the fundamental contribution which Raphael and his school made to the formation of the grand style of the sixteenth century. Although from an expressive point of view the *Saint John the Baptist in the Desert* is charged with emphasis, from a compositional point of view it attests to an absolute mastery of the human form and the ability to fill a large space with a single figure.

A group of works, chosen above all for their small to medium size, takes us to the first decades of the sixteenth century in Florence, to the formation of a Florentine classicism with the *Madonna of the Well*, once attributed to Franciabigio, and an opposition movement generated in the sphere of Andrea del Sarto's school which gave rise to early Mannerism. Here we find Pontormo, with a relatively youthful work like *The Expul-*

PONTORMO (Jacopo Carrucci)
(Pontorme, Empoli, 1494 - Florence, 1556)

Portrait of Cosimo the Elder

Oil on wood
86x65
1518-20

Pontormo was the most complex and restless exponent of Tuscan Mannerism. All his work was a tormented search for an ideal standard which painting intrinsically conserved, without needing to draw on nature or history.
In this work, of a celebratory and evocative character, he draws on German portrait painting, and on Dürer in particular. Many elements in the painting give it an unreal quality: the waxy face devoid of any vitality, the weightless body concealed beneath the bulky, bright red robes, and the funereal tone of the abstract, symbolically dark background. The laurel sapling alludes to the living and dead branches of the Medici family.

GIORGIO VASARI
(Arezzo, 1511 - Florence, 1574)

Portrait of Lorenzo the Magnificent

Oil on wood
90x72
16th C.

Giorgio Vasari, one of the most famous interpreters of the second period of Mannerism, was a painter, an architect, but above all an art historian; his "Lives" of the artists marked the beginning of historiography and the end of theoretical treatise-writing. As a painter Vasari experimented with just about all genres, from portraits to religious and mythological themes. This painting of Lorenzo the Magnificent is distinguished by its intensely plastic colour, although the chiaroscuro is understated. The form is rendered with decision, almost with hardness, a quality discernible in the hands with their protruding veins and rather woody knuckles. Unlike Bronzino, who always placed his characters in an abstract fixity, Vasari seeks to introduce in his Lorenzo the idea of movement, positioning the figure obliquely and breaking the outlines, as can be seen in the ermine trimmings of the tunic.

BRONZINO (Agnolo di Cosimo)
(Florence, 1503-1572)

Portrait of Cosimo I

Oil on wood
71x57
ca. 1545

This painting, slightly wooden and less polished than all the other portraits with which Bronzino consigned the members of the Medici family to posterity, must now be regarded as the original of a long series of replicas. Perhaps the most noteworthy aspect of the painting is the skilful rendering of the armour, the flashing reflections of the metal and the hand resting languidly on the helmet.

Bronzino, Portrait of Eleonora of Toledo
with her Son Giovanni: detail.

BRONZINO (Agnolo di Cosimo)
(Florence, 1503-1572)

Portrait of Eleonora of Toledo with her Son
Giovanni

Oil on wood
115x96
ca. 1544-1545

This is another splendid example of the
celebratory art of one of the most famous
and esteemed court painters. The painting
portrays the beautiful Eleonora of Toledo,
daughter of the Viceroy of Naples and first
wife of Cosimo (1539). The noblewoman is
portrayed together with Giovanni, one of
the eight children she bore for the Grand-
duke. Sumptuous in the stiffness of the
precious brocade dress, Eleonora rises
before us with an almost architectural
majesty. The outline is extremely fine and
precise, and the modelling is essential,
allowing no shadows or expressive lines,
but only the impassive majesty of the
perfectly smooth, alabastrine flesh.
Eleonora's dress is probably the one she
wore as a bride, since she was found buried
with these very clothes during an
identification of her tomb in 1857.

sion from Earthly Paradise and with the so-called "*Charity*" (in reality a
Madonna and Child with the Young Saint John), which belongs to his
maturity, and Rosso Fiorentino with his *Musician Angel*. In other rooms
of the Gallery more monumental works by all these artists are displayed,
from which we can gain a deeper understanding of the complex problems of the time.

As is known, the inventors of the great sixteenth-century *maniera*,

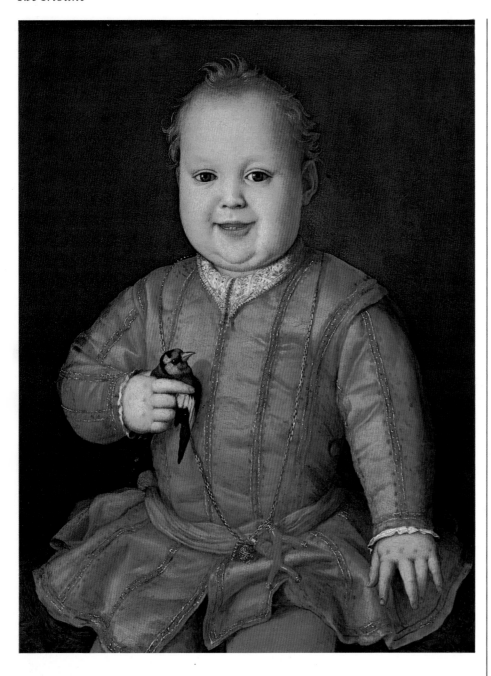

BRONZINO (Agnolo di Cosimo)
(Florence, 1503-1572)

Portrait of Giovanni de' Medici as a Child

Oil on wood
58x45.6
ca. 1545

The painting is remarkable for the crispness of the line and the almost stony polish of the composition, which was probably the prototype for a large number of later replicas.
The boy is dressed in a sumptuous red satin tunic with gold trimmings. His smile reveals two small teeth and in his chubby hands, portrayed with striking naturalism, he holds a colourful little bird.

which grew out of a close and reciprocal interaction between Florence and Rome, were Francesco Salviati and Giorgio Vasari. The latter was its official celebrator with his *Lives of the Most Excellent Painters, Sculptors and Architects*, the first edition of which appeared in 1550 and the second in 1568. In the Tribune today are some extremely fine examples of Giorgio Vasari's art, like the *Allegory of the Immaculate Conception*, a replica of the altarpiece in the church of SS. Apostoli in Florence (1541), and *The Prophet Elisha*, a replica of the painting in the church of San Pietro in Perugia (1566). By Francesco Salviati we have a *Christ Carrying the Cross* and the monumental *Charity*, in which the fusion between Michelangelesque *contrapposto* and Raphaelesque grace lead to the creation on a monumental scale of a *linea serpentinata* formed by the woman, on whom the spiralling lines of the surrounding putti converge. When we recall that in the original arrangement of the room works of this kind were placed next to Greco-Roman statues and small bronzes by Giambologna, we can perhaps better appreciate the effect of contrasting forces which, against the background of the four elements of nature, the Tribune must have represented.

BRONZINO (Agnolo di Cosimo)
(Florence, 1503-1572)

Portrait of Bia, illegitimate daughter of Cosimo I de' Medici

Oil on wood
63x48
ca. 1542

The painting portrays Bia, one of the two illegitimate daughters of Cosimo I, who died in 1542 when she was only five years old. It is one of the loveliest portraits executed by Bronzino for the Medici family. The girl, who wears a medallion with the profile of Cosimo around her neck, is portrayed with an expression of lucid fixity, in perfect accord with the enchanted happiness of childhood, and her very slight smile creates a magical air of suspense. The background, abstract as in many other portraits by Bronzino, is of an almost enamelled lapis lazuli.

BRONZINO (Agnolo di Cosimo)
(Florence, 1503-1572)

Portrait of Bartolomeo Panciatichi

Oil on wood
104x84
ca. 1540

Here the influence of Parmigianino may be more obvious, in the elongated figure and the vigorous line which creates broken surfaces on the sleeves of Bartolomeo Panciatichi. The imposing, idealized structure behind the portrait refers to fifteenth-century styles, while the lucid surfaces of colour define once again all the ideal and intellectual splendour of this man of the court: a work, therefore, totally in keeping with the taste and mentality of the Florentine painter.

BRONZINO (Agnolo di Cosimo)
(Florence, 1503-1572)

Portrait of Lucrezia Panciatichi

Oil on wood
102x85
ca. 1540

As is typical of Bronzino's art, the lady is dressed sumptuously in warm pink satin and dark velvet. A book is held between her aristocratic hands and her severe, pure face is utterly devoid of any naturalistic beauty. The artist makes this lady of a refined and cultured Florentine society an idealized symbol of chaste beauty (note the delicately, but also chastely gathered hair) and high spirituality.

Bronzino, Portrait of Lucrezia Panciatichi: detail.

PONTORMO (Jacopo Carrucci)
(Pontorme, Empoli, 1494 - Florence, 1556)

Madonna and Child with the Young Saint John *

Oil on wood
89x74
ca. 1528

The composition is a great plastic concentration, echoing
Michelangelo's Tondo Doni. The elongated forms derive from a
typology of a heroic nature, possibly drawn from Michelangelo's
Medici tombs in San Lorenzo, but Leonardo's influence is also
still present, in the affectionate attitude of the Madonna bending
towards the Child.
The figures are solid and well-defined, and the chiaroscuro,
rendered with feeling, moulds the golden flesh surfaces with a
yellowish light.

PONTORMO (Jacopo Carrucci)
(Pontorme, Empoli, 1494 - Florence, 1556)

The Expulsion from Earthly Paradise

Oil on wood
43x31
ca. 1535

Although not all scholars are in agreement, there is presently
almost unanimous accord over the attribution of this small work
to Pontormo. The panel is linked stylistically to a drawing with
the "Creation of Adam and Eve" kept in the Prints and Drawings
Collection of the Uffizi, which shows the influence of
Michelangiolesque anatomy yet is further enriched by an
expressiveness drawn from the study of Albrecht Dürer's
engravings.

PONTORMO (Jacopo Carrucci)
(Pontorme, Empoli, 1494 - Florence, 1556)

Leda and the Swan

Oil on wood
55x40
1512-13?

The work was already in the Tribune in 1589, although without a
precise attribution, which oscillated between Andrea del Sarto,
Pontormo and Perin del Vaga. Even today the attribution is
controversial; however, traditionally the work continues to be
considered a youthful work by Pontormo, still influenced by
Leonardo's style.

DANIELE DA VOLTERRA (D. Ricciarelli)
(Volterra, 1509 - Rome, 1566)

Massacre of the Innocents

Oil on wood
51x42
1557

This artist was responsible for the application and popularization of Michelangiolesque forms, which appear both in altarpieces and in civil and religious architectural decorations. Daniele da Volterra, famous for his "Deposition", one of the highest artistic expressions of sixteenth-century Roman art, had no further success and thus remained an indistinct presence in the cultural environment of the court of Paul III Farnese following the sack of Rome.
Vasari informs us that from around 1557 Daniele nurtured the idea of abandoning painting in order to devote himself to sculpture. In this work Daniele's intentions are plainly visible. There is in fact an expanded constructional form which allows him to paint athletes' bodies and to assemble the figures in sculptural groups. However, as regards the architectural structure of the scene, Daniele draws on the Raphaelesque prototype, a perspective effect created by the pavement, the imposing flight of steps and the monumental loggia.

ROSSO FIORENTINO (Giovan Battista di Jacopo)
(Florence, 1495 - Fontainebleau, 1540)

Musician Angel

Oil on wood
47x39
1521

Rosso was born in Florence but worked there only until 1523, when he left the city for Rome
and subsequently France, where with Primaticcio he decorated the Pavilion of Pomona and
the Gallery of Francis I at the castle of Fontainebleau.
Having received his training in a Florentine circle culturally influenced by Andrea del Sarto
and by the controversial Pontormo, he shows here his own personal vein. The musician angel
is represented with a vivacity and movement that is particularly noticeable in the tawny hair,
sprinkled with red and white, a mane of coiling curls that seem to quiver in response to the
music. Even the pointed wings seem to stand up as tautly as the chords of the mandolin.
A charming work that responds to the taste of the public for sentiments of grace and
tenderness, it is perhaps the one that has most determined the popular diffusion of the art of
Rosso Fiorentino. Recent reflectographic analyses have shown that the painting is a
fragmentary part of an altarpiece with the Virgin and Saints. These examinations have also
revealed, below right, partly abrased, the signature and date.

GIORGIO VASARI
(Arezzo, 1511 - Florence, 1574)

The Prophet Elisha

Oil on wood
40x29
16th C.

This composition is a typical example of a painting for private worship, a genre that was popular with Vasari. It is a copy of the work painted for the church of San Pietro in Perugia in 1566.
In spite of the modest size of the work, the artist insists on elaborating a composition of great complexity and refinement, characteristics which would reappear in the profane paintings of the Studiolo executed thirty years later.

GIORGIO VASARI
(Arezzo, 1511 - Florence, 1574)

Allegory of the Immaculate Conception

Oil on wood
58x39
1541

This is certainly one of the most accomplished paintings of a religious subject produced by Vasari, in spite of its being complicated by allegorical symbols composed with the help of contemporary intellectuals. The group of Mary transported by small angels is certainly the result of Vasari's reflections on the works of Raphael, which he saw in Rome. The allegorical group in the lower part of the painting, on the other hand, is inspired by Michelangelo's dramatic dynamism, while he draws on Rosso for the contorted poses of the numerous figures.
This allegorical academicism, however, is diluted in the misty atmosphere, and in a general pictorial effect of extraordinary quality.
This small painting displayed in the Gallery is the replica of a large work which Vasari executed in 1540 for the chapel of Bindo Altoviti in the Florentine church of SS. Apostoli.

THE 16TH CENTURY

Maria Grazia Ciardi Dupré dal Poggetto

Giorgio Vasari was certainly right when he celebrated the sixteenth century as that in which the figurative arts in Italy reached perfection. Italian art achieved complete mastery both of style and of the human form in movement and repose. The formal beauty was such that it enabled the attainment of a series of symbolic meanings, which were frequently extremely complex and of an eminently intellectual nature. Beauty and intelligence were fused in what seemed an unrepeatable synthesis. Although the Italian campaigns were the lamentable cause of a gradual loss of political independence, they also resulted in the sweeping and rapid triumph of Italian art and culture in Europe and later, through Spain, in the rest of the world.

In tracing the events which led to this great achievement, and in particular their origins, it is impossible not to recall the introduction to the third part of Vasari's *Lives of the Most Eminent Painters, Sculptors and Architects*. Although printed in 1550 and written during the preceding years, Vasari's *Lives* were based on a series of artistic facts which were already quite clearly interconnected.

"It was Leonardo who originated the third style or period, which we like to call the modern age; for in addition to the force and robustness of his draughtsmanship and his subtle and exact reproduction of every detail in nature, he showed in his works an understanding of rule, a better knowledge of order, correct proportion, perfect design, and an inspired grace. An artist of great vision and skill and abundant resources, Leonardo may be said to have painted figures that moved and breathed". It is clear that here Vasari was not thinking of the artist's early works, like those at the Uffizi (even if these qualities are already discernible in them); he was thinking more of the mature works, starting with the *Last Supper* in the refectory of the convent of Santa Maria delle Grazie in Milan, the Florentine works which date from the early years of the century, like the *Saint Anne* now at the Louvre, and the cartoon for the *Battle of Anghiari* for the Salone dei Cinquecento in Palazzo Vecchio.

Having introduced Leonardo, thereby defining the fundamental elements of the sixteenth-century style, Vasari proceeds to highlight another essential theme characteristic of the new century. By mentioning Giorgione second, he shows he has understood that in the sixteenth century a culture and style developed that were no longer regional, but national.

The passage which follows that on Leonardo is extremely relevant and worth quoting in full:"Somewhat later followed Giorgione of Castelfranco, whose pictures convey a gradual blending of tones and a tremendous impression of movement achieved through the finely handled use of shadow". Vasari, who had worked for some years in Venice, was well acquainted with paintings such as *The Tempest*, the *Three Philosophers* of Vienna and the *Sleeping Venus* now in Dresden. "In no way inferior to his in strength, relief, charm and grace were the paintings of Fra Bartolomeo of San Marco. But the most graceful of all was Raphael of Urbino, who studied what had been achieved by both the ancient and the modern masters, selected the best qualities from all their works, and by this means so enhanced the art of painting that it equalled the faultless perfection of the figures painted in the ancient world by Apelles and Zeuxis, and might even be said to surpass them were it possible to compare his work with theirs".

Proceeding with Vasari's preface we are struck by the extraordinary clarity with which he distinguishes tendencies and discerns strengths in the artistic environment of central Italy, while the birth of the great Venetian artistic tradition, with Titian, is passed over in silence. This is because the Venetian school existed largely outside that national moment which during the first twenty years of the century involved Leonardo and Giorgione on the one hand, and Raphael on the other, and which was renewed during the second half of the century due to the dominant, unifying influence of Michelangelo. Within central Italy Vasari notes the connections between Raphael and a group of artists who differed widely among themselves, such as Andrea del Sarto, Correggio, Parmigianino, Polidoro da Caravaggio, Rosso, Sebastiano del Piombo, Giulio Romano and Perin del Vaga.

"But the man whose work transcends and eclipses that of every other artist, living or dead, is the inspired Michelangelo Buonarroti, who is supreme not in one art alone but in all three. He surpasses not only all those whose work can be said to be superior to nature but also the artists of the ancient world, whose superiority is beyond doubt". Thus writes Vasari, in a tone which is part poetic and part prophetic. With Michelangelo, indeed, Italian art reached not only perfection but was elevated to a superhuman sphere. The abrupt and violent rift which Michelangelo opened up between himself and his contemporaries is clearly reflected in the Gallery in the distance separating the *Tondo Doni* and the paintings of mainly Florentine contemporary artists. This distance would have been even greater had the city of Florence still possessed the famous cartoon for the *Battle of Cascina* which Michelangelo was to have frescoed on a wall of the Salone dei Cinquecento in Palazzo Vecchio.

A logical consequence of this distance was that Michelangelo's influence — both directly, and more importantly indirectly, through Raphael — became a significant determining factor from 1530 onwards. It is well known that Michelangelo's powerful, plastic, dynamic energy was an irresistible attraction for Raphael from the time he was a young man. This tendency was increased when they were both in Rome and working for the Popes, and so had the opportunity to meet more often. Raphael's Roman style is clearly marked by Michelangelo's influence, and as such takes its place in the Italian and European art of the sixteenth century.

In 1568, as a result of the rapid proliferation of events in the artistic world, Vasari published a new edition of his *Lives*, partly rewritten and with large additions. Although the preface remained unchanged in the second edition, the great Venetian painters of the sixteenth century

CORREGGIO (Antonio Allegri)
(Correggio, 1489 - 1534)

Rest During the Flight into Egypt

Oil on canvas
123.5x106.5
After 1515

Correggio grew up in the Emilian environment, although the inspiration at the source of his more well-founded humanism was Mantegna, whose mythological subjects, complex, often obscure images and mysterious evocation of antiquity exercised an immense fascination for him.
In this work Correggio goes beyond the seductiveness of Mantegna, in the general style, seeking instead a perfect compositional balance in the figures, and in the refined use of light. There is also a tangible hint of Leonardo's vision, which Correggio adapts in an intensely lyrical vein, as can be seen in the expressions of the figures and in the delightful naturistic touches.

Correggio, Rest During the Flight into Egypt: detail.

appeared in the series of individual biographies.

In this short introduction I do not wish to give the impression that sixteenth-century art developed uniformly. On the contrary, few centuries have witnessed such a rapid succession of changes, or the simultaneous existence of widely differing trends. This is all the more true in the sixteenth century because the spheres of activity in the figurative arts were in expansion. They acquired a much broader subjective space, which would have been unthinkable in earlier centuries. The relationship between artist and psyche became more deeply marked. Private and public space too began to expand for political, economic and, above all, religious reasons. This is clearly not the place for an in-depth study of the latter; suffice to say that religious factors had an enormous bearing on developments in the artistic world. It was a period that witnessed the assertion of absolute monarchies and expanding states based on a central administration, the creation of an adequate bureaucratic structure, and therefore a service sector. It was a period which saw the consolidation and reconstruction of the courts and of feudal aristocracy, and which saw the economic assertion of the countries of the Atlantic seaboard and the waning of Mediterranean supremacy. It was above all a century marked by the deep religious division which would torment Europe for centuries to come, a division which developed within Christianity through the Reformation. Finally, it was a period during which the Roman Catholic Church achieved that immense reorganization and reform which goes under the name of the Catholic Counter-Reformation.

Each of these factors had extremely important consequences for art, not only as regards content, but also stylistic choices.

Let us remember that although the above-mentioned political, economic and religious changes affected the whole of Europe, in Italy the situation was one of even greater conflict. The political subdivision of the country into regional states, or even single cities, fostered the flour-

CORREGGIO (Antonio Allegri)
(Correggio, 1489 - 1534)

Adoration of the Child

Oil on canvas
81x77
1518-20

This work dates from the period of the artist's full maturity and shows how Correggio abandons for a moment the magniloquent style of dramatically charged painting and devotes himself with equal fondness and ability to the development of the chromatic qualities of light, immersing his figures in a mellow, suffused, tender atmosphere.
The soft plasticism of the figures shows that the artist has fully assimilated the teachings of Raphael, although the painting is particularly noteworthy for the splendid and quite uncommon gesture of human affection made by the Madonna as she watches over her baby.

CORREGGIO (Antonio Allegri)
(Correggio, 1489 - 1534)

Madonna and Child in Glory

Oil on wood
20x16. 3
1512-15

The most striking aspect of this work by
Correggio, in terms of formal beauty and
emotional intensity, is the pair of angels
with musical instruments and the tender
rapport between the Madonna and Child.

ishing of many different schools with distinct characteristics. The pre-
eminence of Rome and the papal court as the major artistic centre, not
only for Italy but for Europe, was actively disputed by Florence, though
in vain; by the beginning of the following century Florence had become
little more than a regional art centre. Universal art, the Baroque, would
be born and would develop in Rome.

This complex situation favoured some extremely important developments in the art of the sixteenth century. Correggio is a case in point.
The Gallery possesses two outstanding masterpieces by the artist, the
Rest During the Flight into Egypt and the *Adoration of the Child*. Correggio was a provincial, living almost all his life in the house where he
was born. Yet few artists have revealed such a thorough knowledge of
the major Roman influences of Raphael and his school. Through
Raphael he also discovered some of the most subtle aspects of Leonardo's art. At the same time he was the greatest exponent of problems
which were typically northern, or rather Lombard: *plein air*, atmospheric effects of light and shade, foreshortenings, and the mobility of
the human figure immersed in that only seemingly invisible fluid called
air.

These problems had been partially perceived and resolved in the new
world of fifteenth-century humanism, both by Mantegna (*plein air*, fore-

VINCENZO FOPPA
(Brescia, ca. 1427 - 1515/16)

Madonna and Child with an Angel

Tempera on wood
41x32. 5
ca. 1479

The most recent studies have revealed that Foppa's cultural background, initially thought to be Paduan, was fundamentally Lombardic. The artist, who had an eventful life, was highly esteemed by the Sforza family, and was a protégé of Duke Galeazzo Maria.
This "Madonna and Child with an Angel" is a revealing expression of Foppa's complex cultural personality. The space in which the figures are inserted — clearly North European in character, with the little window providing light and the typical Flemish window-sill — is undoubtedly a spiritual space, one which invites us to enter ethically into the painting. Foppa then delineates his subject with clear, sharp colour tones, constructing the planes of the composition with a forceful and essential line.

Raphael, Guidobaldo da Montefeltro: detail.

shortening, illusionism), and by Vincenzo Foppa. Foppa, bound by his prevailing naturalistic interests, was the anti-heroic interpreter of Mantegna. In his splendid *Madonna and Child with an Angel* (left to the Gallery in the Contini-Bonacossi bequest) note the silent, powdery play of light and shade on everyday reality.

As for Correggio, we need only look at a painting like the *Adoration of the Child* to understand how a brushstroke of extraordinary mobility and fluency, both of pigment and of light, blends the human figures into the landscape. When transferred to a cupola, as at Parma first in San Giovanni Evangelisti, and later in the cathedral, the spatial continuum thus created unites heaven and earth. Correggio has for some time now been recognized as the father of the Baroque.

The natural development of sixteenth-century painting from Foppa's preliminary statement was interrupted by the arrival in Milan of Leonardo da Vinci and Donato Bramante from Urbino. Both had a far-reaching impact upon the artistic culture of Lombardy at the end of the fifteenth and beginning of the sixteenth centuries. Mainly through Leonardo's influence a school was founded which included many artists. Some of these were of modest standing, such as Giampietrino (by whom the Gallery possesses a *Saint Catherine of Alexandria*, a painting in a style

RAPHAEL SANZIO
attributed to
(Urbino, 1483 - Rome, 1520)

Portrait of Guidobaldo da Montefeltro

Oil on wood
70. 5x49. 9
1507-09

The authorship of this portrait has long been the object of debate. Presently, though not without some uncertainty, the attribution to Raphael prevails, and in fact many of the master's characteristics are present in this portrait of Guidobaldo, whose pose here expresses a serene and elevated humanity.

SODOMA (Giovanni Antonio Bazzi)
(Vercelli, 1477 - Siena, 1549)

Christ at the Column

Tempera on wood
85x60
First half of 16th C.

This artist from northern Italy was initially influenced by the teaching of Leonardo, especially the master's use of chiaroscuro, which he rendered in a much more vulgar and uninspiring way. However, his cultural development culminated in Rome, where he went in 1508 and in 1513 to paint the ceiling of the Stanza della Segnatura and the Stories of Alexander at the Farnesina. From then on Sodoma was identified among the Mannerists inspired by Raphael, although he distinguished himself from the ranks by his marked predilection for facile sentimentalism.

RAPHAEL SANZIO
(Urbino, 1483 - Rome, 1520)

Portrait of Elisabetta Gonzaga

Oil on wood
52. 5x37. 5
1504-05

For this painting too, there have been various attributions, the authorship of Raphael still being a matter of some debate. The portrait shows the perfectly frontal figure of a calm and dignified noblewoman. The compact and polished oval of her face is defined with a pure line, and the smallest details are observed in the simple yet refined arrangement of her hair. Behind Elisabetta, here portrayed as the symbol of a highly civilized age, is a clear, well-constructed landscape.

typical of Leonardo), others, like Boltraffio and Bernardino Luini, were highly talented. Leonardo's dense *sfumato* and deep chiaroscuro were transmuted by these painters, in a typically Lombard manner, into a painting of light greys with almost impalpable gradations. True to their authentic tradition, they transformed Leonardo's *sfumato* into a phenomenon of natural light.

Sodoma, a native of Vercelli who moved to Siena as a young man, in the sense of his artistic training also belongs to the Lombard school. The Gallery possesses one of his masterpieces, the *Standard of the Company of Saint Sebastian of Camollia*, executed in 1525.

The northern culture of the artist is reflected in the landscape, and in the richness of the description, while the *sfumato* effects reveal his training in the school of Leonardo; there is also the strong influence of Raphael in the Madonna and Saints, and that of Jacopo Sansovino and Michelangelo in the figure of Saint Sebastian in the foreground. As a result Sodoma cannot be tied down to a precise regional definition. For this reason he was able, with Beccafumi, to become one of the founders of Sienese painting in the second half of the sixteenth century. As such, Sodoma's personality is fully represented by his *Christ at the Column*, painted in Siena around 1540.

After Leonardo, the first artists who, already at the end of the fif-

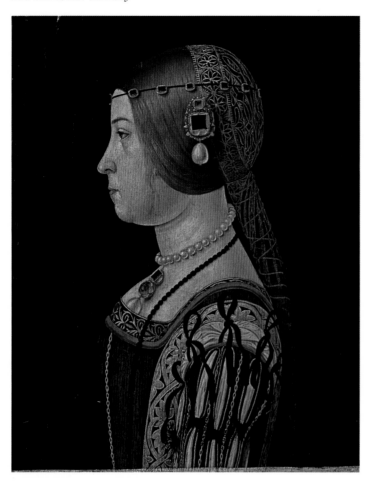 

teenth century, were to produce a new classical vision were the Dominican Fra' Bartolomeo della Porta, a follower of Savonarola at San Marco in Florence, and his lay companion Mariotto Albertinelli.

It was a solemn vision, yet simple, plastic and at the same time rich in colour and light, monumental and harmonious, both in composition and in size.

The *Visitation*, painted in 1503 by Mariotto Albertinelli for the church of Saint Elizabeth in Florence, with its predella divided into three sections depicting the *Annunciation*, the *Nativity* and the *Circumcision*, has been celebrated by Wölfflin as a perfect example of the classical art of the sixteenth century due to its simple yet monumental structure, the harmonious draughtsmanship and composition, the perfect fusion of the modelling, and the airy relationship with a space that is not descriptive but almost architectural in its simplicity.

Similar results had been achieved some years earlier by Fra' Bartolomeo on the doors of a tabernacle with the Annunciation on the back and the Circumcision on the front. In his painting of the *Vision of Saint Bernard* from the Badia Florentina, a year later (1504), Fra' Bartolomeo showed himself to be worthy of Vasari's recognition of him as the founder of this school, over Albertinelli. His way of colouring was much softer, blended, full and at the same time fluid; and the composition, although distinguishable in the confrontation between the two groups, is richer from the point of view of its characters, more lively and vivid in its gestures and sentiments, the dense colour of the paint throwing them into relief against the very light background of the sky and a distant village.

We have to wait for Raphael's *Dispute over the Sacrament* in the Sala

ALESSANDRO ARALDI
(Parma, ca. 1460 - 1528/29)

Portrait of Barbara Pallavicino

Oil on wood
46. 5x35
2nd decade of 16th C.

Alessandro Araldi is a painter about whom little is known. The portrait of this unknown young woman, supposedly Barbara Pallavicino, has the cold, refined beauty of a cameo, and a certain stiffness in its position of clear profile.

GIOVAN AMBROGIO DE PREDIS
(Milan, ca. 1455 - after 1508)

Portrait of a Man

Oil on wood
60x45
15th/16th C.

Giovan Ambrogio De Predis, painter and miniaturist, became the official court painter of the Sforza family, the members of whom he portrayed in numerous miniatures. In this portrait the soft chiaroscuro of Leonardo is plainly visible, but De Predis fails to assimilate the depth of Leonardo's vast and fundamental contribution to art.

BERNARDINO LUINI
(Luino, ca. 1460 - 1532)

Herodias

Tempera on wood
51x58
1527-31

The absence of biographical information on this painter makes a reconstruction of his cultural background somewhat difficult, although his airy perspective constructions would certainly suggest a link with the Venetian school.
Luini was a prolific artist of easel paintings, mostly of religious subjects, with which — as this Herodias reveals — he arrived at a type of classicizing painting, rich in chiaroscural intensity, the prelude to an almost North European-style pathos.

della Segnatura to find another composition marked by such a new and modern classicism. This composition is a demonstration of the great debt which Raphael owed to Fra' Bartolomeo. Raphael arrived in Florence not long before these masterpieces were finished, and in time to admire Leonardo's *Saint Anne* cartoon and see Leonardo and Michelangelo at work on the cartoons for the *Battle of Anghiari* and the *Battle of Cascina*. At the time Raphael was but a precocious and promising young pupil of Perugino, as his early works testify.

The first break away from Perugino's influence can be seen in some paintings which are rightly attributed to the beginning of Raphael's stay in Florence. The *Man with an Apple*, also identified as Francesco Maria della Rovere, and Elisabetta Gonzaga (exhibited respectively in Rooms 26 and 23), became part of the Medici Collections through the Vittoria della Rovere inheritance in 1631. The Madonna of the Goldfinch, datable around 1506, shows how much progress Raphael had made in Florence. The memory of Perugino is now distant, for he has absorbed the influences of Leonardo da Vinci, Fra' Bartolomeo and Michelangelo.

Raphael was fairly active in Florence during the first ten years of the sixteenth century; among other things he painted many portraits, of which two — those of Maddalena and Agnolo Doni — are in the Galleria Palatina. Raphael had a considerable influence on Florentine artistic culture. This can be seen in the work of some of the major Florentine artists who were active during the first two decades of the century, such as Giuliano Bugiardini, whose *Portrait of an Unknown Woman*, is directly modelled on Raphael's portrait of Maddalena Doni. Andrea del Sarto also developed artistically through the influence of Fra' Bartolomeo and Raphael, and continued to look to Raphael during the latter's Roman period.

As for Granacci, in spite of the many experiences he assimilated, there is no doubt that the twin influences of Fra' Bartolomeo and Raphael upon him were lasting and positive. This is clear from the panel with the story of *Joseph Led into Prison*, which was part of a series of painted chairbacks, executed not only by Granacci, but also by Andrea del Sarto, Pontormo and Bachiacca, for the wedding chamber of Pier Francesco Borgherini in about 1515.

Alfonso Berruguete, the great Spanish Mannerist painter, although a protégé and certainly a follower of Michelangelo, was much inspired by the artistic circle of Fra' Bartolomeo, Andrea del Sarto and Granacci. In his *Madonna and Child* he uses a compositional model borrowed from Raphael. Our discussion of Berruguete inevitably leads to Michelangelo. The figure of Salome in *Salome Carrying the Head of John the Baptist*, in the counterbalanced movement which produces the effect of mild rotation, is drawn from Michelangelo's models on the ceiling of the Sistine Chapel.

As is well known, almost all Michelangelo's painting was done in

MARIOTTO ALBERTINELLI
(Florence, 1474 - 1515)

Predella with Scenes from the Life of Christ

Oil on wood
23x150
1503

The predella of the altarpiece with "The Visitation" shows three stories from the life of Christ: the Annunciation, the Birth of Christ and the Circumcision. Despite the small size of the three compartments, Albertinelli succeeds in constructing austere, essential spaces which display a great formal balance. The small, full figures are firmly and vigorously placed in scenes which respect the most rigorous perspective laws of the Florentine Quattrocento.

MARIOTTO ALBERTINELLI
(Florence, 1474 - 1515)

Visitation *

Oil on wood
232x146
1503

Mariotto Albertinelli, the pupil of Cosimo
Rosselli, ran a workshop with Fra'
Bartolomeo, and like him shared an interest
in the painting of Perugino, whose
illuminating example is apparent in this
work, unanimously considered to be his
masterpiece. However, we cannot fail to
notice also the monumentality of the
figures and the geometrically divided
landscape, influences, these, of Fra'
Bartolomeo. The spatial breadth is still
characteristic of Perugino, but the narrative
content is more vigorous.

RAPHAEL
(Urbino, 1483 - Rome, 1520)

Male portrait *

Oil on wood, 51x37
ca. 1505-1506

The attribution of this painting and the identification of the person portrayed have been particularly troubled. In the Gallery's inventory of 1704 it is recorded as a Portrait of Martin Luther executed by Holbein, due to the undoubted characteristics of Northern portrait-painting that the work reveals. In the 19th century scholars engaged in passionate debate over both the identity of the person portrayed and on the name of the artist. It was thought then that it was a portrait of Verrocchio, painted, according to Vasari, by Lorenzo di Credi. This was the most widely accepted hypothesis, until in the first decades of the 20th century a Portrait of Perugino was hypothesized, executed by Raphael, an authorship now almost unanimously accepted. The recent restoration, which has revitalized the brilliant, luminous colours, has also revealed the presence of a very high-quality carmine-coloured brushwork drawing, characteristic of Raphael. The identity of the subject - who seems to have been portrayed from life, a fact that would exclude Verrocchio, who died in 1488, but also Perugino, with whom it bears only a vague resemblance - remains unknown.

Rome. The fresco of the *Battle of Cascina*, for which the artist prepared the famous cartoon (subsequently lost), was never painted. The Gallery does, however, possess the circular painting with the *Holy Family*, also known as the *Tondo Doni,* which is the only certified surviving painting on wood by the great master. It was executed in Florence in about 1504 for the same Agnolo Doni who had had his portrait painted by Raphael.

The painting is an admirable synthesis of the explosively innovative elements in his art, an art which was new not only in relation to the past, but above all when it was compared to that of his contemporaries. One of the great Renaissance myths — the exaltation and centrality of man — has here its supreme realization. The theme of the *Tondo Doni* is profoundly Christian. Humanity would recover its state of grace (the naked men in the background), and its relationship with the God-created world, with the birth of Christ, the man-God. While Leonardo untiringly investigated nature and laboriously explored the mysteries of mankind, while Raphael was approaching a magnificent equilibrium between man and nature, Michelangelo transformed both man and

RIDOLFO BIGORDI known as
RIDOLFO GHIRLANDAIO
(attributed)
(Florence, 1483 - 1561)

Female portrait ('The Nun')

Oil on wood, 65x48
ca. 1510

The portrait of this fine unknown woman - known in the 19th century as "Leonardo's nun", since as a work by Leonardo it was purchased by Ferdinand III in 1819 - has been attributed in the course of time both to Perugino, to Piero di Cosimo and, from the end of the 19th century, to Bugiardini. Recently Antonio Natali has attributed the work to Ridolfo del Ghirlandaio. Two views open from the loggia over the city and show real places in Florence: on the left the arcade of the Ospedale di S. Paolo, in Piazza S. Maria Novella; on the right the area towards Porta al Prato.

FRANCESCO GRANACCI
(Florence, 1477 - 1543)

Joseph Presents his Father and Brothers to the Pharaoh *

Oil on wood
95x224
ca. 1515

A pupil of Ghirlandaio, Granacci seems precociously to have assimilated ideas from the activity of Michelangelo — who was his friend — although he later fell back more modestly on the monumental breadth of figures in the style of Fra' Bartolomeo. His finest achievements can be seen in works like this, with a narrative content, full of highly individual stylized touches inspired by Pontormo.

nature into powerful symbols: in his art, concept and physical reality became one and the same.

Thus, movement always had a tremendous symbolic violence and at the same time a 'terrible' physical evidence. From an exclusively formal point of view, Michelangelo's art overthrew the frontality of classical art and introduced a new way of representing figures that was three-dimensional. The spiral obtained through twisting movements and *contrapposto* was the geometrical shape which Michelangelo prefigured as the symbol of creation. Michelangelo was the first to use abstract elements in a symbolic way, such as the lines and directions determined by a gesture, a movement or a position within space. At a subjective level — except in this early work, which is not without a certain optimism, and this partly because it was destined for a wedding chamber — Michelangelo sought to express in such terms his dramatic vision of human weakness and his no less desperate hope in the grace of God. This brief glimpse into the depths of Michelangelo's spiritual world is enough to understand why his art, with rare exceptions, is interpreted in formal terms. In this sense his influence was enormous.

The stylistic innovations introduced by Michelangelo in this roundel, (and still more in that abstract composition of powerful nudes, the car-

ROSSO FIORENTINO
(Giovan Battista di Jacopo)
(Florence, 1495 - Fontainebleau, 1540)

Moses Defends the Daughters of Jethro *

Oil on canvas
160x117
1523 (?)

In this work, with its powerful nudes and multiple planes, Rosso, now at the height of his maturity, gives full expression to his charismatic and extravagant personality. A carefully planned compositional structure and a precise system of rules and symmetries correspond to the tumultuous drama of the narration. The splendid female figure on the right closes the composition perfectly, counterbalancing the grim and rather obscure naked figure on the left.

The painting, which concludes Rosso's Florentine period, is a work of exceptional ability, in which a Michelangiolesque plasticism is enclosed and compressed into almost abstract structures with disconcerting touches of modernity.

MICHELANGELO BUONARROTI
(Caprese, 1475 - Rome, 1564)

Holy Family with the Young Saint John
(Tondo Doni) *

*Tempera on wood
diam. 120
ca. 1507*

Sculptor, painter, architect and poet, Michelangelo was the perfect embodiment of a true genius. To say this does not mean merely to formulate an aesthetic judgement on his art, but also to formulate a historical judgement, since Genius, in 16th-century culture, was the supernatural force that inspired the spirit of men to great deeds. All of Michelangelo's work was a continuous, consuming striving toward the spiritual, to pure transcendence: a supernatural force, Genius, animated him and made him constantly aspire to the sublime.
Surly, stand-offish, and persistently dissatisfied with himself and with others, he was the first artist in the history of art to be a loner, hostile to the world around him. His early works aroused the great admiration of Lorenzo the Magnificent, who took him into his house in Via Larga as if he were his own son. Here Michelangelo became acquainted with Poliziano and the other humanists of the Medici circle and from them he assimilated the neo-Platonic doctrines that were of such fundamental importance in his life and works.

toon for the *Battle of Cascina*) were revolutionary in the field of painting. For Michelangelo, a pigment was not a paste formed of colours with which the surface was subsequently modelled, but rather pure dyes produced by grinding different kinds of powders without mixing them. Supreme over all else is Michelangelo's *disegno:* the way the drawing is developed in space and only subsequently brought back to a two-dimensional plane gives it an almost magnetic quality. Because of this Michelangelo's figures are constantly in motion. The condition of human existence is the inner struggle between good and evil, mind and matter. The first movements occur therefore within the human figure: they are the *contrapposti*, the balancing contrasts, which give rise to the twistings and are joined together into a spiral.

The character and style of Michelangelo's painting, in the innermost essence of their overwhelming novelty, remained extraneous to the general problems of the time. Yet they fascinated the new generations, not only in Italy, but throughout Europe. What was most striking was the predominant use of *disegno* and the dynamics of *contrapposto*.

Few artists understood the true nature of Michelangelo's vision and succeeded in making it the basis of their personal interpretation. They were, essentially, Pontormo, the Spanish painter Alonso Berruguete and the Sienese artist Domenico Beccafumi, and, in certain instances, Rosso Fiorentino. It was a laborious conquest, one which became conscious and effective only late in the decade. The Gallery has an example of this

The Tondo Doni was executed for Agnolo Doni and Maddalena Strozzi, presumably, as recently indicated, for the birth of their daughter Maria (8 September 1507). A key for the dating is the nude behind Joseph, a reference to the Laocoon, discovered in Rome in January 1506 and much-admired by Michelangelo. It is a highly celebrated work, executed when Michelangelo had only just turned thirty but was already establishing himself as one of the greatest artists of his time. It is remarkable not only for the exceptional technical virtuosity, the thorough knowledge of anatomy, the variety and skill of the composition, but above all for the characterization and vigorous individuality of the figures. There is a lively rapport between the background figures, which are aligned in two different directions, and the compact, twisting central group of the Holy Family, which seems moved and animated by an invisible force, both in the swirling drapery and in the general rotating motion of the bodies, arms and heads.

To emphasize distance and depth the vision of the figures becomes progressively out of focus. It was a fundamental work that acted as an element of attraction, but also of crisis, for many artists of the period, and represented a true archetypal model of composition in painting throughout the sixteenth and seventeenth centuries.

The interpretation of the symbolism of the painting is still the object of debate: it is probable, however, that the figures of nudes in the background represent humanity before the Law (that is, before God the Almighty consigned the Commandments to Moses), united, through the young Saint John, with Mary and Joseph, who symbolize humanity *sub lege*. The Child, so boldly towering above the Madonna, is humanity *sub gratia* and is crowned by the band indicating the ancient symbol of victory. The Tondo is the only surviving painting on wood that we know with certainty was by Michelangelo.

RAPHAEL SANZIO
(Urbino, 1483 - Rome, 1520)

Self-portrait

Oil on wood
47. 5x33
ca. 1506

Whatever its provenance, this painting is certainly not one of the most exciting or noteworthy among the artist's many masterpieces. Although it still symbolizes the traditional, popular image of the painter from Urbino, many doubts have been raised over the authenticity and autography of many parts of the portrait. There is in fact a tendency to see it as a copy of the self-portrait which Raphael included in the fresco of the "School of Athens" for the Vatican Apartments.

RAPHAEL SANZIO
(Urbino, 1483 - Rome, 1520)

Madonna of the Goldfinch

Oil on wood
107x77
1506

In this extremely popular work Raphael succeeds in producing a perfect synthesis of Leonardo's broad, open composition and the compact, restricted one typical of Michelangelo. The pose and the gently shaded face of the Virgin are in fact in the style of Leonardo, whereas the central group is contained within a pyramid of Michelangelesque stamp. The landscape shades off into blue transparencies, with a horizontal line running the entire width of the painting (Tondo Doni), but here, instead of Michelangiolo's stone parapet, there is a soft, grassy bank studded with slender young trees, an edge which also marks the break between the light of the background and the area in shadow. The light reappears in the foreground to light up the Virgin's face and the small naked bodies of the tender young children.

in the painting with *Moses Defends the Daughters of Jethro* by Rosso Fiorentino. Here, the real theme of the painting is a world of struggling new shapes; the reality is a group of figures reduced to stereometric and abstract fragments: the theme becomes conceptualized and distanced from the representation of reality. Rosso seems to be saying that reality can only be reproduced within the conscience and mind of the artist; only then can a creation be new and not merely a reproduction. The result is one of extraordinary modernity. But it must have been an arduous achievement because in 1528, when he executed the *Madonna and Saints*, a painting of supreme refinement, Rosso manifested an acutely critical, unprejudiced and imaginative personality, but one still that was culturally and stylistically linked to the classical Florentine artistic circle represented by Fra Bartolomeo, Mariotto Albertinelli, Andrea del Sarto, Granacci, et al. In this he may be compared to Alonso Berruguete.

In the meantime Florentine classicism was continuing to develop above all through the work of Andrea del Sarto, who was inspired particularly by what he knew of Raphael's Roman style (i. e. starting with the Room of Heliodorus in the Vatican). This Raphaelesque phase is illustrated in the Gallery with masterpieces like the *Portrait of Julius II*, and the *Portrait of Leo X*. Another series of masterpieces dating from this period — the *Madonna of the Chair*, the *Portrait of Baldassare Castiglione*, and the *Vision of Ezekiel* — are in Palazzo Pitti. While the portrait of Julius II belongs to the period of the *Mass of Bolsena*, the portrait of Leo X, with cardinals Luigi dei Rossi and Giulio de' Medici, is one of his last works. An ample and forceful monumental structure, a deeper sense of life, a naturalness which is at once marvellous and eternal: all this is conveyed with a modelling that is rich in colour, smooth and refined, within a confidently designed composition.

In the *Madonna of the Harpies* Andrea del Sarto works a significant change, producing, like Raphael, a composition which is monumental and simple at the same time. The characters have greater dignity and at the same time a more evident tenderness. The pigment is enriched by denser and more vibrant colours, and the chiaroscuro is heightened. Even so, Andrea del Sarto does not reach the level of Raphael's extraordinary naturalism, constrained as he is by more abstract and academic models.

In later works — especially the two which are displayed in the Gallery, the *Saint James* and the *Four Saints*, which come from the Romitorio church at Vallombrosa — he achieves an ever-increasing monumentality, but continues to use the unmodified schemes of symmetry, harmony and centrality typical of classical compositions. The results are nonetheless of an outstanding quality, and quite justify the central position which Vasari reserved for the artist in the realm of sixteenth-century classicism. He had a widespread influence on his contemporaries and, in the last decades of the century his art was an inspiration for younger anti-Mannerist generations who would pave the way for a new seventeenth-century classicism. One of Andrea's most faithful followers, although this in no way eclipsed his own personality, was Domenico Puligo. In his *Portrait of Pietro Carnesecchi,* on show in the Gallery, we can observe the influence of the master, and see how Andrea's vision becomes more melancholy and sensitive.

In 1528, when Andrea del Sarto painted the *Four Saints* for the Romitorio church at Vallombrosa, he seemed unmoved by the contemporary tragedy overwhelming Italian civilization. The sack of Rome in 1527 had exposed the extreme weakness of the peninsula's political organization, and in 1529 the siege of Florence and the final defeat of the glorious republic had shown that the ideal of ancient freedoms had been crushed by the Medici restoration, which now assumed absolute power.

If Andrea del Sarto showed himself indifferent to these and other tragic historical events, this was not the case with some of his young pupils — Rosso Fiorentino, Pontormo, and the Spanish painter Alonso Berruguete. The latter returned to his native land in the second half of the second decade, where he became the foremost representative of an intense and tormented reality which was not so much political as spiritual.

However one interprets their painting, Rosso and Pontormo were certainly minds tormented by the inadequacy of traditional artistic methods, by the insufficient expressiveness of classical canons. Their consequent aspiration was to a free, subjective expression, from which authentic moods and states of mind could emerge, even if they were obsessive, painful or profoundly troubled.

These artists have been called Mannerist, that is, painters of manner. The definition is quite erroneous from an etymological point of view,

BACHIACCA (Francesco Ubertini)
(Florence, 1494 - 1557)

Deposition

Oil on wood
93x71
ca. 1518

Bachiacca belongs to that group of minor artists, of popular temperament and background, part-craftsmen, part-artists, free bizarre spirits in the best Florentine tradition, who in the full flowering of the sixteenth century somehow succeeded in prolonging the naturalistic tradition of Tuscan art.
This work, however youthful, shows the interest which the artist nurtured for the painting of landscape. The whole composition — besides being balanced and almost symmetrically divided by the ladders, the crosses and the group of figures — is in fact set in a rural landscape which serves not only as a background to the scene, but is the natural continuation and development of the grassy terrain in the foreground.

ANDREA DEL SARTO (Andrea d'Agnolo)
(Florence, 1486 - 1530)

Saint James ∗

Oil on canvas
159x86
1528-29

In this painting Andrea del Sarto appears to reflect on an archaizing iconography in the style of Fra' Bartolomeo. The figure is large and dominant, yet the proportions between the masses and the space are accurate. Even the extended spreading of the colours seems intended to lighten the weight of the figure, which due to the faint and uncertain light stands alone and isolated against the background surroundings.

ANDREA DEL SARTO (Andrea d'Agnolo)
(Florence, 1486 - 1530)

Madonna of the Harpies ∗

Oil on wood
207x178
1517

The pedestal on which the Madonna is standing bears the date of the work and is decorated with the bizarre sculptures of two imaginary creatures, considered by some to be harpies, by others sphinxes, but as recently demonstrated, in reality locusts. Interpreting the ninth chapter of the Apocalypse of John, the work is imbued with a complex theological meaning. Some critics have seen in Saint Francis the artist's self-portrait and in the Madonna the face of his wife Lucrezia.
But over and above these fanciful and agreeable suppositions this celebrated painting, besides the revival of monumentality in the style of Fra' Bartolomeo, seems to re-echo the technique of bas-relief, already experimented by Andrea del Sarto in the monochrome Stories of the Chiostro dello Scalzo. The very close background plane, in fact, shows a niche where the chiaroscuro thickens and the Madonna is conceived on a pedestal like a statue; the two saints are instead more lively and do not have the consistency of polychrome statues since their plastic definition is produced by the light, which barely adheres to the surfaces. The grey of the stone prevails and an ethereal, almost monochrome glaze covers everything. For centuries — ever since an evaluation by Vasari — the work was considered to be the prototype of classicism instilled into religious subjects, a refined synthesis of Leonardo's 'sfumato', Raphael's harmony, and the plastic monumentality characteristic of Michelangelo. Andrea del Sarto, who Vasari called the "flawless painter", gives here a typical example of intellectual religiousness of clear neo-Platonic origin.

and therefore useful only as a convention. In terms of style, it indicated tendencies which diverged from classical ideals, yet were not entirely opposed to them.

In fact the two Florentine painters (and with them Domenico Beccafumi in Siena, as we shall see) adopted the norms of a new sixteenth-century classicism but modified them so that they expressed not just a universal order dominated by harmony, light and beauty, but the controversial reality of those years, animated by the subjective imagination. Figures became elongated and enveloped in spirals; compositions were imbued with an atmosphere of disorder and revealed signs of disintegration. These were premonitions of the now impending destruction of that spiritual equilibrium which the common classical faith had created, an equilibrium whose canonical presuppositions were threatening to suffocate the free expression of that ego which man was now discovering within himself.

The stylistic and expressive diversity of Rosso and Pontormo, beyond the defiant attitude towards rules, which they shared, shows how the affirmation of a personal freedom of expression was the basis of their artistic activity. Pontormo initially eluded the classicism of Andrea del Sarto by accentuating the *sfumato*, which the master had used to emphasize form to the point of rendering it insubstantial. This is particularly noticeable in the *Portrait of Cosimo the Elder.* Later, over Andrea del Sarto's compositional framework, he superimposed an increasingly intertwined, counterpoised, spiralling composition modelled on Michelangelo, from whom he also borrowed the range of colours, albeit with different intentions.

PULIGO (Domenico Ubaldini)
(Florence, 1492 - 1527)

Portrait of Pietro Carnesecchi

Oil on wood
59. 5x39. 5

This painter, the pupil of Ridolfo del Ghirlandaio, was attracted by the grandiose style of Fra' Bartolomeo and Andrea del Sarto. Although he imitated these masters, he succeeded only in weakening their forms, rendering them mawkish and insufficiently incisive. This painting was traditionally attributed to Andrea del Sarto, but at the beginning of the present century critics succeeded in identifying the person portrayed and the painting's definite authorship was given to Puligo.

PONTORMO (Jacopo Carrucci)
(Pontorme, Empoli, 1494 - Florence, 1556)

Saint Antony Abbot

Oil on canvas
78x66
ca. 1518-19

It is a late work which, with the play of the
scroll below, recalls the portrait of Cosimo
the Elder, while the saint's pose recalls a
Saint Cecilia by Pontormo which was
destroyed in the seventeenth century in
Fiesole. Particularly noteworthy is the
Michelangiolesque energy of the solid,
compact figure, and the saint's visionary
expression drawn from the engravings of
Dürer.

ANDREA DEL SARTO (Andrea d'Agnolo)
(Florence, 1486 - 1530)

Portrait of a Woman with a Basket of Spindles *

Oil on wood
76x54
ca. 1517

Great dignity and extreme tenderness in this superb portrait of a "Woman with a Basket of
Spindles" for a long time thought to be by Pontormo and only recently attributed to Andrea del
Sarto. Tipycal of the latter, in fact, are the slightly rotating planes, aimed at defining a compact
mass in movement, totally remote from the harsh, almost neo-Gothic line which distinguishes
the portrait-painting of Pontormo. The heavy use of chiaroscuro takes nothing away from the
chromatic richness of the clothes whose soft drapery confers to the woman a classic
monumentality.

Pontormo, Martyrdom of Saint Maurice and the Theban Legion: detail.

We have already seen the *Expulsion of Adam and Eve*, a modern interpretation, in the style of Michelangelo, of Masaccio's famous fresco in the Cappella Brancacci. But now we see the stylized yet powerful arching curve of the sombre black mass of *Saint Antony Abbot*, echoed by the luminous flash of the sinuous scroll in the foreground.

As for the *Supper at Emmaus* from the refectory of the Carthusian monastery at Galluzzo (where the frescoed lunettes remain) hardly any other painting portrays so well the dramatic contrast between nature and art, between reality and its transfiguration.

Still later, at the time of the siege of Florence, the *Martyrdom of the Sain Maurice and the Theban Legion* is transformed into a desperate tangle of bodies *in contrapposto*, a pointless massacre in a world of ghosts illuminated by the fading light of sunset.

In the *Birth of the Baptist* the artist uses a convex mirror to create a deformed image of reality. Rosso expresses his protest differently, above all through his use of colour, both in the *Madonna and Child with Saints*, an early work (about 1516-7), and in the *Musician Angel*, which belongs to his maturity. The viscous, fringed brushstrokes and the unex-

PONTORMO (Jacopo Carrucci)
(Pontorme, Empoli, 1494 - Florence, 1556)

Martyrdom of Saint Maurice and the Theban Legion

Oil on wood
66x45
1529-31

Pontormo executed two paintings of the same subject. One is now kept in the Galleria Palatina and dates from 1529-30; the other is the present work of the Uffizi, which some critics believe was painted by Bronzino on a design by Pontormo. It is certain, however, that a drawing executed by Pontormo in around 1522 was at the origin of both these complex paintings. According to tradition, the male figure on the far right of the painting (near the soldier with a drum) is Pontormo's self-portrait.

PONTORMO (Jacopo Carrucci)
(Pontorme, Empoli, 1494 - Florence, 1556)

Madonna and Child with Saint Jerome,
Saint Francis and Two Angels

Oil on wood
73x61
ca. 1522

The painting had already been attributed to
Pontormo in the collection of Cardinal
Carlo de' Medici, but later the name of
Bronzino was added. Since Bronzino was
directly dependent on Pontormo in this
period it is possible that both artists
worked on the composition.
The rather hard drapery, reminiscent of
Dürer, is emphasized with the use of bright,
lustrous colour tones, whose enamelled and
almost metallic pinks and reds could in fact
be by Bronzino.

pected brightness of the colours deform the figures and the space, thus
altering the harmony of the classical vision.

Rosso Fiorentino and Pontormo are not the only representatives of
the crisis of classicism, or of the tormented artistic vicissitudes prior to
the sack of Rome. Mannerism was destined to become a national phenomenon with its centre of activity in Rome (with the notable exception of Pontormo who remained exclusively Florentine). The Sienese
painter Domenico Beccafumi, having learnt the classical rules by
observing Mariotto Albertinelli and Frà Bartolomeo in Florence and
Raphael in Rome, expressed his own awareness of the weakness of
human life and nature, transforming classical compositions into tangled
skeins of soft colours on grounds that were sometimes dark, sometimes
light, but always inconsistent and porous, broken by sudden flashes of
light. The roundel with the *Holy Family* reveals both his classical background, and the ways in which he intended to dissipate its ideals of static grandiosity. The painting of *The Escape of Clelia and the Roman Virgins from the Camp of Porsenna* shows the fulfilment of this process
of dissipation.

Agnolo Bronzino is generally grouped with these artists, although he
actually belonged to a younger generation and operated within the
sphere of a genuine restoration. From an early age, almost as if forsee-
ing the future, he showed a marked tendency towards order, which can

Portrait of a musician: detail
before restoration.

PONTORMO (Jacopo Carrucci)
(Pontorme, Empoli, 1494 - Florence, 1556)

Portrait of a Musician *

Oil on wood
88x67
ca. 1518

For a long time the portrait was thought to be by Andrea
del Sarto, and the person portrayed the esteemed musician
Francesco dell'Ajolle, who was born in 1492 and died in
France in 1530. In reality, the features of this musician,
other portraits of whom exist, were different. Vasari helps
us here, mentioning that in this period Pontormo painted
the portrait of Giovan Antonio Coppali, his pupil, who later
dedicated himself to music. It may be, therefore, that he is
the person portrayed here.
Note the close similarity to the style of Andrea del Sarto.
But in Pontormo there is a greater psychological
introspection, in the almost oval-shaped hand and in the
unexpected shaft of light dividing the face into areas of
light and shadow.

PONTORMO (Jacopo Carrucci)
(Pontorme, Empoli, 1494 - Florence, 1556)

Portrait of Maria Salviati *

Oil on wood
87x71
1543-45

The grand-daughter of Lorenzo the Magnificent and
daughter of the tutor of Giovanni de' Medici, called
Giovanni dalle Bande Nere, she later became the latter's
wife. In 1526, at an early age, she was widowed and
subsequently devoted herself body and soul to the
education of her son Cosimo (the future first Grand-duke
of Tuscany), living in obscurity in the Castle of Trebbio in
the Mugello.
This was not the only portrait of Maria Salviati executed
by the artist. Another version in Baltimore, certainly by
Pontormo, shows Salviati portrayed with a child (probably
Cosimo).

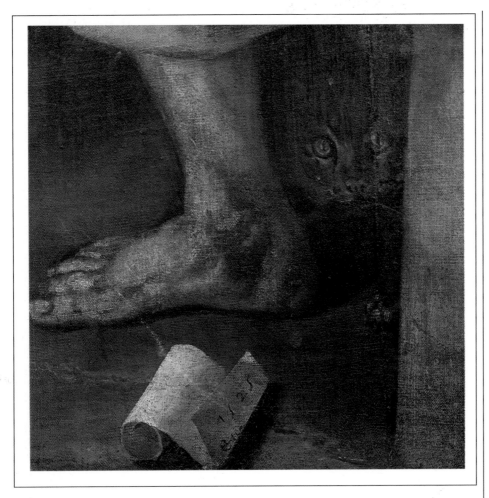

Pontormo, Supper at Emmaus: detail

PONTORMO (Jacopo Carrucci)
(Pontorme, Empoli, 1494 - Florence, 1556)

Supper at Emmaus *

Oil on canvas
230x173
1525

This is one of Pontormo's most popular paintings. Caravaggio, Velázquez and the pre-seventeenth century movement have all been cited in connection with it and its references. Still hovering over it, undoubtedly, is the shadow of Dürer, whose analogous engraving may have inspired Pontormo, but in contrast to Dürer's harsh, angular, North European composition, Pontormo's work takes on an oval, almost abstract form. Note the superbly refined still-life, the almost aristocratic purity of the objects lying on the white linen tablecloth, the transparency of the glasses and the bluish sheen of the metal objects. The bread, on the other hand, is humble, similar to the bread which Pontormo himself said he used in his own frugal suppers. Christ, idealized, has a sturdy young body which is vigorously shown beneath the ample folds of his blue robe.
Pontormo boldly experiments various compositional effects in the painting, as we can see in the figure of the friar on the left, "cut away" below the nose, in the cup-bearer, whose face is almost that of a delinquent, and whose head appears to have been detached from the rest of his body and placed on the shoulder of his companion. A dog and two cats can be seen crouching under the table, their gleaming little eyes looking towards us and increasing the overall sense of mystery. Even the touches of everyday reality are charged with meaning in this painting of the apprehension surrounding the supernatural event. For Pontormo, historical distance has vanished; the faithful are there experiencing the miracle directly.

be associated with the strong influence exerted by Pontormo. The *Madonna and Child with Two Saints* is usually ascribed to Pontormo, but is really more characteristic of Bronzino. The truth is that in his early works he expressed a strong opposition to classical rhetoric, aiming instead at a kind of hyper-realism: the *Dead Christ between the Virgin and Mary Magdalen* reaches such a high level of pathos that every trace of formalism is obliterated. But this was a brief moment. Already in the *Holy Family* he devoted himself to evoking the incorruptible, eternal quality of classical ideals.

In his portraits, too, with some exceptions, Bronzino adopted a similar approach. The difference between artistic (and political) restoration and the free expression of reality can be perfectly appreciated when we compare Bronzino's portraits with Pontormo's *Portrait of Maria Salviati*.

The appropriation of Pontormo's stylistic innovations (with the aim of formal order) by certain artists of the second generation, such as Jacopino del Conte in the *Madonna and Child with the Young Saint John*, should also be seen in the light of this climate of restoration.

We shall see later how the conflict developed between the free expression of artists seeking to explore the dramatic reality which surrounded them, and the celebratory designs of the new political forces. In the second half of the century a third force was to enter into this dialectic: the Church of the Counter-Reformation, with historical and artistic objectives of its own.

In Venice, following Giorgione's establishment of the foundations for a new sixteenth-century style, in the first two decades of the century Titian and Jacopo Palma the Elder gave expression to one of the finest celebrations of classicism in the history of painting, worthy of being compared to the achievements of Raphael in Rome.

This flowering of art in Venice had much in common with parallel developments in central Italy, although it was an art with totally independent means and sometimes different ends. It was the achievement of a perfect classical vision which, with pauses and alternating phases, continued to evolve up until the death of Paolo Veronese.

Towards the middle of the century in Venice another artistic current emerged which absorbed certain stylistic elements of painting in Tuscany and Rome. This current, whose two main exponents were Jacopo Bassano and Tintoretto, represented an alternative to the intensely classical Venetian tendency, without either suffocating it or diminishing its vital impetus.

One of Titian's first works, the *San Marco* palette, executed in 1510, marked the beginning of the first classical period: from then on Titian found a worthy companion in Jacopo Negretti, called Palma il Vecchio, a naturalized Venetian painter originally from Bergamo. In the Gallery we have an expression of this phase in his *Resurrection of Lazarus*. If we compare this work with the paintings of two Tuscan painters of classical tendency, Fra Bartolomeo and Mariotto Albertinelli, we see immediately that although containing more figures it is more poised and solemn in its composition. In spite of this, while in the paintings of the two Tuscans the figures press into the foreground with their ample shapes and lively movements, here the atmosphere envelops them, blending them into the landscape, and contributing to the creation of a harmonious reconciliation between man and nature.

Yet it is to the second decade of the sixteenth century that the greatest masterpieces of Venetian classicism belong: *Sacred and Profane Love* (now in the Galleria Borghese in Rome) and the *Bacchanal,* in the Prado Museum, both by Titian. The Uffizi also has a masterpiece, *Flora,* which arrived as a result of an exchange with the Imperial Gallery of Vienna in the early eighteenth century. If this splendid female figure really represents a reinterpretation of the classical myth, one has to admit that never before had the rediscovery of antiquity been transfigured into such a new, vital and modern vision. In terms of technique the painting was also an expression of the disconcertingly total modernity achieved by the artist. Rendered entirely with colour, which becomes tone with the variation of the light, it reveals to our eyes the exalting and inviting world of the senses; we can almost smell the exquisite fragrance of so much beauty, and feel the softness of the skin and the silken quality of the clothes.

Confronted by the luxuriant splendour of Titian's world, a portrait like *The Sick Man* shows such a subtle concentration of melancholy and unease as to induce us into considering it an example, not of Titian's art, as it is now generally seen, but rather of the persistence and growth of that vein of profound and undefined pessimism which had coagulated in Venice in the years which saw the painting of Giorgione pass from the *Laura* (now in Vienna) to the *Old Woman* (Academy, Venice). This particular mood found its heir in Sebastiano del Piombo, to whom the portrait has also been attributed.

The strident contrast of this melancholy vein and saturnine spirit with the triumphal quality of Venetian painting and the ruling political class, forced the painter to move away from Venice to Rome.

Titian, as we know, was a great portrait painter: with strokes of colour faces full of character and intensely vital figures were brought to life on canvas. An example of this is his *Portrait of a Knight of Malta*, which belongs to the same period as the *Flora*. The result is intensely modern, being comparable at that time only with the superb portraits of Raphael, such as that of Baldassare Castiglione now at the Louvre.

In the second decade of the sixteenth century Palma il Vecchio also entered a phase of more mature classicism with the *Sacra Conver-*

BRONZINO (Agnolo di Cosimo)
(Florence, 1503 - 1572)

Holy Family with the Young Saint John

Oil on wood
117x93
ca. 1540

This work, Vasari informs us, was executed on the commission of
Bartolomeo Panciatichi and this is confirmed by the family coat-of-arms
which can be seen on a high tower forming part of the background
landscape.
The painting has a structure which is dynamic, abstract, yet at the same time
frozen by sharp outlines, typical of Bronzino. Everything is harmoniously
arranged in a great compositional balance, albeit of considerable complexity.
In the foreground the group of the Virgin and Saint Joseph is built up with
revolving movements, which are restrained below by the extremely smooth
bodies of the two children. The delicate face of the Madonna, her almost
chiselled hair, and the pose and form of her hands, closely resemble
elements in Bronzino's famous portrait of Lucrezia Panciatichi.

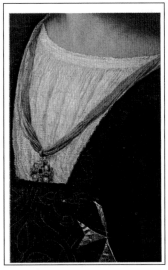

Portrait of a knight of Malta:
detail before restoration.

TITIAN VECELLIO
(Pieve di Cadore, ca. 1488 - Venice, 1576)

Portrait of a Knight of Malta *

*Oil on canvas
80x64
ca. 1515*

Like Bronzino, the other great portrait-
painter of the period, Titian was well aware
of the social importance of the portrait;
both artists in fact painted the people of
their time who counted most.
At the end of the nineteenth century it
was suggested that this noble knight was
Stefano Colonna.
Although the numerous repaintings have
posed problems regarding its certain
attribution — the knight shows a
spirituality of a Giorgionesque type in the
idealized structure of the face, and in the
fixed, melancholy expression — the
painting shows an ample and solemn
general style, the space is created by the
movement itself of the masterfully curved
arm, and clearly speaks the language of
Titian, as does the splendid white shirt
with its tiny pleats and the sumptuous,
austere gown decorated in gold.

sazione, and in the following decade with *Judith*. In the latter painting,
although his subject is clearly inspired by Titian's *Flora*, he shows full
independence at a formal level. In spite of the delightful quality of the
colours, the figure assumes a geometric and abstract dignity, while the
cold background is devoid of the that reverberating murmur of nature
in the *Flora*.

The great classical period of Titian and Palma il Vecchio also involved
other painters: one of these was Sebastiano Florigerio, whose masterpiece, the *Portrait of Raffaele Grassi* is in the Gallery. The painting
shows an awareness of the accomplishments of Titian's and Palma's portraiture during the 1620s and 1630s.

This new phase, in which Titian created portraits in which the glory
of the powerful of the Earth was both sublimated and refined, is represented by the portraits of the Dukes of Urbino, *Francesco Maria I della
Rovere* and *Eleonora Gonzaga*, paintings which the Gallery acquired
from the Ducal Palace of Urbino with the inheritance of Vittoria della
Rovere. Florigerio, not quite grasping the intense, flashing, chromatic
and tonal transfiguration of Titian's portraits, immerses his monumental
figure in the warm but already shadow-filled air of a late afternoon.

In contrast to what happened in Rome, the fate of Venetian classicism

TITIAN VECELLIO
(Pieve di Cadore, ca. 1488 - Venice, 1576)

Portrait of Francesco Maria della Rovere *

Oil on canvas
114x103
1536-38

The signed painting was executed by the
artist between 1536 and 1538 and came to
Florence with the Della Rovere inheritance
in 1631.
The painting, which has recently been
restored, shows fully the characteristics of
Titian's portrait-painting in the nobility and
striking realism of this proud, stern-faced
warrior who looks at us unswervingly in
his glorious shining armour (which it
seems the duke sent personally to Titian so
that he could paint it as realistically as
possible).

TITIAN VECELLIO
(Pieve di Cadore, ca. 1488 - Venice, 1576)

Portrait of Eleonora Gonzaga della Rovere*

Oil on canvas
114x103
1537

Commissioned possibly as early as 1532,
and executed by the artist in 1537 during
the duchess's stay in Venice, this portrait
also represents a living figure and not an
idealized evocation.
Eleonora is there, in a regal pose, almost
seeming to stretch out her bejewelled hand
to receive the customary homage. Her
dress, executed with the patience and skill
of a craftsman, is exceptionally refined.
The lazy little dog dozes, while against the
background of a splendid lowering sky rise
the gentle hills of a melancholy landscape.

231

Titian, portrait of Eleonora Gonzaga della Rovere: detail.

Venus of Urbino: detail before restoration.

lay in the hands of Titian, an artist who had an extremely long life. The great painter's wide-ranging experience enabled him to enrich the classical vision with an overwhelming humanity and a continually renewed vital energy which was essentially modern in tone. Titian's paintings in the Gallery attest if not completely, certainly in a highly significant way, to his grandiose and sumptuous experimentalism. The *Venus of Urbino* marks that same stylistic phase — grander, more plastic, more secure, more sweetly harmonious in the greater richness of planes, movement and spaces — which we saw previously in the portraits of the Della Rovere couple.

A group of later paintings, dating from between 1542 and 1552, shows how Titian too seems to be increasingly attracted by the human personality of the characters he painted. To bring this out to the full he has no hesitatation in reducing the range of colour tones and darkening the surroundings, thus almost completely removing the play of shadows. The result is the extremely powerful figure of *Caterina Cornaro*, queen of Cyprus, and the decidedly impenetrable *Bishop Ludovico Beccadelli*.

If we compare Titian's portraits with those of Tintoretto and Veronese, we see how inquisitive, aggressive and essentially critical, rather than triumphalist, Titian's vision and his concept of the portrait are. The same energy and the same use of a brown-based, yet forceful range of

TITIAN VECELLIO
(Pieve di Cadore, ca. 1488 - Venice, 1576)

Venus of Urbino *

Oil on canvas
119x165
1538

Titian, like Raphael and Michelangelo, belonged fully to the age of the Renaissance for his idea of humanity, which was so rich and complete that it succeeded in being transformed into ideal. Rooted in the Venetian tradition, however, Titian expressed these values in terms of pure colour, and even resolved formal and compositional problems with tonal and chromatic combinations.

This is an extremely fine composition. It invites us to dwell on more than just the warm, golden figure of this young woman with her cascading curls and the attractive, carefully studied movement of her arm, inspired by Giorgione's Venus of Dresden. In this period Titian had reached his full cultural and artistic maturity and thus had come to a pictorial sense of synthetic sensuality. Observe the way the sheet has been painted, with masterful blends of colour, the small dog lazily curled up asleep, the amusing touch of the two maids rummaging in the chest, the world outside the window, and the malicious but at the same time ingenuous expression of the young Venus. There is an intimacy in this scene of almost domestic simplicity which places the whole composition in a warm, human, temporal reality.

colours, also characterize a painting with a mythological theme, *Venus and Cupid,* a subject which was popular with both the artist and his client (in this case Paolo Giordano Orsini). Venetian portrait-painting was dominated by the influence of Titian and Palma il Vecchio in the first half of the century, as is seen in two other works: the portrait of *Doctor Coignati*, painted in 1534 by Paolo Pino, who based his model on portraits by Titian and Del Palma of the second and third decades, and the *Gentleman* by Francesco Beccaruzzi, which was inspired by a more advanced phase of Titian's portraiture.

In the Gallery, developments within the Venetian school were interrupted to make way for the principal artistic tendencies which appeared in northern Italy, especially in the Po valley, during the first half of the century. The Uffizi possesses an important series of paintings which provide a fairly representative picture of this particular artistic phenomenon.

In the first half of the century the main centres of art in Emilia were Parma, where Correggio worked, Bologna and Ferrara. In Bologna, in the midst of classicizing tendencies, Amico Aspertini succeeded in asserting his own independent personality. Active from the early years

SEBASTIANO FLORIGERIO
(Conegliano, ca. 1500 - 1543)

Portrait of Raffaele Grassi

Oil on canvas
127x103
1st half of 16th C.

The few works by this painter to have survived immediately remind us of Pordenone because of the impassioned way the figures are arranged and a characteristic tendency to make the forms ample, almost swollen, thus giving us the presentiment of a freer, almost seventeenth-century use of the line.
In this painting, which for a time was thought to be the portrait of the famous architect and sculptor Sansovino, was later recognized as Raffaele Grassi, father of the painter and architect Giovanbattista.

FRANCESCO BECCARUZZI
(Conegliano, ca. 1492 - Treviso, before 1563)

Portrait of a Man

Oil on canvas
108x92
Mid-16th C.

Beccaruzzi belongs to the school of Treviso, although his far from well-defined personality has often resulted in his works being confused with those of more famous masters. He was in fact comparable to Pordenone, Titian and Bassano, and particularly in portrait-painting his position was always highly ambiguous, although in this male portrait, thanks to a correct range of colours, it is at least agreeable.

PALMA IL VECCHIO (Jacopo Negretti)
(Serina, Bergamo, ca. 1480 - Venice, 1528)

Resurrection of Lazarus

Oil on wood
94x110
1508-10

The painting is one of the very few signed works by Palma, who leaves his name unusually along the edge of the sarcophagus of Lazarus.
The subject is also rare and unusually dramatic, given that the artist far preferred to paint portraits with touches of religious history.
Little is known about the original provenance of this painting, which may have been executed for some convent or church suppressed by the Napoleonic reforms.
The composition is somewhat affected, undoubtedly with influences of Mannerist origin, possibly absorbed through Lotto or the young Titian, elements which in later works would lead the artist to an increasingly turgid, academic style.

of the century, Aspertini was the exponent of an early and determined contestation of classical norms, which he did however continue to draw on, modelling his style on that of Raphael.

The *Adoration of the Shepherds*, donated to the Gallery by Berenson, shows a knowledge of Raphael's style in the period of the Vatican Stanze. But the artist gives it a profoundly anti-classical interpretation, quite evident in the striking alteration of proportions (the figures are short and bulky), the lack of compositional balance, and in the dialectic and elusive relationship with space. In the following decades he accentuated these tendencies, enlarging the human figures considerably, especially through the use of billowing drapery. He created a tendency which was subversive of classicism, analogous to that later expressed in Tuscany by Rosso Fiorentino and Pontormo, but here with specific characteristics of the Po valley.

In fact it is from the local tradition that anti-classical elements and dimensions emerge. This began with the Bolognese miniature of the first half of the fourteenth century and continued up to Giovanni da Modena, the master of International Gothic painting in Emilia. Amico Aspertini's influence also spread outside Bologna. It played an important role in the early development of the art of Ludovico Mazzolino of Ferrara, and with the passage of time the influence evidently increased, as we can see in his *Adoration of the Shepherds* dating from between 1520 and 1524, the *Circumcision*, executed shorly after 1525 and the *Massacre of the Innocents* of around 1530.

On the other hand, the classical tendencies which, in the passage from the fifteenth to the sixteenth centuries, had been coagulated in the person of Francesco Francia at Bologna, found in Ferrara an eminent exponent in Benvenuto Tisi, known as Garofalo. His painting of the *Annunciation* in the Gallery, reveals his complete adhesion to Raphael and, at the same time, a considerable knowledge of early Venetian classicism, particularly of Giorgione. Garofalo keeps this tendency alive throughout the span of his artistic activity, beyond the middle of the century. His knowledge of the successive developments of Venetian art — although consistently interpreted in a classical light — is revealed in the copy of Titian's *Christ and the Tribute Money*, which can presumably be attributed to him.

A painter who showed similar tendencies, Dosso Dossi, was working in Emilia at the same time as Garofalo. He too took Francia as his starting-point to arrive at a delightfully classical result. From the second decade of the sixteenth century onwards, this great painter, drawing on Titian, gave a modern look to the sixteenth-century classicism of Ferrara. The rich colouring and charged vitality of Titian, whose tonal propensity made possible a continual intercourse with nature, in Dosso took on a specific intonation: it became richer in mystery, more uneasy and oppressive.

In his painting of the *Rest During the Flight into Egypt* Dosso places his figures in the setting of a dense wood directly derived from Titian's *Sacred and Profane Love* or the *Bacchanal*, although he fails to obtain from them the natural and serene sense of perfect harmony between man and nature. The *Portrait of a Warrior* shows in a more evident manner the transition towards a vision which diverges from Titian's classicism. This is not only connected with the spirit of the new humanism, but is also an omen of the impending crisis of a civilization such as that of the Este court which, in spite of its many contradictions, had kept alive the ancient ideals of chivalry during the Renaissance. A comparison between Dosso's portrait and Titian's *Knight of Malta* could not be more revealing.

In the climate of a society which had already explored and exhausted every possible symbolic experience, a masterpiece like *Witchcraft*

AMICO ASPERTINI
(Bologna, ca. 1474/75 - 1552)

Adoration of the Shepherds

Oil on wood
44. 5x34
1515

A painter and sculptor educated in the school of Costa and Francia, Aspertini was attracted by fanciful, bizarre forms, elements certainly drawn from North European engravings which were widespread at the time.
In this "Adoration of the Shepherds" the fantastic construction concealing an apse enriched with various elaborate decorations, the figures twisting and darting vivaciously in the most unusual directions, and the tiny, unreal landscape, are enough to convince us that Aspertini was an extremely unusual artist with a decidedly individual and inimitable style.

LUDOVICO MAZZOLINO
(Ferrara, ca. 1480 - 1528)

Adoration of the Shepherds

Oil on wood
79. 5x60. 5
ca. 1520-24

In this work by Mazzolino the sharpness of line typical of the North European tradition is evident. Observe the *linea serpentinata* with which the fragile figures are constructed. Certain whimsical touches of the narrative are probably due to the influence of a painter like Aspertini, whose presence is also visible in the fairy-tale mountain landscape which can be seen in the background and in the unreal cotton-wool cloud supporting a complex composition of angels in glory.

appears. This is a complex allegory of life which is played out entirely at a gaming-table, while music is made through a series of ritual gestures and an artificial light illuminates the faces and searches out their expressions.

It is worth remembering that Ferrara and its court, which for half a century from 1460 onwards had fostered some of the most significant artistic and cultural achievements of the Northern Renaissance, found its sublimation in the literary field too in these years with *Orlando Furioso* by Ludovico Ariosto.

In a painting intended for public devotion, like the altarpiece of the *Virgin and Child with Saints John the Baptist and the Evangelist*, executed for a church in Codigoro, which came to the Gallery in 1913, Dossi shows his desire to give Titian's model (one thinks of the *Madonna and Saints* in the church of San Francesco in Ancona, painted in 1521) a stronger sense of reality: the two saints walk towards us to announce the message of the coming of Christ and tower before our eyes, leaving the image of the Virgin far behind.

Subsequent developments in the artistic life of Emilia are linked to

LUDOVICO MAZZOLINO
(Ferrara, ca. 1480 - 1528)

Madonna and Child with Saints *

Oil on wood
29. 5x22. 8
1522-23

This work, which was probably bought by Prince Ferdinando, is a typical example of the artist's predilection for large, richly decorated backgrounds.
The painting is distinguished by the accentuated sumptuousness of the ornamental motifs — sphinxes, voluted brackets, bas-reliefs. Mazzolini constructs here an intricate and highly refined series of gold brushstrokes which he uses for the setting, the door-jambs and on the robe of Saint Joachim.

LUCA CAMBIASO
(Moneglia, 1527 - Madrid, 1585)

Madonna and Child *

Oil on canvas
74. 3x59. 5
ca. 1570

This "Madonna and Child" is distinguished by a particularly intimate composition and by the originality of the iconography, which transforms the Virgin, almost completely in shadow and devoid of all her traditional symbols, into an ordinary mother cradling her child. However, the divine child expresses its sacred uniqueness by being transformed into a wonderful radiant glow, which also becomes the only source of light for a work whose dark shadows and intense feelings, and the unexpected, emotional apparition of light, would certainly have been popular with the Romantics.

the spread of Roman Mannerism, which, as is well-known, became widespread after the sack of Rome in 1527. A group of great painters became the protagonists of this stylistic tendency in which Italian art won over not only the princely courts of the peninsula, but also, at a European level, the court of the King of France. After the sack of Rome, Rosso Fiorentino and Benvenuto Cellini moved to France and at Fontainebleau created the monument of a new age. Primaticcio and Niccolò dell'Abate, two Emilian painters who with Parmigianino and Girolamo da Carpi formed part of the Tuscan-Roman Mannerist movement in northern Italy, worked here for many years.

Girolamo da Carpi shows closer ties with the current which had its exponents in the pupils and assistants of Raphael in his later works, such as Giulio Romano and Perin del Vaga, to mention the most important. We have already seen a *Madonna and Child* by Giulio Romano which is highly significant in this respect. Perin del Vaga is present in the Gallery with two youthful frescoes, *The Sacrifice of Seleucus* and *The Founding of the Temple of Jove on the Capitol*, which follow the style of Raphael's school in the Vatican loggias. These are solid and well-spaced compositions, with static and plastic groups of figures, which are monumental in effect in spite of their balanced relationship with the surrounding space. Girolamo da Carpi belongs in the main to this stylistic area, even if, in *Jesus in the House of Mary and Martha*, with which he is represented in the Gallery, the figures retain a certain agility of late fifteenth-century stamp. The *Adoration of the Shepherds*, on the other hand, following Longhi's suggestion, is to be ascribed to

Madonna and Child: detail before restoration.

BECCAFUMI (Domenico di Giacomo di Pace)
attributed to
(Valdibiena, Siena, ca. 1486 - Siena, 1551)

Escape of Clelia and the Roman Virgins from the Camp of Porsenna

Oil on wood
74x122
1530x35

Before the restoration to which this panel of a wedding chest was subjected in
1955, there were very few elements which suggested the authorship of Beccafumi.
An examination of the stylistic characteristics which emerged after the restoration
then pointed to Beccafumi, an expert decorator of chests. The subject of the work,
which the painter treated elsewhere, would also tend to confirm his authorship.
From a chronological point of view the work comes from one of the most intense
and mature periods of the artist's production. This Clelia, fleeing the camp of
Porsenna with her companions, belongs to Beccafumi's "classical" repertoire and as
with his other figures and with the scenes which serve as a background to them,
here the painter chooses twisted, muscular bodies, liquid, enamelled colours, highly
dramatic cobalt blue and sea greens, and imposing architectural structures set in
stark, barren landscapes.

LAVINIA FONTANA
(Bologna, 1552 - Rome, 1614)

Jesus Appears to Mary Magdalen

Oil on canvas
80x65. 5
1581

This is the first woman painter officially recognized in the Uffizi Gallery. Her painting is serene, lacking excesses of any kind, either in the construction of forms or the creation of impressive luministic effects, so popular with other painters of her time. She was realistic as much as was necessary, modern as much as was necessary and conformist as much as was necessary. This was only natural, however, since she lived peacefully at home, dividing her time between the loving care of her family and her interest for painting.

Francesco Salviati. The composition is in fact monumental, organized in broad, flowing lines within a flattened pyramid. Although the figures have a fairly marked classical, Raphaelesque component, they express a dynamic potentiality which comes from Michelangelo.

Parmigianino was the most important of the Emilian Mannerists, and one of the greatest painters of all time. The Uffizi Gallery has two of his masterpieces (it also had a third, the *Turkish Slave*, which arrived with the collection of Cardinal Leopoldo dei Medici in 1675 and has been in the Pinacoteca Nazionale di Parma since 1928). The *Madonna and Child with Saints*, known as the *'Madonna di San Zaccaria'*, reveals how he united an artistic training based on the painting of Correggio (the soft colours, the distant landscape fading into the horizon...) and a renewed influence both of Raphael and of those artists who, impelled by the necessity of giving form to an element of greater perfection than beauty, strived for that 'grace' which was obtained through a stylistic technique of an exquisitely mental nature — the line. This therefore assumed an elongated, spiralling movement. In sculpture Cellini had realized a similar artistic ideal.

The first and most important painter of grace was Parmigianino, as we can see from another of his famous works, the painting known as the *Madonna with the Long Neck*. The theme provides the occasion for a harmonious interweaving of lines, for a musical development of pro-

PARMIGIANINO (Francesco Mazzola)
(Parma, 1504 - Casalmaggiore, 1540)

Madonna and Child with Saints, known as "Madonna di San Zaccaria" *

Oil on wood
75. 5x60
ca. 1530

From the time of his very early works Parmigianino broke away from Correggio, his master, being attracted variously by Raphael, by the light effects of Beccafumi and by the bizarre touches of German engravings. In this work, however, executed after his stay in Rome, there is an unexpected return to the art of Correggio, discernible in the poetry which emerges from the warm, golden colour blends, almost creating a fantastic pictorial vision, and in the ability to capture spontaneous family affections. However, this pervading tenderness is crystallized immediately, intellectually, in the relationship between these human emotions, the refined images of the finely rendered background, and the serious, contemplative face of the saint in the foreground.

PARMIGIANINO (Francesco Mazzola)
(Parma, 1504 - Casalmaggiore, 1540)

Portrait of a Man ∗

Oil on wood
88x68. 5
4th decade of 16th C.

Traditionally thought to be Parmigianino's self-portrait, the painting was compared by later critics to other documented self-portraits, and it was seen that the facial features in no way corresponded. This must therefore be considered a simple portrait of the artist's Bolognese period.
Whoever the unknown person is, the face, illuminated by a chiaroscuro which lends a noble, dignified air, is handsome and intense.
Behind the figure we can just make out a mysterious allegorical scene in the roundel (whose function is not only decorative); the scene remains undeciphered due to the highly original arrangement of the composition, which shows only half of it.

DOSSO DOSSI (Giovan Battista Luteri)
(Ferrara, ca. 1489 - 1542)

Portrait of a Warrior ∗

Oil on canvas
86x70
ca. 1530-40

Dossi was the first Emilian artist to engage in controversy with Venetian culture. He came into contact with the circle of Giorgione and Titian, and was acquainted with Ariosto, or at least showed great enthusiasm for Orlando Furioso (1516). He was, in short, a man of his time.
The art of Dossi gives us images of expanded masses, bright colours, and abstruse, bizarre light effects. This painting, however, which at first sight looks classical and traditional, requires individual explanation. The figure, portrayed here with the emblems of a man at arms, reminds us of Giorgione, it's true — which may cause confusion in the attribution of the painting because of the male face stricken with a suffused melancholy — yet the metallic flashing of the light makes the figure alive and at the same time rather disturbing: a strange assemblage of reality and fantasy.

longed, rippling rhythms, which glide over surfaces of refined and brilliant colour. The figures are pure evocations of grace, an ideal in which physical and spiritual beauty coincide: the suggestion of a smile pervading the faces of these characters is the almost palpable sign of it. In his *Portrait of an Unknown Man* Parmigianino reveals the profundity of the psychological dimension of the ideals of grace and elegance, ideals which represent a true escape from a distressing reality and an inexorable melancholy. This gentleman, dressed in a large black cloak from which only the pale, melancholy face, elongated hands and white collar emerge, takes refuge in a rarefied penumbra without finding protection therein.

The other great Mannerist of those years, Niccolò dell'Abate from Modena — only a few years younger than Parmigianino — is represented only by his *Portrait of a Young Man*. This is still fairly significant, however, when compared with Parmigianino's *Portrait of a Man*, because it shows the many nuances which existed within the existential drama of sixteenth-century man.

On a stylistic level what unites these artists to each other, and to their Florentine, Sienese or Spanish colleagues, is their visit to Papal Rome. Ever since Michelangelo painted the vault of the Sistine Chapel, and Raphael frescoed the Vatican Rooms and loggias, Rome had become the centre of the artistic world of Italy, and later of the whole world. The

profound crisis provoked by the Protestant Reformation, and the political clash with the Hapsburg Charles V which led to the sack of Rome, only partially obscured this supremacy.

An artistic training in Rome following a preparatory education in the provinces, was a formula common to many Italian artists. One such was Battista Franco, who was born in Venice, came into early contact with the Roman environment, and later returned to his homeland. In the *Ascent to Calvary,* signed and dated 1552, all these experiences can be seen, making the artist an important channel for Roman culture in Venice.

Returning to Venetian painting, we shall resume the story towards the middle of the century, with artists effectively a generation younger than Titian, even though they were painting beside the master from about this time. But before doing so we must dwell briefly on some artists who, although Venetian by birth, expressed tendencies which were different from those traditional in that environment, and who were consequently constrained to emigrate prematurely. They were Sebastiano del Piombo and Lorenzo Lotto.

Of the first we have already spoken, in differentiating him from Titian and in confirming his authorship of the *Sick Man*. In this painting he shows a deep attachment to Giorgione: in the Venice of the second decade this meant going against the current, not adhering to the first triumphal conquests of Titian's classicism. To be like Georgione meant being interested in the secrets of form and existence in increasingly obscure atmospheric situations.

A subsequent encounter with Raphael led Sebastiano del Piombo to results of a more expansive and classical breadth of vision, like the so-called *'Fornarina'*. In the later *Death of Adonis* the composition may appear to be in the style of Titian, but in fact the clear difference between the two artists is perfectly evident. In Sebastiano's work the female forms are softly moulded by the *disegno* and by the shaded chiaroscuro, while a grey, hardly triumphal, evening light draws a uniform veil over the scene.

Lorenzo Lotto also left Venice early only to return not long after, and then leave again and return again. This repeated coming and going continued throughout his life, undoubtedly for fairly complex reasons. Behind these escapes there was also a profound dissent with Titian of an expressive and stylistic nature. Lorenzo was about ten years older than Titian and had known Giovanni Bellini as an old man. He belonged therefore to a world rooted in profound social and intellectual freedom and in the morality of the profession. His paintings almost always depicted religious subjects, which he interpreted in the light of a wide knowledge of man and existence in both their everyday and eternal manifestation. These became the main elements of Lotto's painting. He hardly ever painted profane subjects; his portraits, on the other hand, were executed with deep humanity. All this put him in profound conflict with the rampant triumphalism of Venetian society and condemned him to solitude.

Lotto's other paintings in the Uffizi bear precious witness to his multiple experiences. In his *Susanna and the Elders*, signed and dated 1517, the articulated movements of the figures, the fluidity of the drapery and the soft plasticity of the bodies show the importance of the Roman experience, which was certainly connected with Raphael's close circle. The Northern, and more specifically the Germanic influence is present in the distribution of space, and in the emphasis of the highly expressive gestures, which are of a didactic character.

In the *Sacra Conversazione*, signed and dated 1534 — which came to the Gallery with the collections of Grand Prince Ferdinando — all these elements are sublimated, passing from a didactic tone to that of a

Witchcraft: detail before restoration.

DOSSO DOSSI (Giovan Battista Luteri)
(Ferrara, ca. 1489 - 1542)

Witchcraft (Allegory of Hercules) *

Oil on canvas
143x144
ca. 1535

The official painter of the Este court, Dossi painted the family portraits, filled castles with paintings and frescoed villas. This routine, which for other painters might have seemed mortifying, did nothing to extinguish the vivacious and brilliant vein of the artist.
Dossi is always consistent. He flushes the flesh tones of his characters with orangey, reddish colours, he places them in risqué situations, with bare-chested women in convivial surroundings and almost obscene merry-making men with such highly characterized faces that they are almost caricatures. The faces of the women and that of the faun are drawn directly from a cultured classical tradition which is inserted into the Mannerist context. The other characters, emerging from a humid, obscure background, are anything but stereotypes: healthy faces reddened by feasting, grimaces, a variety of attitudes. The only note of light — quite unreal — which stands out from the prevalently ruddy tones, falls directly onto the breasts of the woman holding a bowl of fruit.

DOSSO DOSSI (Giovan Battista Luteri)
(Ferrara, ca. 1489 - 1542)

The Virgin Appears to Saints John the
Baptist and John the Evangelist

Oil on wood transferred to canvas
153x114
1520-30

This painting, from the Duomo of
Codigoro, had never been analyzed
thoroughly, partly because of its poor
condition. Today, all the stylistic qualities of
the painter from Ferrara can be recognized,
from the typology and composition to the
imposing, forceful presence of the two
young saints, full of dynamic energy. The
same is true of the colours, where the
choice, the modulation and the
combination of tones is perfectly
characteristic, as is the delightful
glimmering of the luminous landscape in
the background, painted with consumate
ease.

direct relationship with an intimately experienced reality. Two very
large figures with a symbolic function represent Anne and Joachim, the
ancestors of Mary and hence representative of all humanity; they dominate the small, fragile figures of the Virgin and Child, who cling together, intimidated by their future destiny. The renewed contact with Venetian culture transforms the modelling into skeins of soft, delicate colour.

A group of painters working in the first half of the sixteenth century
were fellow protagonists of Venetian artistic developments: they were
Paris Bordone, Domenico Campagnola, and Dossi's friend from Friuli,
Bernardino Licinio. Collectively, they were all influenced by Titian to a
greater or lesser extent. The works in the Gallery are too limited to the
portrait genre to give us a complete idea of these artists' work. The only
artist to emerge, both through a more personal style, and through a
more direct relationship with reality, is the author of the *Portrait of a
Man*. This painting was once unjustly attributed to Alessandro Oliverio
from Bergamo, but Roberto Longhi has more accurately traced its cul-

SEBASTIANO DEL PIOMBO (Sebastiano Luciani)
(Venice, ca. 1485 - Rome, 1547)

Death of Adonis ∗

Oil on canvas
189x285
ca. 1511-12

Of the many painters who assimilated and vulgarized the contemplative, romantic manner of
Giorgione, Sebastiano del Piombo was inspired by the monumental form and by the
possibility of making it solemn with the use of colour. It is precisely in this contained
plasticism that we find the result of the integration of the two pictorial cultures. This painting
shows a still Giorgionesque atmosphere — the view of the lake and the sunset — in which
three superb examples of sculptural nudity are inserted: a doleful Venus, and her attendant
maidservants, who turn abruptly to silence a bearded Pan who is continuing to play his flute.

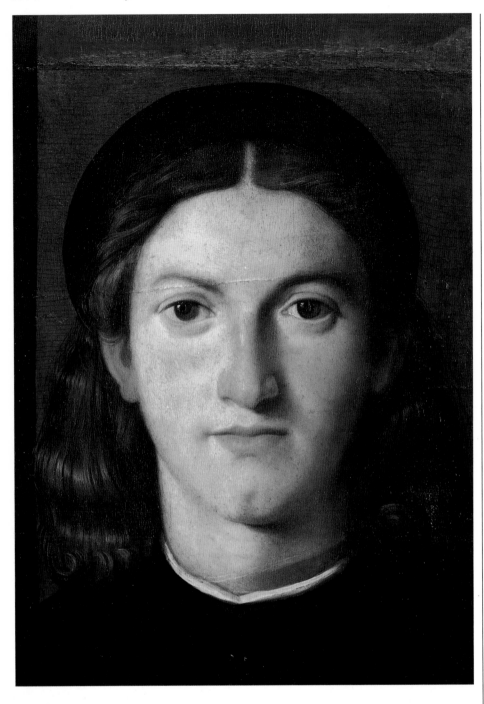

LORENZO LOTTO
(Venice, ca. 1480 - Loreto, ca. 1556)

Portrait of a Youth

Oil on wood
28x22
1505-06

In 18th-century inventories the painting appeared as the portrait of Raphael, executed by Leonardo da Vinci, an assumption based on the soft, atmospheric modelling, the intense psychological penetration, and the traditional iconography of Raphael, who had always been seen as a delicate, elegant and refined youth. Recent X-rays, however, have revealed a previous portrait, completely different from the one executed.

LORENZO LOTTO
(Venice, ca. 1480 - Loreto, ca. 1556)

Susanna and the Elders

Oil on wood
66x50
1517

The composition is characterized by its raised perspective and is divided in two by the brick wall, which seems almost to form a proscenium for the performance of a religious representation. The characters are arranged on this "stage" in dramatic poses, which, although perhaps somewhat strained and rhetorical, are undoubtedly effective.
The charming open landscape gives the composition a delightfully archaic quality — quite intentional — which serves to balance the dramatic impact of the scene in the foreground.

ture to the influence of Dosso. Brusasorci and Muziano we shall refer to later since their art belongs to subsequent movements.

Immediately after 1550, and on into the second half of the century, the focus of artistic activity returns to Florence, and to a small group of foreign paintings. These not only acquaint us with certain aspects of European painting, but also recall the importance and success which foreign artists began to have in Italy, and particularly in Florence, above all in the fields of portraiture and landscape painting. Van Valkenborch's *Country Dance* falls into the latter category.

Among the portraits there are those of an intimate, bourgeois type, which derive (even if distantly) from the Flemish Van Eyck school: the *Portrait of Cornelius Gros* by Christoph Amberger, and the *Portrait of Viglius von Aytta*, which, if it is indeed by Frans Pourbus the Elder, reveals a lesser-known aspect of this painter. The *Portrait of Francis I of France on Horseback* entered the Gallery very early on, together with that of Henry II, the husband of Caterina dei Medici, queen of France. This work, by François Clouet, is a splendid example of the typ-

ical formal display portrait which the major European powers commissioned for purposes of dynasty, representation and prestige. Two essential components are combined in the planning of this portrait: Italian monumentality (the same idea of the condottiere on horseback had been reproposed and re-elaborated within the context of Italian humanism) and Flemish micrography (the detailed representation of the garments and accoutrements).

In the middle of the century, in connection with debates arising within the Catholic Counter-Reformation, there began to prevail, even in normal usage, ideals of abstract simplicity, even austerity, which were to find expression in Cosimo I dei Medici's Sumptuary Laws. An important expression of this phase is the *Self-portrait* of the Utrecht painter Antonio Moro, dated 1558. Two different influences come together in the making of this portrait: the general scheme and the monumental quality of the human figure are Italian, while the Northern influence — inappropriately Dutch — is revealed in the attention to the quality of the light which envelops the subject and softens his haughty expression.

Alongside these North European portraits is one by the Spanish painter Luis de Morales. It is a work typical of both this artist and the Spanish environment, which is distinguished from the rest of Europe by an almost limitless religious passion pervading all social classes. Despite the fact that Morales is considered a typically Spanish painter, this painting, with its very simple compositional scheme, falls within the Italian stylistic matrix.

Around the middle of the century work began in Florence on the decoration of Palazzo Vecchio, which had been chosen as the seat of the reigning family and of central power. At this time the sixteenth-century style — that which Vasari in his *Lives* called the "third style" — had reached its most complete and perfect formulation, at least in the aspirations of the artists. There was an awareness of having produced something that was more complex than the simple concept of classical beauty, of having elaborated and codified the ideal of grace.

The two protagonists of this phase of painting were Georgio Vasari and Francesco Salviati. Both dominated Florentine artistic life in the mid-century decades, although Salviati maintained closer ties with Rome than Vasari, who let them go almost completely after 1550. The real artistic training of these painters took place in Rome, where they were able to supplement their early Florentine education with a profound knowledge of the Roman phase of Raphael and his school, in particular Giulio Romano, who immediately after Raphael's death frescoed the masterpiece of the *Stories of Constantine* in the room dedicated to the Emperor. These two artists elaborated a style which comprised both their individual emphasis and their diversity. It was a style based on *disegno* and on chiaroscuro in the best Tuscan tradition, but also a refined, silken colouring derived from Raphael on the one hand and Parmigianino on the other. Essentially what the Tuscan-Roman artists strived for was the transformation of formal perfection into the ideal of grace.

One cannot judge the entire art of Vasari or Salviati by their few small, but highly refined paintings in the Gallery, such as *Vulcan's Forge* by the former, or *Artemisia Mourning Mausolus* by the latter. One must visit both the state rooms and private quarters of the ducal apartments in Palazzo Vecchio. There, in the Sala dell'Udienza, Francesco Salviati painted the *Stories of Camillus*, and Vasari, with his workshop, planned and carried out the decoration of the Salone dei Cinquecento (1567-71), the Quartiere di Leone X (1556-62) and the apartments adjacent to the first floor, as well as the Quartiere degli Elementi and the Quartiere di Eleonora di Toledo on the upper floor.

In the chapel of Eleonora's apartment is Agnolo Bronzino's master-

MARTIN VAN VALCKENBORCH
(Louvain, 1535 - Frankfurt-am-Main, 1612)

Country Dance

Oil on wood
48x35
16th/17th C.

The painting, generally attributed to Pietro Brueghel (although with no really reliable evidence), is today assigned to this little-known painter from Louvain.
It is a characteristic genre scene, datable from between the end of the sixteenth and beginning of the seventeenth century, infinite variations of which exist in Flemish painting of this period. The naturalistic touches, the realistic quality of the landscape and the representation of common folk, clearly reveal the great distance between it and the cultivated Italian painting of the same period.

JEAN PERRÉAL
attributed to
(?, ca. 1455 - 1530)

Portrait of a Lady

Oil on wood
37x27
End of 15th C./beginning of 16th C.

In the early years of the twentieth century this portrait was assigned to Lukas Cranach. Only more recently has the name of Jean Perréal been raised, a painter often identified as the Master of Moulins, a name which concealed the identity of a painter active in French and Dutch circles at the end of the fifteenth century.
His first canvases reveal the influence of Hugo Van der Goes, whom he interpreted with a less insistent psychological tone and with a more ample general sense of space, possibly due to the influence of Italian art. The quality of intense realism typical of Flemish portrait-painting is softened in the work of this painter into a broader, more monumental vision both of form and space.

piece — the cycle of frescoes with *Stories from the Old Testament* and the altar triptych with the *Descent from the Cross* and the *Annunciation*. These works, which date from between 1542 and 1564, are stylistically close to a small painting on copper, the *Allegory of Happiness*. Powerful, abstractly drawn bodies are arranged in a series of *contrapposti* which, linking up, create sluggish spirals which weigh down the space, filling it and destroying it. Aesthetic formalism, as a conceptual representation of the universe, could not have been given a more radical expression. There is also a small painting by Bronzino on a devotional theme, the *Descent from the Cross*. Since this was painted around 1590, through it we can recognize the painter's late phase, linked to the new climate of the Counter-Reformation, where he is anxious, like the old Michelangelo and the old Ammannati, to put his art at the service of the Church. *Disegno* and chiaroscuro no longer powerfully shape the bodies, but rather soften their plastic presence; gestures and movements become absorbed and sorrowful.

In 1573, when the pictorial and sculptural decorations for the Studiolo of Francesco I were finished, there was a strong feeling that the "third style" was nearing the end of its historical course. Here, indeed, alongside the old masters (Salviati was not present since he died in

FLEMISH SCHOOL OF THE 17th CENTURY

Head of Medusa

Oil on wood
49x74
ca. 1620-30

This is a highly original composition, already fully seventeenth century in style, which with an unusual angle and use of perspective emphasizes above all the horror of the slimy hair of the monster bristling with metallic little snakes.
The large upturned head, which dominates the entire surface of the painting, is a lugubrious classicizing iconography, twisted into a tragic mask-like grimace; it seems thus to unify the natural sense of the disquieting unease of the vision of death with the cultivated citation drawn from classicism.

1563; Vasari was to die in 1574), a new generation of artists was emerging: Poppi, Naldini, Alessandro Allori, Santi di Tito, Butteri, Fei, etc. These were the artists who became the protagonists of Florentine artistic developments at the end of the century. Even the anthological collections of small paintings show that from this time on the unified tendency was being overwhelmed by multiple currents.

Some painters pursued the ideals of the "third style" within a climate of still greater refinement, like Poppi, whose *Three Graces* can be seen in the Gallery. Others projected Mannerism into the infinite atmospheres and vast landscapes of Northern painting, like Jacopo Zucchi in *The Ages of Gold, Silver and Iron*. Zucchi was a superb representative of the international phase of Italian Mannerism.

Santi di Tito is also represented in the Studiolo of Francesco I. He was the protagonist of a break with Italian Mannerist culture and an artistic reform of classicism founded on the great models of the early sixteenth century (Fra Bartolomeo, Mariotto Albertinelli, Andrea del Sarto), to which he added a greater and more humane attention to reality, a sign of new times.

The most representative painter of these years was Alessandro Allori, both for his multiple experiences and his multi-faceted achievements. The small number of his works displayed is sufficient evidence of this. While availing himself of Bronzino's models, he makes the figures in his portraits more human and approachable (as in the portrait of Bianca Cappello and the so-called *Torquato Tasso*, possibly Ludovico Capponi).

In his compositions Alessandro Allori shows an initial experience of Michelangelo's art, which was soon after combined with a tendency towards greater simplicity of composition and form and a more airy relationship with the background landscape. At times these two tendencies co-exist (as in the two youthful drafts for the *Stories of Saint Lawrence*); at others they diverge. The painting on copper of *Saint Peter Walking on the Water*, or 'The Little Boat' and *Venus and Cupid* seem to attain a greater simplicity, but the complications return in the altarpiece with *The Wedding Feast at Cana*, signed and dated 1600, which was formerly in the church of Sant'Agata in Florence and is now in the Gallery's deposits. *Hercules Crowned by the Muses* is a painting of a substantially Mannerist character, as is another painting on copper, the *Sacrifice of Isaac*, signed and dated 1601.

Although there are no paintings by Santi di Tito in the Gallery, there are two by one of his principal followers, Jacopo Chimenti called Empoli. In his *Drunkenness of Noah* and *Sacrifice of Isaac*, datable around 1595, the ideals of Santi di Tito's reforms are realized with a completely new fullness of light and colour. The compositions are simple and prevalently frontal, and the gestures are studied in relation with classical rules of expression.

During the last twenty years of the century, other strains of artistic reform in addition to that of Santi di Tito contributed to mark the end of the Mannerist age. One of these was linked to the work of the Veronese artist Jacopo Ligozzi at the Medici court and in churches and convents in Florence and Tuscany. His works are characterized by classical, airy compositions, with a pictorial spreading which mostly made use of colour and was full of light and shade effects.

Andrea Boscoli, the author of *Saint Sebastian* and the *Wedding Feast at Cana*, presents a painting rich in splashes of colour, executed without the intermediate design stage but directly with fluid brushstrokes.

All these painters found the courage to break the rules of a style which was by this time becoming academic (the Accademia del Disegno was founded in 1565), by observing Venetian painting, and occasionally making the journey to Venice.

The painting of Cigoli, with its rich colours, presupposes a direct

FRANÇOIS CLOUET
(Tours, ca. 1610 - Paris, 1572)

Portrait of Francis I of France on Horseback

Oil on wood
27. 5x22. 5
ca. 1540

There are many singular elements in this famous portrait: the refined taste for the sumptuous dress, the precision of the colours (characteristically Flemish), the clearness of the outlines, the precision of the details (characteristically Mannerist); all aspects which do not distance the portrait-painting art of François Clouet (son of the similarly well-known Jean) from that of the Fontainebleau school. Clouet's Mannerism is not derived from an imitation of Florentine painters, such as Bronzino, but is rather a spontaneous Mannerism, and therefore fresher and more vital, assimilated from some great master of the north, faithful to a great realism and the precision of the modelling.

The identification of the person portrayed as Francis I of France is relatively recent (1769). It is based mainly on the concrete possibility that the painting arrived in Florence with the rich dowry of Christine of Lorraine, grand-daughter and heir of Catherine de' Medici, the queen of France.

GIORGIO VASARI
(Arezzo, 1511 - Florence, 1574)

Vulcan's Forge *

Oil on copper
38x28
1st half of 16th C.

In this work Vasari succeeds in filling a small surface with a complex and highly sophisticated composition, interesting above all for the symbolism and allegories associated with the various characters of the crowded scene.

It is exaggeratedly rich in cultural references, a composition which although complex is lacking in clarity. There are simply too many views, too many figures, and above all too many light reflections on the modelled poses of the bodies, which, if justified by the fact that the scene is set in a forge, seem also to have a precedent in the painting of Gherardi.

knowledge of the Venetian school, and of Titian in particular. For example, in the altarpiece with *Saint Francis Receives the Stigmata*, signed and dated 1596 (which comes from the convent church of Sant'Onofrio), the figure of the saint is immersed in nature, in the shadows of the wood, in the explosive force of the light — all effects obtained with the use of colour.

The crisis of Mannerism was manifested in Florence by two partially parallel phenomena: a return to the ordered, harmonious, reassuring world of early Florentine classicism (that of Mariotto Albertinelli, Fra' Bartolomeo and Franciabigio), and the discovery of Venetian painting with all its irresistible anti-intellectual, naturalistic charge. The same phenomena crop up in other regions, as we can see from the Lombard painter Girolamo Muziano (*Portrait of a Man*) and Ippolito Scarsellino (*Judgement of Paris)* from Ferrara. The former reclaims certain aspects of sixteenth-century Lombard activity, while the latter joins up with the great Venetian painters of the early and middle sixteenth century, from Titian to Paolo Veronese.

We must now return to Venice where, just as Titian was reaching his own explosively dramatic maturity, a new generation of important

Vulcan's forge: detail before restoration.

CECCHINO SALVIATI (Francesco de' Rossi)
(Florence, 1510 - Rome, 1563)

Artemisia Mourning Mausolus

Oil on wood
35x24. 5
ca. 1545

The virtuosic design of Salviati, a typical representative of cultured Florentine Mannerism, is unfailing in this splendid Artemisia, whose majestic figure — imposing but at the same time rigorously constructed with a firm and incisive line — repeats an archetype popular with sixteenth-century Tusco-Roman artists, that of the twisted, rotating figure, accentuated here by the circling arm and the fine folds of the nervously fluttering garment.
The Mannerist figure, in scientific language, is 'serpentinata', a word which conjures up the image of an elastic substance that can be elongated in any direction and certainly underlines the impression of an uncertain and unstable state of the spirit.

BRONZINO (Agnolo di Cosimo)
(Florence, 1503 - 1572)

Allegory of Happiness

Oil on copper
40x30
1567 (?)

This complex allegory represents Happiness (in the centre) with Cupid, flanked by Justice and Prudence. At her feet are Time and Fortune, with the wheel of destiny and the enemies of peace lying humiliated on the ground. Above the head of Happiness is Fame sounding a trumpet, and Glory holding a laurel garland. This Happiness, with the cornucopia, is a triumph of pink and blue; the naked bodies of the figures are smooth, almost stroked by the colour as if they were precious stones — round and well-defined those of the young women, haggard and leaden that of the old man.

ALESSANDRO ALLORI
(Florence, 1535 - 1607)

Portrait of a Woman *
Allegory of Human Life (on the reverse)

Painting on copper
37x27
2nd half of 16th C.

What strikes us in this portrait is the convincing
compromise between the formal purity acquired from
Bronzino, the predilection for enlarged forms drawn from
Michelangelo, and the balanced, rhythmic spatial models of
Raphael, for Allori was a truly skilled alchemist in
combining these various influences in a dignified way.
The lady portrayed is certainly Bianca Cappello, already
painted by Allori in a fresco which now hangs in the
Tribune of the Uffizi. On the back of the portrait is an
allegorical scene, the "Dream of Human Life", which the
artist has rendered in an unnecessarily complicated
fashion.

ALESSANDRO ALLORI
(Florence, 1535 - 1607)

Saint Peter Walking on the Water

Oil on copper
47x40
End of 16th C.

In this work, as often occurs in the painting of Allori, the
composition is slightly over-emphatic. Saint Peter, kneeling
in the foreground, enveloped in his billowing garments,
seems in fact to be acting on a stage. The setting, instead, is
made pleasant and gracious thanks to an almost archaic
use of perspective, to that sea rising high on the horizon,
ruffled by light foaming waves, and to the small boat,
tossed by the waters, brimming with small figures.

EMPOLI (Jacopo Chimenti)
(Florence, 1551 - 1640)

Sacrifice of Isaac

Oil on copper
32x25
Last decade of 16th C.

A particularly accomplished draughtsman, Empoli presents us here with an austere composition, one which succeeds in avoiding the least hint of sentimentalism, yet is nonetheless psychologically charged. The figures are well-constructed, well-finished and dignified, and the faces are expressive, each stricken by the enormity of the dramatic event. The landscape is simple and naturalistic, and not at all schematized.

JACOPO LIGOZZI
(Verona, 1547 - Florence, 1627)

Sacrifice of Isaac

Oil on wood
51x37. 5
ca. 1596

Born in Verona into a family of artists and craftsmen producing silk, tapestries and arms, Ligozzi did most of his painting in Florence. He showed in his works an initial adhesion to a Mannerism of Michelangiolesque stamp, only later to become an interpreter and popularizer of Venetian painting with its emphasis on colour. With this work we are probably at around the halfway stage in the stylistic development of the artist, who has produced here a somewhat complicated and over-emphatic construction, with twisted, elongated figures arranged in a kind of ideal pyramid. The forms are pleasant and accurate, indicative of an excellent 'disegno' — a technique in which Jacopo Ligozzi excelled, together with pastel drawing and tempera — and remarkable compositional balance.

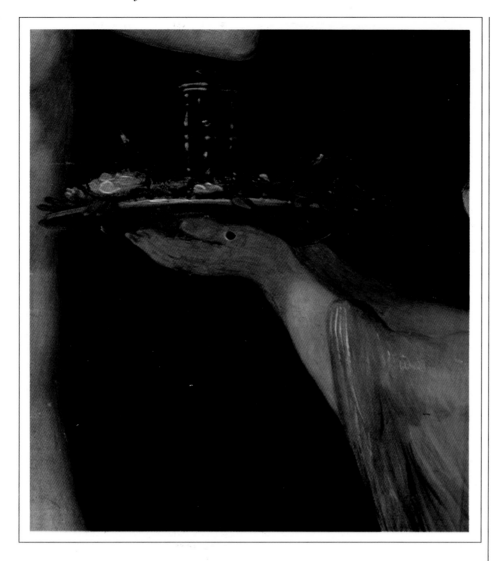

Italian school of the 16th century, Fortune: detail.

painters was establishing itself. The leading figures were Jacopo Tintoretto, Jacopo Bassano and Paolo Veronese, each in turn the founder of a family of artists in the persons of their respective sons and grandsons. Tintoretto's principal assistant and follower was in fact his son Domenico, while Bassano found in his son Francesco, and even more in Leandro, men who would continue his own art without repeating it. The same relationship developed between Paolo Veronese and his son Carletto Caliari.

One of Domenico Tintoretto's paintings, the *Miracle of Saint Augustine,* can be seen in the Gallery. Leandro Bassano's qualities emerge in his *Family Concert*, which has a fairly modern and original compositional style. The four paintings of the Tribune are a significant sample of Carletto Caliari's art.

Like Titian himself in his maturity, the three great masters of the new generation were forced to reckon with the grandiose, complex and dialectic structure of Tuscan-Roman Mannerism.

It should be remembered that this movement reached Venice through the presence there of several of its exponents. The Florentine architect and sculptor Jacopo Sansovino moved to Venice after the sack of Rome in 1527 and remained there until his death, giving new direction to Venetian architecture and sculpture of the sixteenth century. The painters Francesco Salviati, Giuseppe Porta and Giorgio Vasari, the exponents of Tuscan-Roman Mannerism in its mature phase, arrived in Venice between 1529 and 1531. Finally, confronted with the provocation of the sweeping triumph of this movement, Venetian painting could not but yield to the stimulus of a profound revision, not of its fundamental

ITALIAN SCHOOL OF THE 16th CENTURY

Fortune

Oil on wood
46x27
End of 16th C.

On the back of the painting are two strips of iron ending in rings, a sign that the panel was originally part of the door of a piece of furniture or a mirror.
The painting shows a young woman representing Fortune, standing on a globe while generously distributing worldly symbols to her gamblers. She deliberately turns her back on the hour-glass and roses (symbols of the transience of life) being offered to her on a tray by an unknown winged figure, identifiable perhaps as Time or Death.

values, but of the stylistic and expressive tendencies which had accumulated during the first twenty years of the century.

If Titian's acquaintance with central Italian art proved to be an opportunity to deepen and widen his artistic vision, for Jacopo Bassano and Jacopo Tintoretto, who were in their twenties during the years 1535-40, it became an essential aspect of their stylistic formation. About ten years later the same happened for the even younger Paolo Veronese.

Their relationship with an art which had originated in a totally different cultural environment was highly dialectic, so much so that in all three artists it produced extremely original results, which differed profoundly from one to another.

In the Gallery these three painters are represented with a certain discontinuity. Only three paintings by Jacopo Tintoretto on historical themes are on show (the *Miracle of Saint Augustine* being by Domenico): *Christ* and the *Samaritan Woman at the Well*, which come from the Contini-Bonacossi collection, and *Leda and the Swan* (from the Noè Walker bequest). These paintings progressively document the artist's late phase (first the *Leda*, then the two Contini-Bonacossi canvases) when, with ever-increasing rigour and creative tension, he combined the complex compositions of counterpoised figures of Michelangelo origin, drawn from his Mannerist experience, with the progressive use of night and artificial light breaking through the darkness (as in the *Christ* and the *Samaritan Woman at the Well*), or of increasingly grey natural light, turning to evening, broken by the last glimmering rays of daylight.

There is also a marvellous series of portraits by Tintoretto at the Uffizi, which we list here in chronological order, the *Portrait of a Man with a Red Beard*, the *Portrait of a Man in a Fur Cloak*, the *Portrait of a Venetian Admiral* and the *Portrait of Jacopo Sansovino*. These portraits show that Tintoretto started from a knowledge of Titian's mature style, taking in both the grandiose compositional structure and the dense colour pigments, although in Tintoretto this density tends to be swamped by the effect of darkness, and to disintegrate due to the sudden disarming gleams of light. Tintoretto's painting loses the characteristics of tonality in order to emphasize the contrast between light and shade.

Jacopo Bassano has a quite different character. He came into contact with the Mannerism of central Italy through Francesco Salviati, possibly taking some aspects directly from Parmigianino and Primaticcio, who had been Salviati's point of reference. This is particularly clear in the *Madonna and Child with the Young Saint John* (which came into the Gallery with the Contini-Bonacossi bequest). From a compositional viewpoint, it is constructed on the diagonal crossing of elegant, undulating lines; in effect everything is resolved at the level of colour: the flesh-tones gleam softly, ready to dissolve into the dark, dense background of the awning. In this sensual contact with matter, which is typically Venetian, the gestures and faces too no longer conform to extraneous and predetermined models, but become natural and spontaneous. It is not surprising therefore that this artist — perhaps the most elegant of the Venetian painters in a Mannerist sense — executed pieces which for his own times had an almost disconcerting reality. The painting *Two Dogs*, for example, seems to anticipate Velázquez, even in its subject, of which it is unique in the sixteenth century. In the Gallery it is Bassano's late phase which is mainly represented. Through the influence of Tintoretto, and even more of Titian, he tends to adopt the dark light of dying sunsets or even nocturnal light.

The assistance of his son Francesco is also remarkable in the Uffizi paintings, in *The Building of the Ark* (now in the deposits), and in *Moses and the Burning Bush*, while the *Annunciation to the Shep-*

CIGOLI (Ludovico Cardi)
(Castelvecchio di Cigoli, 1559 - Rome, 1613)

Saint Francis Receives the Stigmata

Oil on wood
247x171
1596

This is a work with a high pietistic content, which interprets fully a sort of anti-Mannerist reaction of a religious-moralistic nature. Leaving aside the facile emotivity generated by the emphatic pose of the kneeling saint and the mystical, theatrical smoke which heralds the divine event, the painting is a work of extreme austerity, and avowedly prosaic even from a technical point of view, considering that the artist, breaking with the Tuscan design tradition, executed it in the Venetian style, almost entirely with colour.

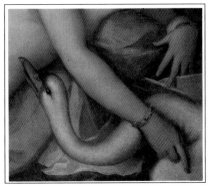

Leda and the Swan: detail before restoration.

Ludovico Cardi da Cigoli, Saint Francis Receives the Stigmata: detail.

herds is more generally attributable to his workshop. These paintings, although not entirely autograph, are nevertheless highly informative about one of Jacopo Bassano's innovations, and hence his importance in a historical sense. This was his ability to transfer religious subjects — including those which were soon to become the most important in the seventeenth-century — to the natural plane of the popular scene; this would later be called the pastoral genre.

This transposition was total, for Bassano, including as it did both style and narrative development. He used the complex and articulate compositions of mature Mannerism to tell stories about village and country

TINTORETTO (Jacopo Robusti)
(Venice, 1518 - 1594)

Leda and the Swan *

Oil on canvas
162x218
ca. 1570

Tintoretto was born in the year in which Titian painted his celebrated "Madonna dei Frari", and spent his youth in a cultural climate animated by the troubled conflict with Mannerism, which had infiltrated Northern Europe and was definitively putting an end to the followers of Giorgione. Tintoretto's entire stylistic development was characterized by the progressive abandonment of Venetian colour, and also of classical form, in order to reach the new expression of luminarism, a painting full of gleaming lights and shadows. In this "Leda and the Swan", a scene set with originality in a rich and comfortable interior, Tintoretto presents us with a work of his maturity, probably executed with the assistance of his workshop. It is a composition of great dignity, executed by a master of consumate experience, who carefully calibrates the two figures, emphasizing the splendour of the naked body and drawing attention to the magnificent velvets. However, the undeniable heaviness of the forms and the monotony of the colours are clear evidence of a certain academic fatigue.

SCHIAVONE (Andrea Meldolla)
attributed to
(Sebenico, ca. 1500 - Venice, 1563)

Portrait of a Man in a Fur Cloak

Oil on canvas
95x76
1570-80

The portrait, which is traditionally attributed to Tintoretto, under whose authorship the "Man in a Fur Cloak" continues to be listed in official catalogues of the Gallery, has recently been attributed to Schiavone on the basis of a convincing comparison with an autograph male portrait in the Arnot Collection in London. Schiavone is generally a little-known artist, whose source of Mannerist inspiration was Parmigianino. He tended, in fact, to identify the mark of the outline with the light, and make the colour fluid, and in this indefiniteness blurred the image to the point that it became a mass of colour in a space full of shadows and lights. He was a master of no great consequence, who succeeded in developing his own genre painting in a sort of post-Giorgionesque intimism, seeking somehow to counter the sumptuous constructions of Mannerist art. If we wished to make a parallel with the literature of Schiavone's time we would think of the development and success of pastoral idylls, of Tasso's "Aminta" and the early works of Tintoretto.

TINTORETTO (Domenico Robusti)
(Venice, 1560 - 1635)

The Miracle of Saint Augustine

Oil on canvas
186x108
Beginning of 17th C.

Jacopo Robusti — called Tintoretto from the work of his father, who was a cloth-dyer — had eight children by the noblewoman Faustina Episcopi, three of whom, Domenico, Marco and Marietta, followed in their father's footsteps. Domenico was certainly the most well-known of the three. It would be pointless to attempt a comparison between father and son, between the important expressive innovations of the former and the achievements of a good though not excellent level of the latter. The boldness of the perspective in this Saint Augustine healing the cripples is undoubtedly typical of Tintoretto, but of Jacopo's dramatic force only the appearance of the light and shadow contrasts and the emphatic chiaroscuro have survived.

life, with men who moved in the night, aware of having been raised to the rank of protagonists of history.

To this moment of dazzling encounter between Venetian tonality and luminarism, and the highly evolved formal world of Mannerism, can be traced the formation of a very great painter, not of Italian origin, but of Italian training, who became the leading representative of Spanish painting in the second half of the sixteenth century — El Greco. The Gallery has on show a signed masterpiece of his — a canvas portraying *Saints John the Evangelist and Francis* — which reveals clear evidence of his Venetian education (based on Jacopo Bassano and Tintoretto), although here El Greco uses both his models in a highly original way to produce an exsaggerated, visionary transfiguration of reality.

Of the three great artists of this generation, Paolo Veronese, who was the youngest, having been born in 1528, revealed from the start a distinct mental and cultural personality. In the ten years which separate him from Bassano and Tintoretto, the Mannerist crisis of sixteenth-cen-

TINTORETTO (Jacopo Robusti)
(Venice, 1518 - 1594)

Portrait of Jacopo Sansovino

Oil on canvas
70x65. 5
ca. 1566

The famous artist was portrayed by
Tintoretto at an advanced age. Tintoretto
invariably preferred the faces of old people
in his portraits, almost as if his profound
humanity and remarkable ability to enter
into the psychology of his subject were
strengthened in rendering the weary and
intense features of the aged.
Sansovino is portrayed with the tools of his
trade in his hand, and is illuminated by a
golden light which subtly highlights the
details of his beard and thin hair. The eyes
are attentive, and seem to observe with
keenness and a certain irony the painter
who is portraying one of the most eminent
sculptors and architects of the sixteenth
century.

tury Venetian painting had lost all its drama. For him the foreshortenings, the *contrapposti,* the rotations and spirals are suitable instruments
for the execution, at a compositional level, of his vision of a magnificent,
grandiose, dynamic world, situated in a space whose boundary is the
surface colour which the created world reveals to our eyes. His compositions are, as a result, solid, well-spaced, monumental, and at the same
time airy, animated, urgent. Not since the second decade, that is since
Titian's early classicism, had Venice seen such classical paintings.

In the *Holy Family with Saints Barbara and John,* which the Gallery
acquired with Cardinal Leopoldo de' Medici's inheritance, the composition has a rich harmony of *contrapposti,* while the extremely bright light
enhances the colour effects and the quality of the materials; the background has the vagueness of an area of colour slowly becoming more
compact. If the *Holy Family with Saints Barbara and John* emanates a
delightful sense of intimacy (it was certainly intended for a private
home), the *Annunciation* shows Paolo Veronese's gifts as a painter of history and as a fresco-painter of large spaces. Even in this not particularly
large canvas he reveals his talent for spectacular scene-setting, which he
later exploited in the large-scale decoration of churches (like San Sebastiano in Venice) and villas (for example the Barbaro at Masèr).

TINTORETTO (Jacopo Robusti)
(Venice, 1518 - 1594)

Portrait of a Man with a Red Beard *

Oil on canvas
52. 5x45. 5
1546-48

This is a work which at first sight might be
confused with any other dignified portrait
of the copious production of the late
sixteenth century. However, a closer look
reveals qualities of considerable
psychological penetration and a nearness to
reality which caused an art theorist of the
second half of the sixteenth century, Sorte,
to write, ' ... in his portraits. . . which he
does from life, he immediately places the
shadows, half-tints and reliefs; the flesh is
well imitated and effected with such
practical vigour, quickness and attention
that it is wonderful to see him work'.

TINTORETTO (Jacopo Robusti)
(Venice, 1518 - 1594)

Portrait of a Venetian Admiral

Oil on canvas
127x99
1570

The portrait is certainly of an admiral, although the precise identity of this dignified noble is still uncertain. The names of Sebastiano Venier, and later of Agostino Barbarigo, the Venetian noble who died in the Battle of Lepanto, have been mentioned, but more recent critics are far from convinced.
It is another of Tintoretto's masterpieces. The atmosphere of the painting is made particularly warm and intense by the purple velvet dress of the figure, whose proud, authoritative air is befitting for a man of leadership. The view of the sea in the background certainly alludes to his profession.

Yet, in spite of the *trompe-l'oeil* perspective, the lateral multiplication of spaces, the breaking through of miraculous clouds from above, the light colour laid on in pure surfaces on which only reflections of light flash with superimposed brush-strokes of a pure colour or white, gives this painting too a form which is geometric, perfect, harmonious and regulated in all its parts. From a complex equilibrium created through a dynamic of movement in no way inferior to Tuscan-Roman Mannerism (the two figures of the Angel and the Virgin are portrayed in *contrapposto* and in torsion) emerges a deep sense of serenity, of tranquil control of the world and of reason. Because of this, Veronese may be considered one of the last exponents of Italian humanism. The demonstration of Veronese's ability to propose a comprehensive synthesis of the world — in the context of the paintings at the Uffizi — is also found in the *Martyrdom of Saint Justina*, a canvas of modest size which advances the same vision of a perfect world in which the natural and sublime are united in harmony.

Veronese's customary use of scenography and organization causes the vision to expand once again in the large painting of *Esther and Ahasuerus*. But he also has an intimistic vein, which leads him to create themes or interpretations which anticipate in a singular way certain sev-

BASSANO (Jacopo da Ponte)
(Bassano, ca. 1515 - 1592)

Annunciation to the Shepherds
Judas and Tamar

Oil on canvas
40x96, 40x95
Second half of 16th C.

Within Mannerism, Jacopo Bassano succeeded in focusing on an aspect which for the most part had escaped contemporary artists, that is, the importance of minor particulars and apparently insignificant secondary details, especially in paintings of a religious or devotional subject, thus showing an acute and extremely mobile curiosity which made him capable of analyzing everything thoroughly. As a result his approach to the religious event was neither didactic, nor ecstatic, nor lyrical, but was rather that of a person who with keen interest observes a scene and rapidly takes notes.

The Annunciation to the Shepherds was a particularly popular theme with the painter, who attempted it several times, characterizing the scene with animals, sacks, vases, pots and other everyday objects. In so doing he created a completely original genre, a balance of religious and pastoral visions which his own children and pupils would continue through the seventeenth century.

Like the Annunciation, the scene of the serious Judah and beautiful Tamar (lit up by the glow of her own mantle) is also set in a gloomy, open landscape. The general style and use of light in the two compositions are very similar.

LEANDRO BASSANO (Leandro da Ponte)
(Bassano, 1577 - Venice, 1622)

The Concert *

Oil on canvas
114x178
ca. 1590

Son of Jacopo da Ponte, Leandro was initially active in his native
city. Later he moved to Venice (1592), where he won some
success particularly as a portraitist, thanks to his lively use of
colour, thick, bright mixtures and rich highlightings. Compared
to his brothers, who were also painters — Francesco the
Younger, Gerolamo and Giovanni Battista — he was the best and
most faithful continuer of his father's art.

EL GRECO (Domenikos Theotokòpulos)
(Candia, 1541 - Toledo, 1614)

Saints John the Evangelist and Francis

Oil on canvas
110x86
ca. 1600

Domenico Theotokòpulos, who was born into an eastern
Catholic community, a minority that was completely alien to the
great cultural movements of the time, owes precisely to this
original cultural background the rigorous intransigence of forms
and content expressed in his works.
El Greco marks a definitive turning-point and a decisive
detachment from any remaining vestige of Renaissance art, due
to his spiritualistic-visionary style which, although shunning the
classicizing myth, certainly did not follow naturalistic paths.
This work perfectly conveys the painter's tendency to express
exaggerated, totally ecstatic images, transfigured by a light which
irrationally breaks down bodily limits, almost making them
emerge from a swirling, unreal vortex which is above all a
dimension of the soul. The large figures of the two saints
dominate a space lacking in any decorative or realistic
adornment. A leaden, smoky sky renders the composition even
more dream-like.

enteenth and eighteenth-century *tableaux de chambre*. A typical example is the tiny *Saint Agatha Crowned by Angels* (20x18 cm). Paolo Veronese was also a great portrait painter, although none of his portraits are displayed in the Gallery.

The annexation of the territories of Bergamo and Brescia to the Venetian Republic attracted a large part of the artistic forces of these two Lombard provinces towards Venice. However, the Lombard tradition had elaborated specific, original qualities of its own which prevented its being colonized by the overpowering art of Venice. The sixteenth-century schools of Bergamo and Brescia are not well represented in the Uffizi: however, a painting like the *Transfiguration* by the Brescian painter Girolamo Savoldo is powerful evidence of the fact that although the Lombard tradition was certainly influenced by Titian's painting of the second decade, the interpretation was clearly and decidedly anti-Titian. The evangelical characters, the fishermen, peasants and ordinary people, are painted with the warm colours of Titian; Christ, who lives among them, is treated no differently, although his more delicate features tell us that he is descended from an ancient line. The realism with which the painting is imbued gives it a harmoniously archaic fifteenth-century flavour.

The approach of the Bergamo painter Giovan Battista Moroni is no different as regards the dazzling courtly art of Venice. He is represented in the Gallery by three portraits: the *Portrait of Count Secco-Suardo*, the *Portrait of the Poet Giovanni Antonio Pantera* and the *Portrait of a Man with a Book*. Although Moroni also painted many altar-pieces, he is best-known for his portrait-painting, the activity which brought him fame. His portraits are significant evidence of how a contemporary of Paolo Veronese, while mindful of the light-coloured painting and new compositional formulas developed by this master, could produce quite different results. Moroni replaces the exaltation of great historical characters with his own wish to confer on characters who are neither famous nor rich a calm but profound human dignity. His painting, attentive to all natural aspects, such as the gradations of a very clear light, lend great cordiality to the portrait of Count Suardo, whose full-length courtly model was used by Paolo Veronese to give the figure greater emphasis and monumentality. Here, the figure of the count is portrayed by Moroni in a familiar pose, surrounded by the objects which are dear to him and to which he attaches particular significance. In the other two portraits the painter prefers to use the half-length figure, a format which allows a more intimate, human relationship with the sitter. These portraits are in line with classical traditions and therefore represent an implicit refusal of the formal and thematic rules of Mannerism.

As we have already mentioned, shortly after 1570 the crisis of Mannerism was already in progress, at the same time that it was celebrating its final triumph at an international level. The conditions which led to the crisis were complex, the most important certainly being associated with the Catholic Counter-Reformation and the edicts laid down at the Council of Trent. There were also reasons of a human, cultural and artistic nature, a factor of some weight being the exhaustion of a stylistic formula which was threatening to overreach itself, thereby obstructing a direct contact with nature and with man. This justified the widespread and varied attempts at change and reform which have already been referred to.

The most important of all, as regards its future weight, was that of Federico Barocci from Urbino, who was active in various areas of central Italy and in Bologna. Florence has a considerable number of Barocci's works, some of which come from the Della Rovere Urbino Collections — the *Portrait of Francesco II della Rovere*, the *Portrait of Ippoli-*

PAOLO VERONESE (Paolo Caliari)
School of
(Verona, 1528 - Venice, 1588)

Esther and Ahasuerus

Oil on canvas
208x284
1562-65

It is widely thought that this painting is an old copy or perhaps the work of an imitator of
Veronese, a judgement we might share if we observe the weak, unfocused colour scheme,
which, although certainly inspired by the creations of the Veronese master of the 1560s fails
to reproduce the sharpness of his tones and his masterly blend of colours. In spite of this the
painting is airy, and in its vast, noble, stage-like structure, built up on various perspective
planes, it shows a deliberate theatricality.
In these very years, Paolo Veronese came close to a serene classicism intended not only as an
episodic architectural citation (in this period the artist knew Palladio, Sammicheli and
Sansovino) identifiable in his paintings and frescoes (see those of Villa Maser), but rather as
the fulfilment of his artistic vision.

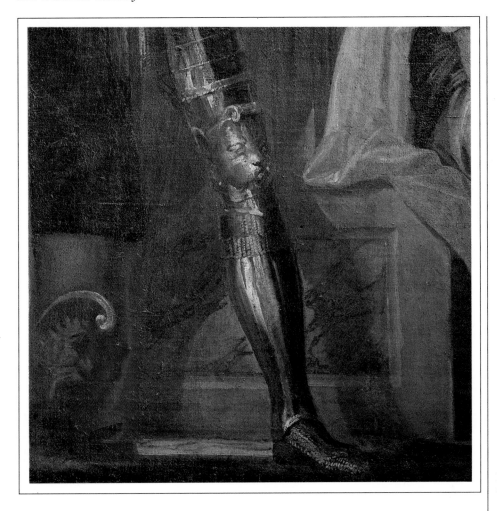

Paolo Veronese, Esther and Ahasuerus: detail.

to della Rovere, the *Visitation*, known as the *'Madonna of the Cat'* (in store) — others of which have come into the Gallery on different occasions from the Medici Collections (*Portrait of a Girl, Noli me tangere*, the *Stigmata of Saint Francis*, the *Madonna del Popolo*).

The *Madonna del Popolo*, which was formerly in the parish church of Arezzo, had been commissioned by the Confraternita dei Laici, and was removed at the behest of the Grand-duke in 1787. The altarpiece, which Barocci painted in 1579, had a considerable influence on various painters of the generation of the Mannerist crisis, such as Cigoli, whom we have already mentioned, and Gregorio Pagani. In it, having superseded his initial Mannerist phase, Barocci takes inspiration from Correggio, anticipating a fundamental attitude of the Baroque and Rococo periods. The *Madonna del Popolo* is already a great Baroque construction: the *contrapposti,* the torsions, the intertwining of bodies and the Mannerist spiral do not combine to create an elaborate formal synthesis, but rather a series of expanding planes which hover and move in space and in the still oppressive air. Galileo had not yet discovered that the universe was far larger than that which it was believed was centered on the earth. Representing the universe beyond the earth would be the task of the Baroque period. Barocci had discovered another of the many ways of escaping the existential Mannerist condition which Correggio offered to new generations. In the *Noli me tangere*, while the outlines of the individual elements widen, thereby allowing them to be immersed in a flow of colour with graduated shading, sentiments too break free from the confines of their rhetorical origins and take on shades of meaning — silences, unspoken allusions, intuited and unexpressed feelings. All these delightful nuances are represented not only with the *disegno*, but also with highly refined shades of colour.

PAOLO VERONESE (Paolo Caliari)
(Verona, 1528 - Venice, 1588)

Annunciation

Oil on canvas
143x291
1556

This youthful Annunciation perfectly exemplifies the style which anticipated the development of Veronese's art into the calmer and more complex schemes of his maturity, in which considerable space is devoted to backgrounds of Palladian and Sansovino-style architecture transformed into sceneries of pure colour.
The light is golden, gay and joyful, and spreads throughout the composition with gleaming reflections, reflections which almost come from the central glory of angels, rather incongruously inserted from above into a space that was constructed horizontally.

Paolo Veronese, Annunciation: detail.

281

GIOVANNI GIROLAMO SAVOLDO
(Brescia, ca. 1480 - Venice or Brescia, 1548)

Transfiguration *

Oil on wood
139x126
ca. 1533

Savoldo has little interest for the dramatic ardour of Titian, but is inspired more by the melancholy contemplation of Giorgione. An introvert by nature, he seeks touches of resplendent luminarism in even the smallest things, and in a highly refined way focuses his interest on that which is less spectacular and more unusual. Savoldo shrinks from oratorical attitudes and dazzling effects. As can be seen in this his only work displayed at the Uffizi, he prefers themes which rather than lending themselves to narration are instead more suited to a sort of intimate poetical digression.

PAOLO VERONESE (Paolo Caliari)
(Verona, 1528 - Venice, 1588)

Saint Agatha Crowned by Angels

Oil on wood
20x18
ca. 1580

Over the centuries many names have been proposed for the identity of this female figure. It was suggested that the woman portrayed was Saint Agnes, later Saint Apollonia, secondary considerations which hardly detract from the intimate grace and delicacy of this small canvas, unanimously attributed to Veronese's maturity.

Even in such a limited space, the technical and pictorial qualities of the work are exceptional: the aerial balance of the small angels, the rapt, contemplative pose of the saint, and the glittering brightness of the clothes, which seem almost to be woven with gold, as light as veils in the sleeves and as resplendent as shining metal in the folds of the skirt.

Transfiguration: detail before
restoration.

FEDERICO BAROCCI
(Urbino, 1535 - 1612)

"Madonna del Popolo" *

Oil on wood
359x252
1576-79

The "Madonna del Popolo" dates from the period immediately prior to the painter's maturity. The influence of Correggio is plainly visible in the sinuous, complex line underpinning the entire composition, in which the arc formed by the crowd below harmoniously links up with the celestial arc formed by the figure of Christ, the Virgin and the angels appearing amid the clouds.
The groups of figures twist and intertwine in continuous, daring contrapuntal chiaroscuro, thus forming, as in Correggio, a garland around the piazza which is almost concealed by the dusty golden sunlight impregnating the throng, the temple and the arcade below the faint blue sky. However, Correggio's model fails to prevent Barocci from affirming his own distinctive style — the bold contrast he makes between the background of diffused light and the dynamic chiaroscural effects of the foreground, the original touch of the teeming crowd, and the almost Rococo caprice of the twisted and light-fragmented forms.

FEDERICO BAROCCI
(Urbino, 1535 - 1612)

Portrait of a Girl

Oil on paper
45x33
1570-75

The young woman of this charming little portrait has been identified as Lavinia della Rovere, the young bride of Alfonso d'Avalos (1583).
The dainty female figure is made quite delightful by her watery gaze, glowing with a discreet light, the freshness of her mother-of-pearl flesh and the incomparable grace of her timid, furtive smile. A full, rounded face, framed by a high frilled collar which is already fully seventeenth-century in style.

THE 17TH AND 18TH CENTURIES

Mina Gregori

The rooms in the Gallery dedicated to the seventeenth and eighteenth centuries are an illustrious record of the participation of the last Medici rulers in the period of European collectionism which had started at the end of the sixteenth century. In the field of Flemish painting once again the Medici collections are an unrivalled nucleus in Italy. Although the historical overview inevitably also includes the paintings displayed in the Galleria Palatina, the importance of the portraits and various large-scale canvases kept at the Uffizi cannot be sufficiently stressed. The eminent masters were Peter Paul Rubens and Anthony Van Dyck. Famous throughout Europe in court circles, and for their figurative interpretation of the Catholic ideology, for a long time the two artists were fundamental points of reference for the development of seventeenth-century schools in northern Europe, including Protestant Holland and England, while their presence in Italy — Rubens from 1600 to 1608; Van Dyck from 1621 to 1627 — was highly stimulating in several cities, especially Genoa, Mantua, Venice and Rome.

In the retinue of Vincenzo Gonzaga, Rubens had been present at the wedding of Maria de' Medici and Henry IV of France, celebrated by proxy in Florence on 5 October 1600. In 1603 he made a second visit to Tuscany. The Medici, however, unlike the Duke of Mantua, to whom they were related, were not patrons of the young Flemish painter.

The first work whose arrival in Florence was widely documented was the canvas with the *Consequences of War*, which was bought by the painter Justus Sustermans, the official portraitist of the Medici court. The painting, now at the Pitti, arrived in 1638, at the same time as the introduction in Florence of the painting of Pietro da Cortona, which was, with the sculpture of Bernini, one of the first organic interpretations in Italy of the artistic tendencies of Rubens.

While in the middle of the century Rubens' painting of the *Madonna della cesta* (Pitti) appeared in the inventories, in the late seventeenth century the intensification of interest in the Flemish painter — also confirmed by the letters of Grand Prince Ferdinando — is represented by various episodes regarding the leading figures in the Medici family most systematically involved in collectionism. In 1617, in response to the interest in drawings of the greatest collector, Cardinal Leopold, the Medici ambassador in Brussels, Francesco Airoldi, sent the sketch in chiaroscuro of the *Three Graces*.

Although Cosimo III, as already noted, was more interested in Dutch masters, in 1686 he acquired two paintings by Rubens — *Henry IV at the Battle of Ivry* and the *Triumphal Entrance of Henry IV into Paris* — which were linked (not only ideally) to the cycle with the *Stories of Maria de' Medici* executed by the Flemish painter between 1622 and 1625 for the Luxembourg Palace. The parallel cycle had originally been planned as a series of ten large paintings celebrating the military feats of Maria's deceased husband, which would occupy another gallery in the building. But the painter would undertake their execution after various difficulties and problems (it was even thought of replacing him with Guido Reni), only in 1628, when he made it known that he had made the drawings for them, and in 1630 when he started to paint the canvases. If Maria's exile was the main cause of his failure to complete the undertaking, it is known that Rubens executed various sketches and six large canvases, five of which we know today, two at the Uffizi, the other three (for the most part not autograph) respectively at the Alte Pinakothek in Munich, the Göteborg Museum and formerly in the Bührle Collection in Zurich. The sketch for *Henry IV at the Battle of Ivry* is in the Bonnat Museum in Bayonne; for the *Triumphal Entranceof Henry IV into Paris*, which according to the plan was supposed to be displayed in the position of honour on the end wall of the Gallery, three sketches are known (the one in the Wallace Collection is clearly inspired by Mantegna's *Triumph of Caesar* which Rubens must have just seen at Hampton Court, where it had been displayed in 1629).

Cosimo III's fortuitous acquisition of the two unfinished autograph paintings — which were at the Abbey of the Holy Sepulchre in Cambrai, and apparently were coveted by Louis XIV who intended to obtain them through an intermediary, Charles Le Brun — had a dual significance. The paintings were important for dynastic reasons because they exalted a monarch with whom, through Maria, the Medici were related, and for artistic reasons because they were by the most famous artist in Europe at the time. They are in fact extremely important examples of Baroque painting and of Rubens' conception of the historico-celebratory picture, in which factuality was exalted and raised to symbolic exemplariness, as *historia* in the classical sense, by the presence of allegorical figures. The Uffizi possesses another example of the historico-celebratory genre — a workshop replica whose importance is limited to its subject, the *Triumphal Entrance of Cardinal Prince Ferdinand of Spain into Antwerp*, an event which occurred in 1635 in which Rubens, who was always involved in political affairs, had placed high hopes.

On their arrival in Florence in 1686 the two paintings with the *Stories of Henry IV* must have appeared extremely modern to Florentine painters. Dating from the 1620s, the energy generated by the large number of figures, the intensity of the chiaroscural *macchia*, and the incredibly free, sketch-like execution, were a precedent not only for the crowded compositions of Pietro da Cortona (which provoked the famous dispute at the Accademia di San Luca), but also for the strongly chiaroscural pictorial quality of the late Baroque. The *Henry IV at the Battle of Ivry*, in particular, corresponds to that moment of the Rubensian evolution which coincided with Flemish painters working in Genoa, like Malò, and Genoese artists like Valerio Castello and, later, Gregorio de Ferrari. If this style also had repercussions on the specialist field of battle painting, for example on Borgognone, in Florence it must also have affected Livio Mehus and Pier Dandini.

The great consideration for the two *Stories of Henry IV* is revealed by their successive placements, in a saloon of Palazzo Pitti and, later, at the end of the eighteenth century, in the Niobe Room, here intended significantly to serve as a backdrop for the celebrated group of ancient stat-

PETER PAUL RUBENS
(Siegen, 1577 - Antwerp, 1640)

Henry IV at the Battle of
Ivry

BEING
RESTORED

Oil on canvas
367x693
1627/30

The subject refers to a decisive episode in the eighth and final religious war in France (1585-93), in which the succession to the throne of Henry III was fought for on 14 March 1590 in the relentless battle of Ivry. Henry IV, who was recognized as the legitimate heir, defeated Charles of Lorraine the Duke of Mayenne, leader of the Holy League, who was supported by the Spanish army.

In this painting Rubens excludes any reference of a descriptive nature, no indication which might help to localize the battle in time or space. The celebration of the episode is not based on a reconstruction of the events as much as on the re-evocation, through the tumultuous movement of masses revolving around the two central horses, of a furious battle in which Henry IV, recognizable by his famous white plume, distinguished himself as a courageous fighter.

PETER PAUL RUBENS
(Siegen, 1577 - Antwerp, 1640)

Triumphal Entrance of Henry IV into Paris

Oil on canvas
380x692
1627/30

This canvas, which came to Florence
together with the previous painting,
belongs to the same unfinished cycle
dedicated to Henry IV and shows the
king, converted and victorious,
triumphantly entering Paris on 22 March
1594 at the end of a long period of
internal struggles. Again renouncing any
reference to time or place, Rubens
illustrates the episode in a complex
allegorical context, creating an analogy
with the triumph of a Roman emperor.
In particular, the group of the crowned
king and the architecture of the triumphal
arch (derived from the Roman prototype
of the arch of Titus), surmounted by
soldiers and horses, arise from an evident
reinterpretation of Mantegna's painting of
"Caesar's Chariot".

ues. For thematic reasons, the Triumphal Entrance of Cardinal Prince Ferdinando of Spain into Antwerp was hung together with these paintings. Although the compositional model of this work is undoubtedly Rubensian, and justifies the gallery reference to the master, the execution cannot confirm the attribution to Rubens; the painting's historical importance, however, is undeniable. Recent research has established that, as was known in the eighteenth century when it was acquired, the large canvas formed part of the festive decorations executed, on the design and partial participation of Rubens, on the occasion of the Cardinal Prince's solemn entrance into Antwerp on 17 April 1635. Of the painters who executed the paintings, whose unrefined execution confirms their occasional and temporary use, in 1634 the *Triumphal Entrance* (Rubens' sketch of which is at the Hermitage) was entrusted to Jan van den Hoecke, as is revealed by the contract. Bodart has suggested that Jacob Jordaens was also involved, and in fact the work appears to be more brightly-lit and expressively emphatic compared to other paintings by Van den Hoecke. An example of it is his *Hercules*, a painting which shows how in the circle of Rubens painters proceeded not only in his wake but also in that of Van Dyck. Its attribution to Hoecke, court painter of the governor of Flanders, Archduke Leopold William, is attested to by the inventories of the Grand Prince to whom it belongs.

The acquisitions of Grand Prince Ferdinand varied in importance, as has been noted, and not only in the case of Rubens. Nonetheless he possessed an important autograph work by him, the *Resurrection* (Pitti), which is representative of the Flemish artist in the second decade, when he was still under the influence of his Roman experiences. According to the family custom of securing when possible private works which were put on sale in Florence (as was certainly the case with the *Holy Family* by Hoecke from Palazzo da Fiorenzuola), the Grand Prince acquired for the Medici collections the *Consequences of War* (Pitti), whose Rubensian authorship is indubitable, and whose allegorical subject had been described by the painter to Justus Sustermans in a letter of 12 March 1638.

Alongside this painting of prime importance, we should also mention the *Portrait of Isabella Brandt* of the Uffizi, which together with other paintings was sent as a gift to the Grand Prince in 1705 by his cultured brother-in-law the Elector Palatine Johann Wilhelm von Neuberg. Ferdinando greatly appreciated the painting, writing that it "surpasses the imagination and is a prodigy of that celebrated paintbrush".

The painting in question was a portrait of the artist's first wife, who died in 1626, and was indeed a masterpiece, one of those top-grade paintings by Rubens which it was easier to see in the collections of northern Europe. Painted on a panel of considerable size and without additions, a recent cleaning has revealed one of the most splendid portraits of Isabella, the last which Rubens executed probably by using a much earlier drawing, now at the British Museum. Among its many qualities are the psychological penetration (the suspicion of a conversational smile), the superlative magical effect of colour (the glow of the reddish panel in the background already adopted by Rubens in his youthful portraits) and of light (the reflections on the chin, the neck and the pearls), the elegance of the pose and the rendering of the hands, all perfectly in keeping with that refinement of which Van Dyck was also an interpreter. The portrait-painting of the two Flemish masters had contributed to spreading it throughout Europe and even Watteau would admire and draw inspiration from it.

Also belonging to the group of paintings acquired by Grand Prince Ferdinando is the large *Allegorical Portrait of Philip IV of Spain on Horseback*, which at the time was thought to be by Velázquez. The painting

JAN VAN DEN HOECKE
(Antwerp, 1611 - Brussels, 1651)

Triumphal Entrance of Cardinal Prince Ferdinand of Spain into Antwerp

Oil on canvas
405x328
1634/35

On 17 April 1635 celebrations were held for the triumphal entrance into Antwerp of Cardinal Prince Ferdinand, brother of Philip IV and archbishop of Toledo, who had just been appointed governor of the Spanish Low Countries. As the tradition of solemn entrances demanded, the city was decked out for the occasion with various stage-like decorations whose conception was entrusted to Rubens. His original sketch for this canvas, which was subsequently executed by Van den Hoecke and placed on the arch of triumph, is now in the Hermitage in St Petersburg. The composition is more or less a reworking of the central part of the "Triumphal Entrance of Henry IV into Paris", and like it is inspired by Mantegna's "Triumph of Caesar" and the "Triumph of Scipio" by Giulio Romano.

PETER PAUL RUBENS
(Siegen, 1577 - Antwerp, 1640)

Portrait of Isabella Brandt

Oil on wood
86x62
ca. 1625

This portrait, one of the most famous of Rubens' masterpieces, shows the artist's first wife Isabella Brandt (1591-1626) and was probably executed shortly before her death. The painting, traditional both in its style and in the pose of an interrupted reading, is based entirely on the quality of touch, a sort of "solo composition" of the brush, which is in places rapid and heavily mixed, in others vigorous and stylized, and in others still soft and "sfumato". It is not unlikely that the conventional motif of the column and the vine tendril have the allegorical significance which is characteristic of them, referring therefore to the constancy and eternity of love.

Peter Paul Rubens, Portrait of Isabella Brandt: detail.

was placed in this room because it was considered to be the most important known copy of the famous portrait of the king executed by Rubens in 1628 and destroyed during the fire of the Alcazar in Madrid in 1734. Although the general conception and the allegorical figures of this representation of the victorious king, borne up and guided by Faith, seem closely dependent, even for their execution, on the model of Rubens (his style had been introduced in Spain), in the figure of the horseman and in the open landscape traversed by a river in which the valley of Manzanarre has been recognized, the naturalistic tradition is discernible. The calmness and density of the landscape and the transparency of the back lighting which has the effect of detaching the horse's hind quarters from the background are substantial alterations of the dynamic atmosphere characteristic of Rubens.

The king's head, dress, and outstretched leg protected by a leather boot pitted and dirtied by the light and shade which accentuate its thickness

Diego Velazquez, Portrait of Philip IV of Spain on Horseback: detail.

DIEGO VELAZQUEZ and workshop
(attributed)
(Seville, 1599 - Madrid, 1660)

Equestrian portrait of Philip IV king of Spain *

Oil on canvas, 338x267
ca. 1645

It derives in part from the equestrian portrait painted by Rubens in Madrid in 1628 and lost in the fire of the Alcazar in 1734. It bears an extraordinary resemblance to Rubens' original, described in the inventory of the royal collections (1636), but in the work of the Uffizi the king is portrayed at a more advanced age and does not correspond with the twenty-two year-old Philip who had posed for Rubens, with a hat decorated with white feathers, a detail that makes this a much more personalized painting. When it figured in the collection of the Marquis of Eliche (who died in Naples in 1687), the portrait now at the Uffizi was described as a copy from Rubens, but the head of the sovereign was believed to be by Diego Velazquez, an attribution that was accepted until the beginning of this century, when it was reascribed to the school of Rubens. Art scholars (Lopez-Rey, 1963) have nonetheless reattributed the portrait of Philip IV to the Spanish circle. The readability of the work after restoration has encouraged the view that Velazquez was the author.
That the Spanish master had carefully studied the painting by Rubens emerges from a comparison with his numerous equestrian portraits of the king - of which we can admire an example in Florence in the splendid old copy of the Galleria Palatina - and even with the "Portrait of Prince Baltasar Carlos" (Prado, Madrid), datable to 1628-29. More typically Rubens is the allegorical insertion of the high part with the allegorical figures of Faith offering the king the laurel of victory and placing the cross on the terrrestrial globe behind the sovereign, Divine Justice hurling thunderbolts and the Indian who symbolizes the New World.
As for the structure of the equestrian portrait, we cannot but recall the models of Giambologna, the Flemish sculptor who with his workshop in Florence had revived the tradition of the equestrian monument ("Cosimo I", 1587-95; "Ferdinando I", 1601-8; "Henry IV", 1600-1614). Vice versa it was precisely a painting by Rubens that served as a model, especially for the pose of the horse in the act of rearing, for the equestrian statue of Philip IV that Pietro Tacca executed for Madrid (1634-42).

and texture, support the attribution to Velázquez with which the painting entered the collection of Grand Prince Ferdinando. Josè Lopez-Rey believes, exactly as is mentioned in a 1651 inventory of the collection of the Marquis of Eliche, from where it came, that the head was executed by Velázquez, who worked on the painting around 1645. Being a court painter, he was probably commissioned to execute with assistants the copy of the royal portrait painted by Rubens. In the middle of the 1640s the king's prestige had been strengthened by his victories against the French and Velázquez enjoyed new favours. The fact that the painting came from the collection of the Marquis of Eliche, son of the prime minister who succeeded Olivares, where it was mentioned in 1651, seems to bear out the hypothesis of Lopez-Rey.

At the end of the eighteenth century, in 1792 to be precise, through

exchanges with the Gallery of Vienna, the *Bacchus Astride a Barrel* came to Florence with the attribution to Rubens. The painting had previously belonged to the prestigious collections of Christine of Hohenstaufen and the Orléans family, and had been purchased by Emperor Charles VI. Although the larger version of the Hermitage (previously in the Richelieu and Crozat collections and coming from Rubens' inheritance) is recognized as a better example of this subject, the canvas of the Uffizi is the only work in the Gallery representing, albeit in a workshop version, the artist's extreme style.

Anthony Van Dyck visited Florence in 1622, during his Italian period. As a recently discovered biography of the painter mentions, he stayed in the city about a month studying the works of art belonging to the Medici family, part of which Ferdinando had already arranged at the Uffizi. The biographer states that the Flemish painter was unable to find an important patron in Florence because Grand-duke Ferdinando II was still young, although his brother Don Lorenzo probably had his portrait painted, a work which today is lost. According to the biography, Van Dyck also met the Flemish painter Justus Sustermans, this being highly probable since the latter had lived in Florence for several years.

The Florentine galleries possess some important works by Van Dyck, primarily the *Portrait of Cardinal Bentivoglio* (Pitti), which has been in Florence since 1653. Executed in Rome in 1622, or more probably in 1623, it can be regarded as the fundamental prototype for Roman portrait-painting. The *Portrait of Charles V on Horseback*, inspired by Titian's version with the *Emperor at the Battle of Mühlburg* (Madrid, Prado) in the light of various considerations can be considered the work of assistants or the product of a workshop executed prior to Van Dyck's Italian period. The dating seems confirmed by the close similarities with an early drawing at Christchurch Oxford, with the sketch for *Saint Martin and the Poor Man* (Washington), this too dating from the end of the artist's first Antwerp period, and with the two large portraits by Anton Giulio Brignole Sale (Palazzo Rosso) and Cornelis de Wael (Antwerp), executed in the Genoese period. Although in a mediocre state of preservation, the painting is of interest — in addition to the allegorizing interpretation (the eagle with the laurel garland of the victor) — for the *abbozzo* style to which Rubens and Van Dyck gave great impulse and which represented one of the most popular techniques in seventeenth-century painting.

The other two portraits also had wide notoriety in the past. The portrait of the medal engraver Jean de Montfort, active from 1596 to 1649 and master of the Mint at the Brussels court, was mentioned in 1704 and was probably purchased, like the preceding work, by Grand Prince Ferdinando. At the end of the eighteenth century it was hung in the Tribune, a fact which confirms its reputation. The work is thought to date from the period which Van Dyck spent in Antwerp immediately after his return from Italy (about 1628); however, a comparison with another smaller-sized version in Vienna suggests that due to certain weaknesses in workmanship the Florentine painting was executed with the help of the workshop. The physical presence of the figure, which occupies almost the entire surface of the canvas, brings the portrait close in conception to the vigour of the great Genoese models. The North European component, amplified through the style of Rubens, also demonstrates what importance the two Flemish artists had for the Dutch portrait.

The *Portrait of Marguerite of Lorraine, Duchess of Orléans* represents Van Dyck's evolution towards silky, silvery tones, in an interpretation which in the fourth decade of the seventeenth century the artist also exported to England, as is confirmed by its similarity with the *Queen Henrietta Maria and her Dwarf Jeffery Hudson* (Washington, 1633). The work is dated by the above-mentioned biography to 1634 and was

PETER PAUL RUBENS
School of
(Siegen, 1577 - Antwerp, 1640)

Bacchus Astride a Barrel

Oil on canvas
152x118
ca. 1640

In this composition, other replicas and copies of which are also known, the complex, lively arrangement of poses and gestures typical of Rubens contains a mixture of figurative and iconographical elements drawn from models which the Flemish master had been able to study carefully. The Bacchanal was a theme frequently represented by the artists of Rubens' circle, especially by engravers, who with monitory captions underlined its moral implications.

Anthony van Dyck, Portrait of Charles V on Horseback, detail.

ANTHONY VAN DYCK
School of
(Antwerp, 1599 - London, 1641)

Portrait of Charles V on Horseback *

Oil on canvas
191x123
ca. 1625

This posthumous portrait was inspired by Titian's "Charles V at the Battle of Mühlberg" (Madrid, Prado). Apart from the age of the emperor — who here is portrayed younger — and his different armour, substantial modifications (compared to the sixteenth-century model) have been made to the pose of the horse, which is no longer in profile but nervously jerking towards the onlooker, and to the background, where a rough seascape has replaced the open valley typical of the Venetian style: a re-elaboration, therefore, according to a typically Baroque vision. But although it is linked to the tradition of equestrian portraits by Rubens and Van Dyck, the painting is really rather weak. A comparison with similar subjects executed by Van Dyck serves to accentuate here a poverty of invention and lack of vigour, especially in the figure of the horse.

Anthony van Dyck, Portrait of Marguerite of Lorraine, Duchess of Orléans: detail.

probably executed in Brussels. In spite of its admirable elegance, it is a 'series portrait': that of her husband, Gaston d'Orléans, is at the Musée Condé in Chantilly. The *Portrait of a Lady* at Kenwood, Iveagh Bequest, corresponds to the biographer's mention of the portrait of her sister Henrietta of Lorraine, executed at the same time; the latter repeats the model of the Uffizi painting with little variation.

Justus Sustermans trained in Antwerp, but was already in Florence at the beginning of the 1620s, establishing contact with tapestry-makers like Pietro Févère; he died in Florence in 1681 as court artist. The *Portrait of Galileo Galilei* is perhaps the most famous work by Sustermans, at least from a historical point of view. Executed from life in 1635, it was sent by Galilei to France, from where it was later retrieved by Vincenzo Viviani to be displayed in the Tribune; thus, the likeness of the great scientist was duly celebrated in a public place. We know almost nothing about Sustermans' relations with Flanders in the Florentine years, beyond his probable encounter with Van Dyck in 1622 and his exchange of letters with Rubens in 1637-38 for the commission of the *Consequences of War*; yet the artist's Flemish roots always seem evident in his paintings. Sustermans, more than is commonly said, contributed significantly to the conversion of various Florentine painters, like Volterrano and Mehus, to a Baroque style.

Caravaggio and Annibale Carracci represented the two poles, both of North Italian origin, of the renewal that took place in Italy at the end of the sixteenth century.

The refined naturalness of the Emilians is worthily represented at the Uffizi, even though the paintings are few in number. Annibale Carracci is credited with the *Venus with a Satyr and Cupids*, a painting which has

ANTHONY VAN DYCK
(Antwerp, 1599 - London, 1641)

Portrait of Marguerite of Lorraine, Duchess of Orléans

Oil on canvas
204x117
1634

This work, which shows great accomplishment in the head and hands, appears rigorously in keeping with the schemes of official portraiture, but is set off by the invention of the curtain raised by the wind, creating an opening towards the background landscape: an unusual touch which Van Dyck had adopted previously only in his youthful "Portrait of Nicolas Rockox", now in St Petersburg.

JAKOB JORDAENS
Attributed to
(Antwerp, 1593 - 1678)

Portrait of a Lady, known as "Jordaens' Mother"

Oil on canvas
68x50

The painting was acquired in 1902 from Professor Emilio Costantini as a work by Rubens, though today opinions are divided as to its authorship. The attribution to Jordaens, for example, is highly questionable, while the name of Sustermans proposed by Van Puyvelde (1953) is quite unacceptable. This unremarkable painting suffered an alteration in the past, being enlarged at the sides and at the top.

JUSTUS SUSTERMANS
(Antwerp, 1597 - Florence, 1681)

Portrait of Galileo Galilei

Oil on canvas
66x56
1635

Elia Diodati, a lawyer from Lucca who was exiled in Paris, had known Galileo during his repeated journeys in Tuscany. It was to Diodati that the great scientist owed the publication of the translation of his "Dialogo sopra i massimi sistemi" in 1635. This portrait, which Galileo had executed by Sustermans, was given to Diodati as a token of his recognition.

been dated to 1588 on the basis of an inscription on the back of an old copy. It was purchased in 1620 and is mentioned by the major Bolognese source, Carlo Cesare Malvasia. The mischievous interpretation of the mythological subject goes beyond the fullness of senses of Titian's late 'poetries', despite the fact that the figure of Venus from behind seems to recall a precise model typical of the Venetian artist. The fusion of superficial truth and Alexandrine spirit in this early work announces not only a new personality, but a revival, on different foundations, of the humanistic, classicizing culture, which seems to end the period of pure Counter-Reformation, such that it is not difficult to forsee Carracci's position when he moves to Rome, and the importance of his frescoes in the Galleria Farnese.

The *Man with a Monkey* was attributed to Annibale Carracci only in the nineteenth century. The intensely Venetianizing workmanship reveals Carracci's interest in the portrait-painting of Venetian contemporaries like the young Palma and Aliense, and in the spread of character heads and portraits in the Venetian area at the end of the sixteenth century. It also prompts the question of whether it would be opportune or not to rectify some attributions in the corpus of Bolognese artists in favour of the Venetians. This is perhaps the case, as Borea sustains, with the *Man with a Monkey*, which, as we have pointed out, has no authoritative historical documentation.

The landscape paintings of the Emilians, who at their origin renewed the tradition of the Venetians and Ferrarese, are splendidly represented by Guercino's *Country Concert*. It is worth mentioning that this work, one of the masterpieces of the Italian seventeenth century, was chosen in 1773 among the paintings to be transferred from Poggio a Caiano to the Uffizi (suggesting that it had belonged to Grand Prince Ferdinando). The freshness of the execution, the humid, gleaming depths of the landscape, and the neo-sixteenth-century re-evocation of the musicians, place the work around 1617, in that early period which favoured the modern rediscovery of Guercino. A different kind of interpretation is needed for the *Landscape with Cupids* by Francesco Albani, dating from around 1630, a highly-praised product of the classical schema elaborated in Rome in Carracci's circle. The rhythm pervading it not only in the line of dancing putti, but also in the trees and their distribution, is a high example of Albani's fragile neo-Attic art.

The Gallery has three early works by Caravaggio, each with its own provenance and individual history. The *Medusa* was sent as a gift to Ferdinando I, probably in the last years of the sixteenth century, by Caravaggio's patron, Cardinal del Monte. Being a tournament shield, it was certainly destined from the very beginning for the Medici Armoury, where for a long time it was kept with the name of its author in a fantastic room which on the basis of inventory descriptions has been reconstructed by Detlef Heikamp. The shield was applied to the arm of a figure in Oriental dress and protected by Oriental armour, raised up on a wooden horse and ready for combat. The apotropaic significance of the *Medusa*, which was referred to in poems dedicated to it by Murtola and Marino, was therefore accentuated, increasing the onlooker's sense of horror which the painter had wanted to provoke in representing the fatal moment with the absolute contemporaneity of the shout and the decapitation. The head was made more strikingly life-like through Caravaggio's shading of the background, which transformed the convexity of the shield into concavity.

The *Bacchus*, which is neither mentioned in the sources nor traceable in the inventories, is one of the most important attributions to Caravaggio, linked to the first years of the 'rediscovery' of Caravaggio in the present century. Until recently the work was associated with a *Bacchus* mentioned by Baglione among the artist's early works, but there is now a

ANNIBALE CARRACCI
(Bologna, 1560 - 1609)

Venus with a Satyr and Cupids

Oil on canvas
112x142
1588

Acquired in 1620 for the Medici collections, this painting, which was already famous in the seventeenth century, was for moral reasons covered over with another canvas of a more chaste allegorical subject through most of the eighteenth century. The recovery of the original painting in 1812 has restored to us a work of great importance in Annibale Carracci's youthful development. If we are to believe the date, 1588, written on the back of an old copy, the painting of the Uffizi falls in a decisive year for the young painter: the time, that is, of his evolution from late Mannerist Bolognese culture, already enriched by Correggio, towards the colour-light synthesis of Titian and Veronese, from which would emerge that neo-Venetianism at the foundation of the Carraccesque "reform".

GUERCINO (Giovan Francesco Barbieri)
(Cento, 1591 - Bologna, 1666)

Country Concert

Oil on copper
34x46
ca. 1617

This painting on copper, more than the numerous other works housed in Florentine galleries, documents a particular moment in the activity of the Emilian artist, for it reveals the interest which the young Guercino cultivated for landscape painting. Both the dignified composition, constructed with side wings converging towards the background, and the sketch-like execution of the trees' foliage recall the landscape tradition typical of artists from Ferrara.

CARAVAGGIO (Michelangelo Merisi)
(Caravaggio or Milan, 1570/71 or 73 - Porto
Ercole, 1610)

Medusa

Oil on canvas-covered wood
diam. 55
1591/92 (Longhi)
1598/99 (Cinotti)
1601 (Heikamp)

It has now been confirmed that this striking painting was commissioned to Caravaggio by his patron Francesco Maria Del Monte in order to make a gift of it to Ferdinando I. The canvas was attached to a wooden shield and displayed in the Medicean Armoury (where it was recorded in 1631) on the arm of an oriental suit of armour which was donated to the Grand-duke, presumably in 1601, by the Shah of Persia Abbas the Great.

The representation of Medusa on a shield or on armour was common in the course of the Renaissance, during which time it lost its original function and became simply a decorative motif or symbol of power.

Michelangelo Merisi, Bacco: detail.

CARAVAGGIO (Michelangelo Merisi)
(Caravaggio or Milan, 1570/71 or 73 - Porto Ercole, 1610)

Bacchus

Oil on canvas
95x85
ca. 1589 (Longhi)
ca. 1596 (Mahon)

This work, discovered and attributed relatively recently by Roberto Longhi (1916), was of fundamental significance in the youthful activity of Caravaggio. Identified originally as "Bacchus with various bunches of grapes", it was dated by Longhi to around 1589. Subsequent documentary research moved the date forward to 1596, to a time, that is, when Caravaggio was already under the protection of Cardinal Francesco Maria del Monte.
As might be expected, the most varied interpretations of this painting have been advanced. According to Longhi, the ironic identification of Bacchus with "this sluggish youth of a Roman tavern" was controversially anti-classicist. Nonetheless, it is impossible to overlook in this work the references — ironic or otherwise — to classical antiquity both in the pose of the arm and in the "Roman style" drapery. The insertion of the bowl of fruit should not be interpreted as a merely descriptive or naturalistic element, since there is now no doubt about the symbolic meaning of the still life, at least in the years of its origin as an independent genre.

tendency to identify the painting mentioned by the biographer as the *Sick Little Bacchus* formerly in the workshop of Cavalier d'Arpino and later in the Scipione Borghese collection ("Borghese has it", recorded Mancini). In fact, the *Bacchus* of the Uffizi is a considerably evolved work among the early paintings. The choice of the classical figure and his representation, which projects him onto the plane of reality, almost as if in an occasional fancy-dress, with the physical presence of the model as had never before happened in painting, are the essential and complementary elements with which the young Caravaggio enriched his favourite themes in Rome (and for the *Bacchus* we can suppose he was already in contact with Cardinal Del Monte). In order to understand them, although the literary, neo-Giorgionesque aura by which they were inspired must be taken into consideration, of prime importance was the resolute determination of Caravaggio (whose declarations on method would be collected by Van Mander) to represent them with a painting that was not idealizing but aimed at 'portraying from life'.

The *Sacrifice of Isaac* came to the Gallery in 1917 and, like the *Bacchus*, was displayed in 1922 at the great exhibition of Italian painting of the seventeenth and eighteenth century in Palazzo Pitti, the first public occasion which consecrated the discoveries and studies of Caravaggio made by Longhi, Lionello Venturi and Marangoni. The painting comes from the Sciarra Collection and it is highly likely that it is the same painting mentioned in the inventories of the Barberini Collection. It is not certain, though not unlikely either, that a payment of 1603 made to the painter by Maffeo Barberini for an unspecified work refers precisely to this painting. Interpreted initially as an early work, the *Sacrifice of Isaac*

remains a problematic issue due to the prevalent connections from a stylistic point of view with the artist's early activity. Other aspects of the painting, however, could give a dating of 1602-1603.

Of the Caravaggesque painters in the Florentine galleries there is no trace in this room except for the half-figure of *Vanity* by Mattia Preti, possibly a fragment of a larger work. And so too the *Neptune Pursuing Coronis* by Giulio Carpioni, like a fine relic, represents those local artistic schools which await (think of the Florentine school primarily) an adequate representation in the planned enlargement of the Gallery, which in the eighteenth century was one of the first in Europe to be organized according to a classification by schools.

Recent research by Pierre Rosenberg has shown that the *Annunciation*, purchased in 1793 as a work by Vouet, is certainly the work of Michel Dorigny, Vouet's son-in-law and follower. If this painting, equidistant between Vouet and Poussin, represents a somewhat diminished variant of French history painting, of far greater importance from a historical and artistic point of view is the *Harbour with Villa Medici* by Claude Lorrain. A recent cleaning has brought to light the inscription 'Romae 1637 Cla'. The imaginary representation of Villa Medici (which belonged to the Tuscan dynasty) as part of the architectural scenery of a ship-filled harbour refers directly to the person who commissioned the work, remembered in the 'Liber Veritatis' as 'the most serene Cardinal de' Medici', who is undoubtedly Carlo, since his nephew Giovan Carlo became cardinal only in 1644 (the painting would later pass into the collection of Cardinal Leopold).

If the grandiose scenographic vision of works like this contributed to the fame of Claude Lorrain as an artist of perspective, the evocative power that springs from it, made up of historical memory, imaginary classicism and suggestive emotions on nature (we find here again the celebrated effect of morning light reflected on water) account for the admiration for and popularity of Lorrain, whose influence, with uninterrupted continuity through Vernet and the English landscape painters, reached into the nineteenth century.

Another anticipator of the eighteenth-century, pre-Romantic 'sublime' was Salvator Rosa. The work displayed is recorded, not by accident, as *Fear*. The classically cloaked figures, the mysterious call of the young man who is reaching them and the tempestuous presence of nature seem to leave the onlooker without an answer. The work expresses the perturbation of an invisible presence which even today conveys an agonizing power.

A brief word must be said about a fragmentary *Angel's head*, which was discovered by Luciano Berti in the deposits and bears an inscription on the reverse with a reference to Bernini. Although only a fragment, its rarity should be stressed, there being very few of his paintings which are not portraits (a small canvas with *Two Apostles* has recently been bought by the London National Gallery), while the pictorial characteristics, with more delicacy and languor, represent the story up until Baciccio.

The interest of the Medici family in the painting of northern Europe, with its analytical exploration of nature, its interior settings and its representation of natural things, is amply reflected in the Florentine collections and concerns particularly, as we can see from the historiographical identification, various members of the grand-ducal family. In the first half of the seventeenth century the interest of the Medici — and Cardinal Carlo and Cosimo II, both sons of a northern woman, Christine of Lorraine, should be remembered — was to a large extent focused on landscapes.

Over and above these considerations, let us turn our attention to two masters who occupied a prominent position in the first phase of the diffusion in Italy of the landscape genre, Paul Bril and Jan Brueghel dei Vel-

CARAVAGGIO (Michelangelo Merisi)
(Caravaggio or Milan, 1570/71 or 73 - Porto
Ercole, 1610)

Sacrifice of Isaac

Oil on canvas
104x135
1591 (Longhi)
1595 (Friedlaender)
1597/99 (Mahon)
1603/4 (Aronberg Lavin)

The painting was donated to the Uffizi in 1917 by John Fairfax Murray, the son of the English
pre-Raphaelite painter who had settled in Florence. It had previously come from the Sciarra
collection in Rome (1812) and, even further back, had appeared in the inventories of the
Barberini properties in 1608.
Some critics have raised doubts about its authorship, claiming that it may be an excellent
copy. Friedlaender (1955) even talks of "pastiche" due to the incongruous combined
presences of disparate stylistic elements. Today the prevailing conviction is that it is the
original of the Barberini "Isaac". Friedlaender has noted that the angel's left hand derives
from that of the angel in Leonardo's "Virgin of the Rocks", a highly significant observation for
it would confirm the hypothesis that Caravaggio nurtured a particular respect for the
Florentine master, who was loved and studied in Lombardy "with an intensity it would not be
exaggerated to call mythical".

luti, here represented in the small format that was especially popular with the latter. The Florentine galleries possess an excellent documentation of the various periods of Paul Bril, from the two *Landscapes* with the deer-hunt and the hare-hunt, among the oldest examples of his activity in Italy, dating from 1595 (the year is sometimes read '93), to the large landscapes that were commissioned and bought by Cardinal Carlo in 1617 and 1618, and in which the vision of the Flemish painter seems to develop in accordance with the classical landscape painting of Carracci's circle. The *Landscape with Hunters* certainly came after the two earlier paintings and can be dated to the last years of the sixteenth century due to the calmer, more classical arrangement of the trees' foliage, the centrality of the fortified house, characteristic of the Roman countryside, and the clearing in the foreground.

Of an even greater quality and importance is the *Wooded Landscape with a Ford* by Jan Brueghel dei Velluti, a painting of the artist's maturity, dated 1607. Executed after his stay in Italy, during which time the painter was used extensively by Cardinal Federico Borromeo, and after his return to Antwerp, it is a little-known yet extremely fine example of Flemish landscape painting. The perfect gauging of the two 'telescopic' views penetrating the wood is typical of those characteristics which differentiate the landscapes of Brueghel dei Velluti from those of painters like Coninxloo and which cannot be explained other than as profoundly northern and un-'Italianizing' interpretations of Italian and Venetian experiences.

Cosimo II summoned various North European artists to the Florentine court, including, almost certainly, Cornelis Poelenburgh. Although most of the works in Florence by this Dutch painter are at Palazzo Pitti (a group which has no numerical comparison with other museums in Europe), the oval *Landscape* painted on copper with Ovid's story of *Mercury and Batto* of the Uffizi corresponds stylistically to the period between about 1620 and 1622, when the artist probably resided in Florence, and it is sufficient to make clear the importance of 'Cornelio Satiro' (as he was called in his Roman years) in the sphere of the landscapist current of Elsheimerian tradition. His paintings show an original classical vision of northern, Elsheimerian origin to which an Italian, Filippo Napoletano, contributed decisively during his Florentine period in the service of Cosimo II. With this painter Poelenburgh shows a close affinity, which confirms the hypothesis of his stay in Florence.

Remaining within the sphere of Italianizing painters, the *Landscape* by Herman Swanevelt and the late *Rest after the Hunt* by Johannes Lingelbach are among the average production of these painters, at levels which are typical of old-established picture galleries like the Medicean one. Of greater interest, although today considered only a derivation from an engraving by Elsheimer and not an original by the German master as was claimed until a few years ago, is the *Mercury and Herse*, whose re-attribution to Jacob Pynas seems convincing. It is worthwhile observing, however, that the Florentine galleries possess a very important painting by this Dutch painter, who today is deservedly distinguished from his brother Jan, the *Preaching of the Baptist* of the Pitti, which places him in the first decade of the seventeenth century among the most original followers of Elsheimer and among those who in Rome were most enriched by different influences.

Another aspect of Medicean collectionism in keeping with the taste of the European princely courts of the late seventeenth century is represented by the series of small-format Dutch paintings and with interior scenes whose history is perhaps more noteworthy than their intrinsic quality. These paintings, in fact, were bought by Cosimo III during his journeys to Holland before coming to the throne in 1670, or even later, or come from the Elector Palatine and his wife Anna Maria Ludovica.

JAN BRUEGHEL THE ELDER
called 'dei Velluti'
(Brussels, 1568 - Antwerp, 1625)

Wooded Landscape with a Ford

Oil on copper
24x35
1607

The youngest son of Pieter Brueghel the Elder, Jan shared with his father the highest
reputation of the family, a veritable dynasty of artists who succeeded in distinguishing
themselves in the most varied pictorial genres.
Specializing above all in the production of landscapes and still lifes with flowers, the artist did
not limit himself to a mere imitation of his father's art, but succeeded in establishing his own
individual style. Critics have only recently taken into consideration this landscape, which is
in fact of a considerably high quality. The composition is characterized by a markedly
horizontal development, which Brueghel preferred for his landscapes, and shows a road in the
middle of a wood, a subject the artist repeated in other works. The delightful little figures,
represented in the most varied positions, are ranged against the trees which are rendered with
remarkable subtlety. Faintly visible in the distance, on the left and right of the painting, are
the houses of a city whose identity remains a mystery, although even the knowledge of its
name would certainly add nothing to the serene harmony of a painting not devoid of a
remarkable realism.

Their authors include the best pupils of Gerrit Dou, one of the initiators of the genre of bourgeois and aristocratic subjects represented with meticulous attention to detail. Gabriel Metsu and Frans van Mieris belong with Dou to the Leiden group. In contrast with the simplicity of Ter Borch they preferred the anecdotal style and the refinement of surfaces, such that it is no surprise to learn that these paintings, which were produced in the sphere of Dutch bourgeois society for whom they were destined, immediately won the favour of the courts, thus proving wrong the modern schematizations of art sociologists. As for the Florentine court, it is known that the sophisticated products and the beautiful, refined materials were appreciated.

Like the small scenes by Metsu and Del Mieris, the surreal truth of the *Fruit and Insects* by Rachel Ruysch also confirms these preferences, which had already found expression in the religious court painting of Carlo Dolci. However, these observations certainly do not exhaust the variety of the Medici collections. They can even be corrected and denied by the presence of paintings which, although of the same genre, are more intense and in certain respects appear forerunners, like *The Cook* by a pupil of Ter Borch, Caspar Netscher, a work which attracts us with its perfect balance of realism and psychological penetration.

The *Woman Playing a Lute* is, together with the *Family of a Rustic Interior* of the Louvre, one of the masterpieces of Cornelis Bega, a painter appreciated today for the subtle and subdued matching of colours, though with full, candid tones — his blues, browns and dusty greys recalling Greuze — and for the sharply delineated figures. His variations, which mark the changes occurring in the middle of the century and which distance him from his master Adriaen van Ostade and other Dutch intimist painters, were once considered a vulgarization of their painting with its blended colours and silky effects. But Bega can be placed at the beginning of a line which would later be successful in the eighteenth century with Horemans, Ceruti, Bouchardon and Greuze.

The scenes of taverns and rustic interiors — another popular theme in North European painting — are represented by an important painting by Jan Molenaer, formerly attributed to Brouwer. The collection does not have the bawdy, excited scenes which made Jan Steen famous, but instead a small painting called *The Luncheon*. Possibly sent by the Elector Palatine to Grand Prince Ferdinando, it should be observed closely: in fact we discover in it a peaceful group of figures seated around a table illuminated by an Italian light of Caravaggesque origin.

If, from the Quattrocento onwards, light, in certain situations, represented the meeting-point of North European painting with Italian painting, the *Groote Markt in Haarlem*, signed and dated 1693 by Gerrit Berckheyde, is the expression of another highly important moment in which this meeting-point was reposed: the birth of the *veduta* painting genre. If Berckheyde and Jan van der Hayden are today considered to be the Dutch precursors of Canaletto, in the *Groote Markt in Haarlem* the cobbled open space which widens out in the foreground, like a picture taken with a wide-angle lens, is the eye's first encounter with a light that inundates the stones and produces material and 'naturalistic' abstractions reminiscent of Vermeer. The perspective painter's spare view noticeable in the buildings, which are clearly defined by the light and shadow, opposes the Vermeerian tradition with an already fully-stated rationalism which indicates the European origins of Venetian *veduta* painting.

Berckheyde's view represents an aspect of Dutch painting that was little known in Italy but of great significance. But the most celebrated works in the room are the three portraits by Rembrandt. The *Self-portrait as a Young Man*, dating from around 1634 (note the later addition at the bottom of the painting) belonged to the important Florentine col-

CORNELIS VAN POELENBURGH
(Utrecht, 1586 - 1667)

Mercury and Batto

Oil on copper (oval)
35. 5x48. 2
ca. 1621

Cornelis van Poelenburgh (or Poelemburgh) trained in the school of Abraham Bloemaert and as a young man made the journey to Italy which had by then become almost a ritual among Dutch painters of his time. His presence is documented in Rome from 1617 to 1625, a city where, under the name "Cornelio Satiro", he distinguished himself as one of the most representative members of the Dutch "Schildersbent".

Poelenburgh's art established itself as a natural continuation of the Italian-style landscape of Mannerist derivation, which was destined to produce numerous followers and imitators. His poetic compositions make use of a refined laying-on of colour and are enriched with decorative architecture and small, clear figures, which are painted in without outlines.

The subject of the work is taken from Ovid's "Metamorphosis", in which it is recounted how the aged Batto, after witnessing Mercury's theft of Apollo's livestock, promises to remain silent in exchange for a heifer; Batto is later turned into slate by the vengeful Mercury when, questioned by the god in disguise, he shows himself incapable of keeping the secret.

RACHEL RUYSCH
(Amsterdam, 1664 - 1750)

Fruit and Insects

Oil on wood
44x60
1711

Daughter of the anatomist Frederick
Ruysch, Rachel showed an extraordinary
aptitude for painting from a very tender age
and when she was still young entered the
workshop of Willem van Aelst, a still-life
painter. Carefully guided by the master,
Rachel soon established herself
independently and later won the favour of
the Elector Palatine as a painter of still-lifes,
usually with flowers and fruit. Her
paintings are impressive both for the lavish
colours, which are of an unusual intensity,
and for the harmonious compositions,
whose complexity and richness extended
to a considerable variety of types. The
floral still-lifes, in whose production she
specialized, are often striking for the rare
and exotic flowers, and the insects
associated with them, which were all
reproduced with scientific precision.

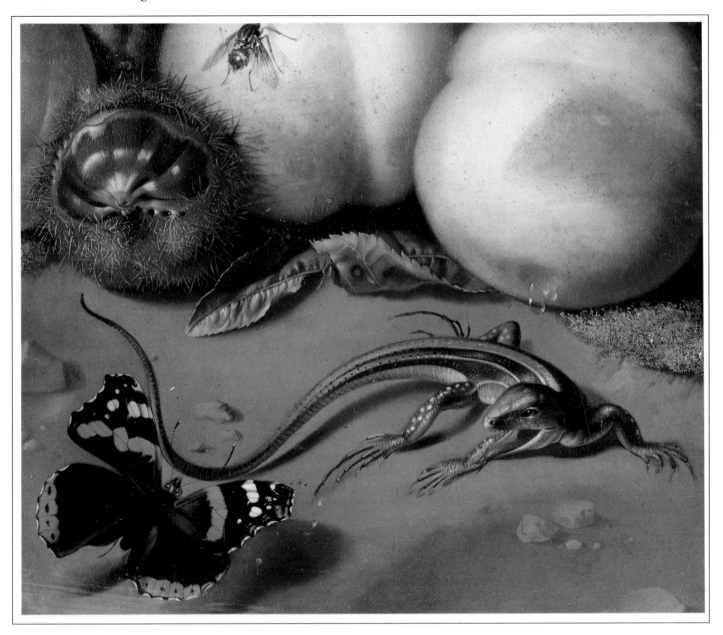

lection of the Gerini family, which it came to as a gift from the Elector Palatine. The artistic and intellectual evolution of the Dutch painter, his study of man's image and destiny, which caused his later works to be rejected by contemporaries, is splendidly expressed — although these paintings await a suitable restoration — in the other *Self-portrait*, which shows him as an old man around 1664 in a pose of relative serenity, and in the powerful, tragic *Portrait of an Old Man* executed in 1665, four years before Rembrandt's death.

The more magical and mysterious aspect of the speculation on reality — in this case the reality of nature — which was expressed in Holland in its first phase with the ingenious Elsheimerian filtrations of the engravings of Esaias and Jan van der Velde and Willem Buytewech, found mature expression in the few paintings and engravings of Herkules Seghers. The *Landscape* of the Uffizi, which entered the Gallery with the attribution to Rembrandt at the beginning of the nineteenth century, a gift of Baroness Hadfield Cosway, was re-attributed to Seghers only in 1871 by Bode and shows his links also towards older Flemish landscapists like Joost de Momper.

The admiration which Rembrandt must have had for these invariably unpopulated scenes, animated by inhospitable rocks and formless ruins, and painted with a new conception of the subject and its composition, is

CORNELIS BEGA
(Haarlem, 1631/32 - ca. 1664)

Woman Playing a Lute

Oil on wood
36x32
1664/65

Son of the sculptor Peter Begijn, or Beggijn, the artist went down in history with the name Bega, which could be a variation of his family name, or may have been a choice forced upon him as a result of his dissolute nature which caused him have brushes with the law. He was a pupil of Adriaen van Ostade, and although he did not equal the latter's fame, and despite being struck down by the plague when still young, he won the esteem of his contemporaries.
While remaining faithful to the themes of this master (family scenes, tavern and domestic interiors) the artist did in fact break away from Van Ostade's style, softening the latter's marked tendency toward caricature with a more subtle humourism through which he created figures that were well characterized but in a dignified way set off by caricature.

Jan Steen, The Luncheon: detail

confirmed by the fact that, as results from an inventory, he possessed eight examples of them, one of which we can assume is the Uffizi painting.

Various authoritative critics believe that the tiny figures on the left are one of the contributions which Rembrandt himself would later make to the painting.

The room dedicated to the eighteenth century is a limited representation of what the Florentine galleries possess of this century, a century which saw the end of the Medici dynasty, and the regency and reforming presence of Pietro Leopold, who in 1790 was succeeded by Ferdinando of Lorrain. Artistic activity was deeply affected by these events, which led to the falling off of the patronage of the last Medici, the decline of centuries-old manufactures and the exodus of artists.

In the regency period the initiative of various families — Gerini, Ginori, Riccardi — and throughout the century the presence of the British colony, stimulated new activity in the fields of engraving, city topography, porcelain, and portraits intended as 'conversation pieces', and allowed the city to acquire the new genre of *veduta* painting (Zocchi, Bellotto) and import classicistic tendencies (Batoni).

JAN STEEN
(Leiden, 1626 - 1679)

The Luncheon

Oil on wood
41x49. 5
ca. 1650/60

Jan Steen was one of the representatives of the second generation of great seventeenth-century Dutch painters. The artist's vast production — more than 500 paintings — ranged from the most unrestrained vitalism to the most genuine family intimism, and was often animated by a humourism whose myriad facets did not shrink in front of the vulgar and the grotesque. In fact, the artist has gone down in history more for the latter characteristics, than for his mythological and religious paintings. Although information about his life is extremely scanty, we do know that his financial situation was precarious, and that in 1672, to make ends meet, he opened a tavern at the Lange Brug in Leiden.

The family scene was a subject which Steen frequently painted, but unlike other versions of this theme, here the artist renounces the crowded, jolly composition and instead captures his characters as they pause and listen to the music being played by the little violinist.

REMBRANDT Harmenszoon van Rijn
(Leiden, 1606 - Amsterdam, 1669)

Self-portrait as a Young Man

Oil on wood
62. 5x54
1633/34

A characteristic of Rembrandt is the variety
of subjects and genres which he painted.
This makes him unique among Dutch
painters of the seventeenth century. It
was precisely in this period, in fact, that his
fellow-countrymen tended to opt for
particular specializations, distinguishing
themselves in a variety of specific
iconographical genres: winter landscapes,
sea views, tavern scenes, church interiors,
etc. Each artist painted a single genre;
very few dedicated themselves to different
themes. In the vast repertoire of
Rembrandt's production, the genre of the
portrait is more typical of his youthful
period (1630-1645). Various of his self-
portraits, as well as portraits of friends and
relatives, date from this period. The
portrait would be a particularly significant
and recurrent genre in his entire activity,
since he would often include portraits in
his religious, mythological and historical
paintings, characterizing gods, biblical
characters and heroes with either his own
features or those of his family. This
painting is one of the first of numerous
self-portraits of the painter. It shows the
artist with a strong-willed expression, in an
extremely natural, unaffected three-quarter
pose; the figure is illuminated by a light
coming from the left whose spreading
glow enlarges the space which serves as a
background.

REMBRANDT Harmenszoon van Rijn
(Leiden, 1606 - Amsterdam, 1669)

Portrait of an Old Man

Oil on canvas
104x86
1665

The work is signed and dated, and although its original provenance is unknown we know that
the painting was in Paris at the beginning of the nineteenth century.
The "Portrait of an Old Rabbi", as it is sometimes called, shows again the artist's interest in
mankind and his inner life. Always attracted by old age, for everything that has something
undeniably characteristic and venerable, the painter gives here yet another display of the new
type of beauty — not classical, but interior — which he created for his aged figures.

JAN VAN HUYSUM
(Amsterdam, 1682 - 1749)

Vase of Flowers

Oil on glass
63x50
End of 18th C.

Son of Justus, a decorator of apartments and gardens, Jan van Huysum was one of the most famous Dutch painters of floral still lifes, establishing himself in a pictorial genre that was already popular and widespread, and taking it to a perfection and virtuosity which was at times even mechanical. However, whereas in French artists, whom the painter was inspired by, ability and technical complexity were also reflected in the sometimes excessive elaboration of the portrayal, Van Huysum stayed within the sober Flemish-Dutch Quattrocento tradition, even though he used specialistic motifs of the seventeenth century (the dark background and the presence of rare species of flowers).

HENDRICK GERRITSZ POT
(Haarlem, ca. 1585 - Amsterdam, 1657)

The Miser

Oil on wood
36x32. 7
ca. 1640/50

The artist was the pupil of Karel van Mander and probably came into contact with Frans Hals, whose large-scale genre scenes he sometimes imitated. His artistic production, however, was oriented more towards portraits and small-sized genre paintings.
This work is of unknown provenance. The initials "HP. " with which it is signed, for a long time deceived critics into thinking its author was Horatius Paulyn. It was Frizzoni, at the beginning of the twentieth century, who changed the painting's attribution in favour of Pot.

JACOB VAN RUYSDAEL
(Haarlem 1628/29 - Amsterdam? 1682)

Landscape with Shepherds and Peasants

Oil on canvas
52x60
ca. 1660-70

Jacob van Ruysdael, like Jan Steen, belongs to the second generation of
great Dutch painters. Possibly a pupil of his father Isaak, a cabinet-maker
and artist, he began painting at a very early age. No real master can be
considered responsible for his artistic formation, although it is certain
that when he became an adult the works of Jan van Goyen and
Rembrandt were already widespread and well-known.
As Gerson affirms, his master was the nature of his home town, where
he spent about half his life. It seems that for a short period he was
acquainted with Meindert Hobbema and before him with Berchem.
There is no evidence of his stay in France, though some of his
landscapes reveal that he travelled widely in Holland and in
neighbouring areas.
It has been said (Gombrich, 1972) that 'it was he who discovered the
poetry of the Northern landscape just as Claude Lorrain had discovered
the poetry of Italian nature. Perhaps no other artist before him had
strived to express his own feelings and moods through images of
nature'. Indeed, even in his early works the artist combines an
undeniably romantic vein with a profound need for order and formal
stability, which is expressed as a continual search for precise rythmic
symmetry.
In the works he executed around the 1650s Ruysdael started to include
in his landscapes various architectural motifs which, while vaguely
resembling Rembrandt or the Italianizing landscapists on the one hand,
on the other can be interpreted as elements created to confer stability
to the structure of the composition.
As regards the subjects, a certain form of "rationalism" is noticeable in
the accuracy of observation and in the absolute respect the artist shows
for the natural elements he represents. It is precisely his "scientific
exploration" of the world of nature that leads Gerson to associate him
with Cornelis Vroom, an heir in turn of the tradition of Adam Elsheimer.
The judgement which Goethe formulated about Ruysdael's art, admiring
his "Jewish Cemetery in Dresden", also carries a less romantic meaning
than is generally believed ('pleasing to the eye and in itself, it stimulates
our innermost sensibility, encourages meditation and lastly expresses an
idea').
Whether he executed imaginary landscapes (where the influence of the
Mannerist landscapist Gillis van Coninxloo is noticeable) or whether he
worked on real landscapes (there are many of his views of Amsterdam
and its surroundings, where he had an atelier and spent the later part of
his life), the artist showed an unrivalled ability to portray reality in all its
aspects. From the foaming water of the waterfall and the stillness of the
marsh to a whole variety of tree species, composite undergrowth, open
clearings, sandy dunes, stormy skies and clear ones, his vast production
(about 500 works) embraces everything without descriptive indulgence.
On the contrary, his melancholy and solitary views are elevated to an
intense lyricism which makes man small and defenceless before nature,
and as a result is not unlike religious contemplation...
The painting in question is signed and was purchased by the Gallery in
1797. Its dating is approximate like many of the works executed by the
artist after the 1650s, a period during which he stopped dating his
works. His works after this period are usually dated on the basis of an
examination of the various styles of dress worn by the tiny figures
which sometimes populate the scenes.
The painting shows a plain with trees, one of those Dutch plains the
painter loved and portrayed various times, skilfully rendering the sense
of distance by raising the observer's viewpoint.

irba s

Although the Uffizi does not have paintings relative to these eighteenth-century episodes of Florentine artistic history, there exist nonetheless various expressions of the first significant approaches to that century dating from the time of Grand Prince Ferdinando, the great discoverer of new talents and new tendencies. In the first decade of the eighteenth century the painters Sebastiano and Marco Ricci, Giuseppe Maria Crespi and Magnasco visited Florence and worked for Ferdinando. Ferdinando understood the importance of the latter artists for new subjects that were an alternative to the Baroque, for scenes of neo-Callottian inspiration, and for amusing Dutch-style genre subjects. This important chapter is represented by two paintings by Giuseppe Maria Crespi, *The Artist's Family*, which he sent to the Prince in 1708, full of allusions which the court was able to understand, and *The Flea*, a later painting whose popularity is attested to by the existence of various replicas.

A work which for various reasons is linked to Crespi and to his innovative scenes of interiors and modern life is *The Confession* by Pietro Longhi, a subject which Crespi had treated in the *Sacraments* series of Dresden.

Of old Medici provenance is the *Flora* by Rosalba Carriera. It is not the only painting by this pastellist, since the galleries also have three portraits of the daughters of Rinaldo d'Este dating from 1723. Compared to these the *Flora* appears to be an earlier work by reason of the intense, meticulous and characterizing chiaroscuro. The way of interpreting the portrait, in close connection with the allegory, was splendidly grasped by Rosalba — the light background, and the delicate colours which can only be compared to the colours of flowers, belong to the eighteenth-century world which Watteau had inaugurated and envisaged.

The provenance of the *Portrait of a Lady in Exotic Dress Reading a Book* remains unknown, although its provenance from Parma has been claimed in connection with the somewhat dubious identification (on the basis of an inscription on the back which also records the date, 1753) of the person reading with Marie Adelaide of France. If the exotic theme and the composition derive from a drawing by Boucher, engraved in 1747, the author of the canvas is the French-Swiss painter and pastellist Jean-Etienne Liotard, an 'outsider' of the eighteenth century because of the original position he assumed in the century's European cosmopolitanism. A careful analyzer of reality in keeping with the Northern tradition he belonged to, in the conception of the portrait, in the intimistic, bourgeois setting, in the singularity of the colours which he avoided matching and combining according to traditional parameters — which placed him in a line which would lead to Degas — Liotard was Chardinian in his taste for the still life which he cultivated particularly in his maturity, was opposed in France but in close relations with the Enlightenment, and was an adventurous traveller and precocious admirer of the exotic as is shown in this splendid Florentine painting.

The grand-ducal collections also provided the two views of Venice by Canaletto, by whom the Florentine galleries also have two *Caprices* bought in 1907 and sometimes attributed to Bellotto. The *View of the Grand Canal* has raised some doubts which do not seem justified. Of the many paintings by Canaletto with a view of the Grand Canal from this viewpoint, this one of the Uffizi is very similar in its framing to the famous version of the Galleria Carrara in Bergamo. Like the other replicas it seems it was executed around 1726-28. The *View of the Ducal Palace* is somewhat later, dating from the 1730s. This view of the wharf with the most important monuments of the city recalls the more famous (and slightly more restricted) version commissioned by the Duke of Bedford in a series of twenty-four *vedute* during his journey to Italy (1730-31). The precise view can be linked to a drawing at Windsor which is

GIUSEPPE MARIA CRESPI
(Bologna, 1665 - 1747)

The Artist's Family *

Oil on copper
28x24
1708

A lively and bizarre family scene, this group portrait was conceived by Crespi in the wake of events which are worth mentioning to understand the irony and wit of Crespi's painting. Beyond the apparent realism, half portrait and half genre scene, the painter addresses himself, with a confidential play of allusions, to the person who actually received the painting, his new patron Ferdinando de' Medici. An episode which occurred in 1706 had indirectly brought Crespi into contact with his future patron. In that year he had executed a "Massacre of the Innocents", now at the Uffizi, for a Bolognese priest, Don Carlo Silva, who had declared his intention to make a gift of it to Ferdinando. But promises over payment were not maintained and for that painting Crespi brought a lawsuit against Silva. After winning the case in 1708, the artist himself donated the "Massacre of the Innocents" to the Prince.

With this amusing family portrait the painter introduced himself to Ferdinando, portraying himself pulling a small cart which is occupied by his second child, Luigi, who later bacame a painter and biographer. The baby is followed by his wife, Giovanna Cuppini, and their first-born child Maurizio. On an easel in the background is a caricature of Silva, the chance intermediary of the fortunate encounter between the artist and his patron.

The painter's family: detail before restoration.

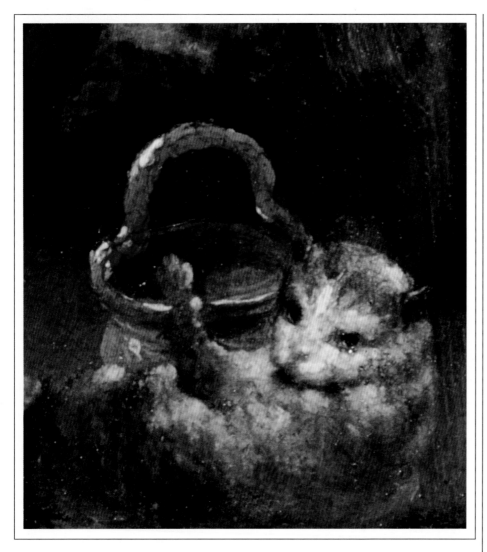

Giuseppe Maria Crespi, The Artist's Family: detail.

probably the basic model for Canaletto's canvases with the representations of the departure and arrival of the Bucintaur for the feast of the Ascension which the painter executed between the end of the 1720s and the beginning of the 1730s. To these themes are linked the engravings of Venetian subjects which Antonio Visentini engraved presumably between 1729 and 1734 and published in 1735.

The old section is completed with two historical portraits of *Vittorio Alfieri* and the *Countess d'Albany* executed in Florence in 1793 by François Xavier Fabre, who left them to the Uffizi in 1824 in compliance with the wishes of the Countess. These paintings are the most famous of the Tuscan activity of this pupil of David, which lasted from 1793 until 1825, and document the beginning of that period. The heroic vision in the style of David, especially in the portrait of the poet, confers a dignified tone which is completely in keeping with his poetry. The galleries also have Fabre's splendid *Portrait of Giovanni Antonio Santarelli* of 1812, not on display, which documents how the painter gravitated in that period in the orbit of Ingres. The portrait of Santarelli may be considered one of the masterpieces of this sphere and of the activity of French painters in Italy at the beginning of the nineteenth century.

In 1793 Ferdinando III had searched for French paintings in order to fill a gap in the collections and at the same time he also intended to enlarge the Bolognese section, which was later enriched with works from the Gerini collection.

Among the most recent acquisitions, that is since 1900, the year in which the controversial painting by Tiepolo entered the Uffizi, the Venetian eighteenth century has represented a constant objective. The two

GIUSEPPE MARIA CRESPI
(Bologna, 1665 - 1747)

The Flea *

Oil on copper
46. 3x34
ca. 1715

Roberto Longhi was the first to suggest that this subject might represent an episode in the series portraying scenes from the "life of a singer". The cycle, executed for an English gentleman, was painted on copper. In this scene we rather get the impression that the choice of the subject was the cue for a representation of popular, everyday life in the North European style. We may recall, in fact, that in the biography of his father, Luigi Crespi mentions a painting depicting "the miserable life of a woman of low repute". As in the "bambòccianti", from whom Crespi certainly drew inspiration, the disagreeable elements in the scene portrayed, in contrast with the details of a life of luxury (the roses, the fashionable little dog, etc.) indicate a moralistic intention.

GIOVAN BATTISTA TIEPOLO
(Venice, 1696 - Madrid, 1770)

Erecting a Statue in Honour of an Emperor *

Oil on canvas
420x175
ca. 1734/36

The canvas, of mixtilineal form, originally decorated a
ceiling of the Archiepiscopal Seminary in Udine.
Independently of whether the execution was
autograph or the result of a joint effort, there is little
doubt that Tiepolo was responsible for the conception
of the work. Compositional arrangements inherited
from Baroque figurative culture are forced by the
painter into a grandiose and fantastic perspective
structure. The steep scaling off of planes and the
broad expanse of sky in the centre are intentional,
since the painting was to be observed from below, but
the result of this daring illusionism goes far beyond
any preliminary considerations, revealing rather a
rococo taste for spatial artifice and fertile decorative
freedom.

ROSALBA CARRIERA
(Venice, 1675 - 1757)

Flora

Pastel on paper
47x32. 5
ca. 1730/40

Trained as a miniaturist, Rosalba Carriera became very
famous and sought-after throughout Europe, and
especially in Paris where she was highly esteemed by
Watteau for her portraits in pastels. This technique,
which she used exclusively, was particularly suitable
for the haziness and lightness of her pictures and also
for her mawkish obligingness towards her sitters. Her
portraits are a typical example of what Diderot called
"flatterie", that is, they tend towards over-
embellishment and idealization.

Alessandro Longhi, Portrait of a Lady: detail

Caprices by Francesco Guardi, the *Arch and Pier* and the *Bridges over the Canal*, entered in 1906 from the collection of Luigi Grassi, the *Caprices* by Canaletto (not on display) in 1907 and in the same year the *Portrait of a Lady* by Alessandro Longhi, whose fine *Portrait of a Prelate* (also not on display) was purchased from the Brass Collection in 1931. The Gallery acquired the *Susanna and the Elders*, an early work by Piazzetta, in 1920.

Although it cannot be said that the Gallery of the Uffizi has pursued a systematic policy of purchases since the last War, two sensational episodes have increased its collections: the acquisitions from the Pallavicino family, in addition to the *Confession* by Pietro Longhi, of two signed works by Chardin, whose importance is in no way diminished by the fact that they are replicas of rather superior versions in the Rothschild Collection and in the Washington National Gallery. In 1974, finally, two historic portraits by Francisco Goya were purchased — *Maria Teresa de Vallabriga on Horseback* and the *Countess of Chinchón*, for long preserved in Florence by the Ruspoli family. With these new acquisitions the Uffizi affirmed its role — for the richness, variety and importance of the works preserved in it — as the foremost National Gallery in Italy.

ALESSANDRO LONGHI (Alessandro Falca)
(Venice, 1733 - 1813)

Portrait of a Lady

Oil on canvas
100x80
ca. 1770

Originally following in the footsteps of his father, Alessandro Longhi found his own direction as a specialist portrait-painter, although his style is always lighter and less acutely and intellectually penetrating than that of Pietro. In this painting of the Uffizi, the face, with its surface smile, without secret thoughts, impenetrable as the white mask attached to the black three-cornered hat, is engulfed by the stunning dress, with its lace frills and intricately embroidered cloak; the climax is the pink ribbon she is wearing round her neck.

CANALETTO (Giovanni Antonio Canal)
(Venice, 1697 - 1768)

View of the Ducal Palace

Oil on canvas
51x83
Before 1755

This view of the Wharf and the Riva degli Schiavoni taken from the Docks of San Marco,
which from the Zecca and the Libreria Vecchia embraces the Ducal Palace and the Prisons as
far as Palazzo Dandolo (now the Albergo Danieli), is one which Canaletto repeated many
times. Today we know of more than ten autograph versions, the most important of which
are those showing the departure or arrival of the Bucintaur in the foreground, instead of the
ordinary plying of boats, as here.
It is highly likely that for this composition Canaletto used the "optical camera", an instrument
which facilitated the control of perspective in such a wide and "unnnatural" field of vision.
The stamp of naturalness is produced in any case by the immediacy of the boatmen's
movements and by the temporary balance created by the boats crossing.

CANALETTO (Giovanni Antonio Canal)
(Venice, 1697 - 1768)

View of the Grand Canal

Oil on canvas
45x73
ca. 1730

Although with the usual animation of boats and gondolas, of minimal silent episodes, this composition, more than others, shows traces of Canaletto's early experience as a painter of stage sceneries, an activity he was involved in until around 1720. The almost central vanishing-point produces a theatrical, geometric opening out of the rows of buildings, or rather their regular convergence like two side wings, such that the stretch of Canal becomes a stage for the action of the boats.

FRANCESCO GUARDI
(Venice, 1712 - 1793)

Caprice with an Arch and Pier
Caprice with Bridges over the Canal

Oil on canvas
30x53
ca. 1780

Guardi was perhaps the most well-known interpreter of
the "caprice", an invented, fantastic, perhaps even bizarre
view. In contrast with the "capricious inventions" of
Piranesi, Guardi's images always remained within the
confines of probability, of visual plausibility, both in the
architectural references and their spatial arrangement.
They are Venetian images, but, as Longhi writes, "of
variable Venices, sandy with silver and rust". The lucidity
of Canaletto is broken up in the sketchy, vibrant touch, and
the depth of perspective is supplemented by the temporal
depth of memory: an old ruined arch, a Renaissance
facade, a Gothic harbour entrance. These "caprices" mark
a decisive change in the taste for ruins, a stepping-stone
between the seventeenth-century yearning for classicism
and the pre-Romantic sense of time, the inexorable ruin.

JEAN-BAPTISTE-SIMÉON CHARDIN
(Paris, 1699 - 1779)

Girl with Racket and Shuttlecock
Boy Playing Cards

Oil on canvas
82x66
ca. 1740

These portraits, acquired recently by the Uffizi, are exact
replicas of two celebrated works by Chardin which were
in Russia in the eighteenth century and are now in the
Rothschild Collection in Paris and in the National Gallery
of Washington.
Note how Chardin succeeds, in the "magical" tuning of
colours, in conveying the extraneousness and disinterest
of the two children from the fact of being exposed to the
painter's attentive eye: both are engrossed in their own
game. It is worth emphasizing the extent to which this
simplicity, this familiarity of situation, this reciprocal
detachment between the figure portrayed and the
observer, marked a significant break with the tradition of
official portrait-painting.

JEAN-ETIENNE LIOTARD
(Geneva, 1702 - 1789)

Marie Adelaide of France in Turkish Dress

Oil on canvas
50x56
1753

The identification of the subject and the date are based on the inscription on the back, "Madame Marie-Adelaïde de France MDCCLIII". The theme of reading was typical of rococo artists from Boucher to Fragonard. But Liotard excludes their tone of sweet sensuality, and instead, with clearer descriptiveness, accentuates the oriental aspect. What strikes us about the figure engrossed in the reading of a French poetical work is the sense of an inner vitality: "calm breathing, eyes fixed on the lines of the page and, further away, on the imaginary horizon springing from the book".

Jean-Marc Nattier, Marie Zeffirine of France:
detail.

JEAN-MARC NATTIER
(Paris, 1685 - 1766)

Marie Zephirine of France

Oil on canvas
70x82
1751

This work, signed and dated, is probably the one which was in the rooms of Marie Josephine of Saxony, wife of Louis, the Dauphin of France, and mother of Marie Zeffirine (1750-55), and was exhibited at the Salon of 1753.

FRANÇOIS-XAVIER FABRE
(Montpellier, 1766 - 1837)

Portrait of Vittorio Alfieri

Oil on canvas
93x73
1793

The painting is signed and dated in the lower right corner, "F. X. Fabre Florentia 1793", and on the reverse bears a famous sonnet written by the poet, dated 18 August 1794.

To glorify the personality of this writer of tragedies, Fabre has clearly added to the faithfulness of the portrait a heroic tone, evident in the facial expression and the pose of the raised arm over which the brown mantle is slung *all'antica*.

Beyond its value as a historical document, the work is also a striking example of the more severely classicistic current which emerged from the school of David, of whom Fabre was a pupil and close follower.

FRANÇOIS-XAVIER FABRE
(Montpellier, 1766 - 1837)

Portrait of the Countess d'Albany

Oil on canvas
93x73
1793

Louise of Stolberg, Countess d'Albany (1752-1824), was a prominent figure in late eighteenth-century Florence, not only and not so much because of her well-known relationship with Vittorio Alfieri, but above all because of the fervent intellectual activity she sustained in her salon, which was frequented by numerous French artists whose "cultural tendencies [led to] the decisive introduction into Florence of neoclassical ideas".

FRANCISCO GOYA Y LUCIENTES
(Fuendetodos, Saragozza, 1746 - Bordeaux, 1828)

Portrait of the Countess of Chinchón

Oil on canvas
220x140
ca. 1797-1800

The stunning dress, of a still Tiepolesque lightness, stands out against a timeless, unidentified background; but what really strikes us in this portrait is the totally unidealized face, and the closed, melancholy, uncomprehending expression which verges on idiocy. This is Maria Teresa de Vallabriga y Borbon, Countess of Chinchón, the daughter of Don Luis de Borbon and Maria Teresa de Vallabriga, and wife of Manuel Godoy, the favourite of Queen Maria Luisa.

Francisco Goya y Lucientes, Portrait of the Countess of Chinchón: detail.

FRANCISCO GOYA Y LUCIENTES
(Fuendetodos, Saragozza, 1746 - Bordeaux, 1828)

Portrait of Maria Teresa de Vallabriga on horseback

Oil on canvas
82,5x61,7
1783

In the summer of 1783 the Infante Don Luis de Borbon, brother of Charles III, invited Goya to stay at his residence of Arena de San Pedro, where the painter executed a series of portraits (possibly sixteen) of Don Luis's family. Goya mentions the equestrian portrait of Maria Teresa de Vallabriga, the wife of Don Luis, in a a letter to his friend Martin Zapater on 2 July 1784.
Although the artist referred to a painting that was unfinished, the reference has been linked to this canvas of the Uffizi, which comes from the collection of the Ruspoli family, who in turn acquired it from Spain through inheritance. Evident in this work is Goya's revival and readaptation of the 17th-century tradition of the equestrian portrait, particularly that of Velázquez.

GIOVAN BATTISTA PIAZZETTA
(Venice 1682 - 1754)

Susanna and the Elders

Oil on canvas
100x135
ca. 1720

There has never been any doubt about the authenticity of this canvas, which came to the Uffizi from Venice, where in 1740 it belonged to the Bonomo Algarotti Collection, nor has its dating ever wavered from the years around 1720. Its close stylistic affinity with the "Saint James being Led to his Martyrdom" from the church of San Stae in Venice, until now dated 1717, has always constituted a valid chronological support.
The work perfectly illustrates the achievements of Piazzetta after his stay in Bologna (1703-1710) which allowed him, together with Giuseppe Maria Crespi, to develop an artistic style that drew inspiration from the Venetian "tenebrosi", and also showed the influences of Antonio Molinari and Guercino.
From an iconographical point of view, it is interesting to note that Piazzetta, diverging from tradition, rather than taking advantage of the subject to work on a female nude, instead chose a moment of the episode which had no artistic precedent: 'it is not the elders who are spying on Susanna or trying to lure her, on the contrary it is the woman who looks apprehensively towards them as they leave the garden, plotting their false accusation of adultery' (Jones 1981).

PLAN OF THE GALLERY

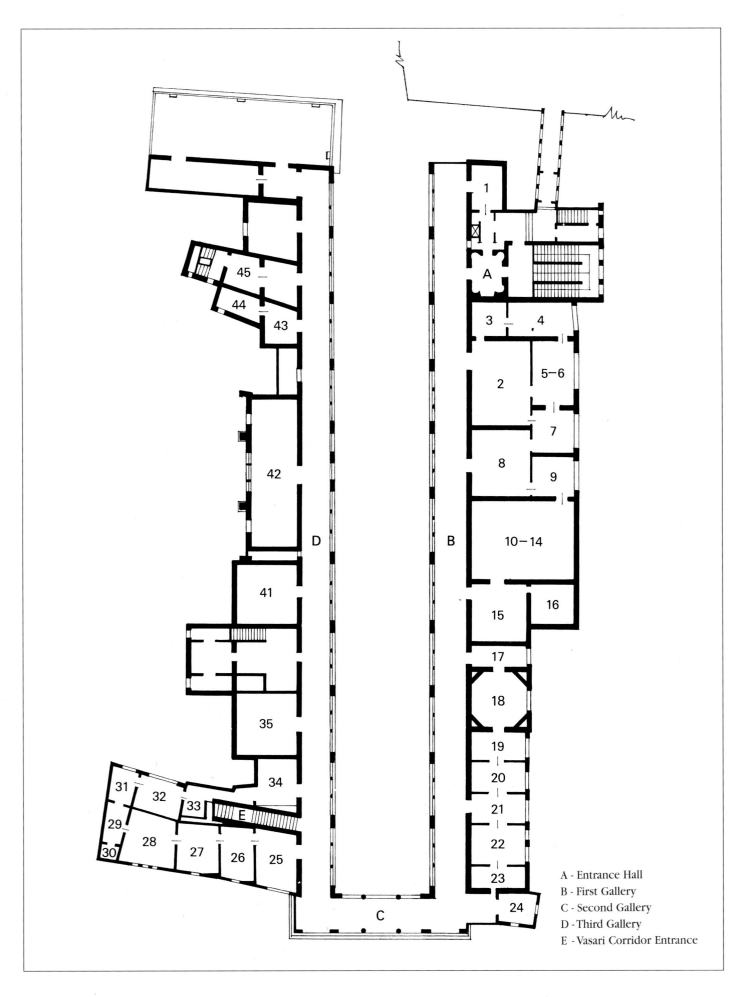

A - Entrance Hall
B - First Gallery
C - Second Gallery
D - Third Gallery
E - Vasari Corridor Entrance

INDEX OF ARTISTS AND WORKS

AUTHORS OF THE CATALOGUE ENTRIES
AND PHOTOGRAPHIC REFERENCES

Alberta Bencini   pp.: 100, 101, 102, 129, 130, 315, 317, 318, 321, 323, 325, 326, 351.

Eliana Pilati   pp.: 24, 26, 28, 30, 33, 34, 36, 37, 39, 41, 42, 43, 44, 45, 46, 47, 48, 53, 55, 56, 58, 60, 62, 64, 67, 69, 70, 71, 73, 74, 75, 77, 78, 79, 81, 82, 83, 85, 87, 88, 90, 92, 93, 94, 95, 96, 97, 99, 104, 105, 106, 108, 109, 110, 112, 114, 117, 118, 119, 120, 123, 124, 125, 127, 132, 135, 136, 137, 138, 139, 141, 142, 144, 146, 148/149, 152, 153, 154, 156, 159, 160, 162, 164, 166/167, 168, 170, 172, 176, 178, 179, 180, 182, 184, 186, 188, 189, 190, 194, 196, 198, 199, 200, 202, 204, 205, 206, 207, 208, 210, 212/213, 214, 216, 218, 220, 221, 222, 224, 225, 226, 229, 230, 231, 233, 235, 236, 238, 240, 241, 242, 244, 247, 248, 249, 250, 252, 254, 255, 256, 258, 259, 261, 262, 263, 264, 266, 269, 270, 272, 274/275, 276, 279, 281, 282, 284, 328.

Claudio Pizzorusso   pp.: 289, 290, 292, 294, 296, 298, 300, 302, 304, 307, 308, 309, 310, 313, 330, 332, 334, 336, 339, 341, 343.

Rita Bianucci   pp.: 85, 135.

Giovanna Giusti   pp.: 53, 60, 104, 208, 224, 297.

Photographic references: the photographs in this volume are the property of Casa Editrice Bonechi archives and are by Antonio Quattrone and Orlando Orlandini. The photographs on the following pages are the property of Scala - Istituto Fotografico Editoriale: 29, 31, 34, 43, 44, 45, 46, 48, 64, 65, 66, 67, 69, 73, 80, 82, 84, 85, 87, 88, 89, 91, 94, 95, 96, 102/103, 106, 107, 108, 109, 110, 113, 116/117, 119, 129, 135, 137, 143, 147, 148, 149, 153, 179, 210, 211, 213, 215, 219, 231, 232, 233, 239, 249, 273, 300, 301, 311, 329, 332, 350, 351. The photographs on pages 16, 59, 60, 77, 104, 258, 309 are from the archives of Antonio Quattrone. The photograph on page 61 is from the archives of Nicolò Orsi Battaglini.

CATALOGUE OF WORKS
IN THE UFFIZI GALLERY

Notes for consultation:

The indexes of artists and works listed here correspond to the state of display at the time of this volume's publication. Any variation can be attributed to the fact that the Gallery of the Uffizi is in continual transformation.

An asterisk (*) indicates that the room in question is presently closed to the public.

The works underlined are reproduced in this book.

LIST OF ARTISTS AND WORKS

Agnolo di Bondone (*see* **Giotto**)

Agnolo di Cosimo (*see* **Bronzino**)

Albani, Francesco (Bologna 1578-1660)
(room 43*)
    Dance of the Cupids

Albertinelli, Mariotto (Florence 1474-1515)
(room 25)
    <u>Visitation</u>
    <u>Predella with Scenes from the Life of Christ</u>

Allegri, Antonio (*see* **Correggio**)

Allori, Alessandro (Florence 1535-1607)
(rooms 18, 33*)
    Portrait of Bianca Cappello
    <u>Portrait of a Woman</u>
    <u>Allegory of Human Life</u>
    (verso of the preceding)
    <u>Saint Peter Walking on the Water</u>
    Hercules Crowned by the Muses
    Venus and Cupid
    Sacrifice of Isaac
    Portrait of Ludovico Capponi

Altdorfer, Albrecht (Regensburg? 1480 c.-1538)
(room 22)
    <u>Martyrdom of Saint Florian</u>
    <u>Saint Florian Taking Leave of the Monastery</u>

Amberger, Christoph (? 1505 c. - Augsburg 1562)
(room 33*)
    Portrait of Cornelius Gros

Andrea d'Agnolo (*see* **Andrea del Sarto**)

Andrea del Castagno (Castagno 1421 c. - Florence 1457)
(Room of San Pier Scheraggio)
    Dante Alighieri
    Giovanni Boccaccio
    Francesco Petrarch
    Pippo Spano
    Niccolò Acciaioli
    Farinata degli Uberti
    The Cumaean Sibyl
    Queen Esther
    Queen Tomyris

Andrea del Sarto (Florence 1486-1530)
(rooms 18, 26)
    Portrait of a Woman with the Young Petrarch
    <u>Madonna of the Harpies</u>
    <u>Portrait of a Woman with a Basket of Spindles</u>
    Vallombrosa Altarpiece
    <u>Saint James</u>

Andrea di Cione (*see* **Orcagna**)

Andrea di Cione (*see* **Verrocchio**)

Andrea Orcagna (*see* **Orcagna**)

Anguissola, Sofonisba (Cremona 1531 c. - Palermo 1626)
(room 34)
> Portrait of an Unknown Man

Antonio Benci (*see* **Antonio del Pollaiolo**)

Antonio del Pollaiolo (Firenze 1431 c. - Rome 1498)
(room 9)
> Hercules and Antaeus
> Hercules and the Hydra
> Portrait of a Lady
> (Antonio e Piero del Pollaiolo) Three Saints' Altarpiece

Araldi, Alessandro (Parma 1460 c.-1528 c.)
(room 23)
> Portrait of Barbara Pallavicino

Aspertini, Amico (Bologna 1475 c.-1552)
(room 29)
> Adoration of the Shepherds

Bachiacca (Florence 1494-1557)
(room 27)
> Deposition
> Predella with Scenes from the Life
> of Saint Acasius
> Christ before Caiaphas

Baldovinetti, Alessio (Florence 1425-1499)
(room 8)
> Madonna and Child with Saints
> Annunciation

Baldung Grien, Hans (Schwäbisch Gmünd ca. 1484 - Strasburg 1545)
(room 20)
> Adam (from Dürer)
> Eve (from Dürer)

Barbieri, Giovan Francesco (*see* **Guercino**)

Barocci, Federico (Urbino 1535-1612)
(rooms 33*, 35*)
> Portrait of a Girl
> Portrait of Francesco II della Rovere
> "Madonna del Popolo"
> Portrait of Ippolito della Rovere
> Stigmata of Saint Francis (copy from)
> Christ and Mary Magdalen
> Self-portrait

Bassano, Jacopo (Bassano ca. 1515-1592)
(room 32)
> Two Dogs
> Judas and Tamar
> Annunciation to the Shepherds

Bassano, Leandro (Bassano 1557 - Venezia 1622)

(room 32)
> The Concert (attr.)

Bazzi, Giovanni Antonio (*see* **Sodoma**)

Beato Angelico (Vicchio di Mugello ca. 1400 - Roma 1455)
(rooms 5/6, 7)
> Thebaid
> Coronation of the Virgin
> Madonna and Child with Saints

Beccafumi (Valdibiena ca. 1486 - Siena 1551)
(room 27)
> Holy Family with the Young Saint John
> Escape of Clelia and the Roman Virgins
> from the Camp of Porsenna
> Self-portrait

Bega, Cornelis (Haarlem ca. 1631-1664)
(room 44*)
> Woman Playing a Lute

Bellini, Giovanni (*see* **Giambellino**)

Bellini, Jacopo (Venice ca. 1396- ca. 1470)
(room 5/6)
> Madonna and Child

Benci, Antonio (*see* **Antonio del Pollaiolo**)

Benci, Piero (*see* **Piero del Pollaiolo**)

Berckheyde, Gerrit (Haarlem 1638-1698)
(room 44*)
> The Groote Markt in Haarlem

Benci, Antonio (*see* **Antonio del Pollaiolo**)

Benci, Piero (*see* **Piero del Pollaiolo**)

Berckheyde, Gerrit (Haarlem 1638-1698)
(room 44*)
> The Groote Markt in Haarlem

Berlinghieri, Bonaventura (workshop; 13th century)
(room 2)
> Madonna and Child with Saints and Crucifixion

Bernini, Gian Lorenzo (Naples 1598-1680)
(room 43*)
> Head of a Youth

Berruguete, Alonso (Paredes de Nava 1488 - Toledo 1561)
(room 25)
> Salomé with the Head of John the Baptist

Bigordi, Domenico (*see* **Ghirlandaio**)

Bigordi, Ridolfo (*see* **Ridolfo del Ghirlandaio**)

Bles (de), Herri Met (*see* **Civetta**)

Boccaccino, Boccaccio (Ferrara ca. 1466 - Cremona ca. 1524)
(room 23)
    Gypsy

Boccaccino, Camillo (Cremona 1504-1546)
(room 34)
    Head of an Old Man

Boltraffio, Giovanni Antonio (Milan 1467-1516)
(room 23)
    Narcissus at the Spring

Bonaccorsi, Pietro (*see* **Perin del Vaga**)

Bordon, Paris (Treviso 1500 - Venice 1571)
(room 32)
    Portrait of a Knight
    Portrait of a Man in a Fur Coat

Boscoli, Andrea (Florence ca. 1560-ca. 1606)
(rooms 33*, 35*)
    Saint Sebastian
    The Marriage in Cana

Both, Jan (Utrecht 1610-1622)
(room 44*)
    Village

Botticini, Francesco (Florence 1446-1498)
    Three Archangels (not on display)

Botticelli (Florence 1445-1510)
(rooms 9, 10/14, Room of San Pier Scheraggio)
    Fortitude
    The Return of Judith
    The Discovery of the Body of Holophernes
    Madonna of the Rose Garden
    Madonna of the Magnificat
    Madonna and Child
    The Birth of Venus
    Pallas and the Centaur
    Madonna of the Pomegranate
    Calumny
    Primavera (Spring)
    Adoration of the Magi
    San Barnaba Altarpiece
    Portrait of a Man with a Medal of Cosimo the Elder
    Saint Ambrose Altarpiece
    Saint Augustine in his Study
    Saint Mark Altarpiece
    Cestello Annunciation
    Coronation of the Virgin
    Annunciation of San Martino

Bril, Paul (Antwerp 1554 - Rome 1626)
(room 44*)
    Landscape with Hunters

Bronzino, Agnolo (Florence 1503-1572)
(rooms 18, 27, 33*)
    Annunciation
    Portrait of Bartolomeo Panciatichi
    Portrait of Lucrezia Panciatichi
    Portrait of Bia, illegitimate daughter of Cosimo I
    Portrait of a Man with a Lute
    Portrait of Eleonora of Toledo with her Son Giovanni
    Portrait of Giovanni de' Medici as a Child
    Portrait of Cosimo I
    Portrait of a Woman
    Portrait of Maria de' Medici
    Portrait of Francesco I de' Medici
    Lamentation of Christ
    Pygmalion and Galatea
    Allegory of Happiness
    Deposed Christ
    Panciatichi Holy Family
    Martyrdom of Saint Maurice and the Theban Legion (Bronzino and Pontormo)

Brueghel, Jan, the Elder (Brussels 1568 - Antwerp 1625)
(rooms 20, 44*)
    Calvary (from Dürer)
    Wooded Landscape with a Ford

Brusasorci (Verona 1492-1569)
(room 31)
    Bathsheba

Buonarroti, Michelangelo (*see* **Michelangelo**)

Burgkmair, Hans (Augsburg 1473-1531)
(room 20)
    Portrait of an Unknown Man

Cagli, Corrado (Ancona 1910 - Rome 1976)
(Room of San Pier Scheraggio)
    The Battle of San Martino

Caliari, Carlo (Venice 1570-1596)
(room 18)
    Original Sin
    The Creation of Eve
    The Expulsion from Paradise
    The Family of Adam

Caliari, Paolo (*see* **Veronese**)

Calvaert, Denijs (Antwerp 1540 - Bologna 1619)
(room 33*)
    Assumption of Mary

Cambiaso, Luca (Moneglia 1527 - Madrid 1585)
    Madonna and Child (not on display)

Campi, Bernardino (Cremona 1522-1591)
(room 34)
    Portrait of an Unknown Man (attr.)

Campi, Giulio (Cremona 1502- ca. 1575)
(room 34)
    Portrait of an Unknown Man (attr.)
    Portrait of Galeazzo Campi
    Portrait of a Musician (attr.)

Caliari, Paolo (*see* **Veronese**)

Canal, Giovanni Antonio (*see* **Canaletto**)

Canaletto (Venice 1697-1768)
(room 45*)
    <u>View of the Ducal Palace</u>
    <u>View of the Grand Canal</u>
    The Tower of Marghera (Canaletto and workshop)

Caravaggio (Caravaggio or Milan ca. 1570 - Porto Ercole 1610)
(room 16, 43*)
    <u>Sacrifice of Isaac</u>
    <u>Bacchus</u>
    <u>Head of Medusa</u>

Cardi, Ludovico (*see* **Cigoli**)

Carpaccio, Vittore (Venice ca. 1460-1526)
(room 21)
    Group of Soldiers and People
    in Oriental Dress (attr.)
    Sibyl (attr.)
    Prophet

Carracci, Annibale (Bologna 1560 - Rome 1609)
(room 43*)
    <u>Venus with a Satyr and Cupids</u>
    Man with a Monkey

Carriera, Rosalba (Venice 1675-1757)
(room 45*)
    <u>Flora</u>
    Portrait of Felicita Sartori

Carrucci, Jacopo (*see* **Pontormo**)

Cassai, Tommaso di Giovanni (*see* **Masaccio**)

Cenni di Pepo (*see* **Cimabue**)

Chardin, Jean Baptiste Siméon (Paris 1699-1779)
(room 45*)
    Girl with Racket and Shuttlecock (being restored)
    <u>Boy Playing Cards</u> (being restored)

Chimenti, Jacopo (*see* **Empoli**)

Cigoli (Cigoli 1559 - Rome 1613)
(room 35*)
    <u>Saint Francis Receives the Stigmata</u>

Cimabue (Florence, records from 1272-1302)
(room 2)
    <u>Santa Trinita Madonna</u>

Cima da Conegliano, Giovanni Battista
(Conegliano Veneto ca. 1460- ca. 1518)
(room 21)
    <u>Madonna and Child</u>

Civetta (Bouvignes ca. 1480 - Ferrara ? ca. 1550)
(room 44*)
    Copper Mines

Clouet, François (Tours ca. 1510 - Paris 1572)
(room 33*)
    <u>Portrait of Francis I of France on Horseback</u>

Codde, Pieter (Amsterdam 1599-1667)
(room 44*)
    Concert

Conti (de'), Bernardino (Pavia 1450 - ? ca. 1525)
(room 23)
    Portrait of a Man

Correggio (Reggio Emilia 1489-1534)
(room 23)
    <u>Adoration of the Child</u>
    <u>Rest During the Flight into Egypt</u>
    <u>Madonna and Child in Glory</u>

Costa, Lorenzo (Ferrara ca. 1460-1535)
(rooms 19, 21)
    <u>Saint Sebastian</u>
    <u>Portrait of Giovanni Bentivoglio</u>

Cranach, Lukas, the Younger (Wittenberg 1515 - Weimar 1586)
(room 20)
    Portrait of Lukas Cranach the Elder

Cranach, Lukas, the Elder (Kronach 1472 - Weimar 1553)
(room 20)
    <u>Adam</u> (being restored)
    <u>Eve</u> (being restored)
    <u>Portraits of Martin Luther and Catherine Bore</u> (workshop of)
    <u>Portrait of a Young Woman</u> (workshop of)
    <u>Portraits of Frederick III the Wise and Johann I Electors of Saxony</u> (workshop of)
    Portraits of Martin Luther and Philipp Melanchthon (workshop of)

Crespi, Giuseppe Maria (Bologna 1665-1747)
(room 45*)

The Artist's Family
The Flea

Daddi, Bernardo (Florence ca. 1290-1348)
(room 4)
Madonna and Child with Saints Matthew and Nicholas
Madonna and Child Enthroned with Angels and Saints
San Pancrazio Polyptych

Daniele da Volterra (Volterra 1509 - Rome 1566)
(room 18)
Massacre of the Innocents

David, Gerard (Oudewater ca. 1460 - Bruges 1523)
(room 22)
Adoration of the Magi
Deposition

De Bles, Herri Met (*see* **Civetta**)

De Morales, Luis (Badajoz ? ca. 1509-1586)
(room 33*)
Christ with the Cross

Domenico di Bartolomeo (*see* **Domenico Veneziano**)

Domenico di Giacomo di Pace (*see* **Beccafumi**)

Domenico Veneziano (Venice ca. 1400 - Florence 1461)
(room 7)
Santa Lucia dei Magnoli Altarpiece

Dossi, Dosso (Ferrara ca. 1489-1542)
(room 29)
Rest During the Flight into Egypt
The Virgin Appears to Saints John the Baptist and John the Evangelist
Witchcraft (Allegory of Hercules)
Portrait of a Warrior

Duccio di Boninsegna (Siena ca. 1255-1319)
(room 2)
Rucellai Madonna

Dürer, Albrecht (Nuremburg 1471-1528)
(room 20)
Madonna and Child with a Pear
The Apostle James
The Apostle Philip
Portrait of the Artist's Father
Adoration of the Magi
Calvary (not on display)

Emilian school (16th century)
(room 29)
Portrait of a Youth

Empoli (Florence 1551-1640)
(room 33*)

Drunkenness of Noah
Sacrifice of Isaac

Fabre, François-Xavier (Montpellier 1766-1837)
(room 45*)
Portrait of Vittorio Alfieri
Portrait of the Countess d'Albany

Falca, Alessandro (*see* **Longhi Alessandro**)

Falca, Pietro (*see* **Longhi Pietro**)

Feti, Domenico (Rome ca. 1589 - Venice 1623)
(room 43*)
Artemisia

Figino, Girolamo (Milan, records from 1524 to 1569)
(room 34)
Madonna and Child with Saints Margaret and Mary Magdalen

Filipepi, Sandro (*see* **Botticelli**)

Fini, Tommaso di Cristoforo (*see* **Masolino da Panicale**)

Flemish school (17th century)
(room 33*)
Head of Medusa

Florentine painter (second half of the 16th century)
(room 33*)
Ulysses on the Island of Circe

Florentine school (mid 13th century)
(room 2)
Madonna and Child

Florigerio, Sebastiano (Conegliano ca 1500-1543)
(room 34)
Portrait of Raffaele Grassi

Fontana, Lavinia (Bologna 1552 - Rome 1614)
(room 33*)
Jesus Appears to Mary Magdalen

Foppa, Vincenzo (Brescia ca. 1427- ca. 1515)
(room 23)
Madonna and Child with an Angel

Foschi, Pier Francesco di Jacopo (Florence 1502-1567)
(room 27)
Portrait of a Man

Fra' Bartolomeo (Savignano 1472 - Florence 1517)
(room 25)
The Virgin Appears to Saint Bernard
Annunciation, Nativity and Circumcision
Portia

Fra' Giovanni da Fiesole (*see* **Beato Angelico**)

Francesco di Cristofano (*see* **Franciabigio**)

Francesco di Stefano (*see* **Pesellino**)

Francia (Bologna ca. 1450-1517)
(room 19)
    Portrait of Evangelista Scappi

Franciabigio (Florence 1484-1525)
(rooms 18, 26)
    Madonna of the Well
    Portrait of a Young Man

French school (16th century)
(room 33*)
    Portrait of Cristina of Lorraine

Friulian friend of Dosso (active in the first third of the 16th century)
(room 29)
    Portrait of a Man
    Allegorical Figure

Fumiani, Giovan Antonio (Venice 1643-1710)
(rooms 36-40)
    The Stoning of Zachariah

Gaddi, Agnolo (Florence ca. 1350-1396)
(room 5/6)
    Crucifixion

Gaddi, Taddeo (Florence ca. 1300-1366)
(room 4)
    <u>Madonna and Child Enthroned with Angels and Saints</u>

Garofalo (Ferrara 1481-1559)
(rooms 29, 30)
    Madonna and Child with Saints Martin and Dorothy
    Annunciation
    Adoration of the Shepherds
    Saint Jerome

Gellée, Claude (*see* **Lorrain**)

Genga, Girolamo (Urbino 1476-1551)
(room 19)
    Martyrdom of Saint Sebastian

Gentile da Fabriano (Fabriano ca. 1370 - Rome 1427)
(room 5/6)
    <u>Adoration of the Magi</u>
    Four Saints of the Quaratesi Polyptych

Gentile di Niccolò (*see* **Gentile da Fabriano**)

German school (16th century)

(room 20)
    Open Book
    Crucifixion with Mary Magdalen and the Patrons

Ghirlandaio (Florence 1449-1494)
(room 10/14)
    Madonna Enthroned with Saints
    <u>Madonna and Child with Angels and Saints</u>
    <u>Adoration of the Magi</u>

Giambellino (Venice ca. 1425-1516)
(room 21)
    <u>Sacred Allegory</u>
    <u>Portrait of a Young Man</u>
    <u>Lamentation over the Dead Christ</u>

Giampietrino (? - post 1540)
(room 23)
    Saint Catherine of Alexandria

Giorgione da Castelfranco (Castelfranco Veneto ca. 1477 - Venice 1510)
(room 21)
    <u>Portrait of a Man in Armour with Equerry</u>
    <u>The Judgement of Solomon</u>
    <u>Moses Undergoes Trial by Fire</u>

Giottino (Florence ca. 1320- post 1369)
(room 4)
    <u>San Remigio Pietà</u>

Giotto (Vespignano 1267 - Florence 1337)
(room 2)
    <u>Ognissanti Madonna</u>
    <u>Badia Polyptych</u>

Giotto di Stefano (*see* **Giottino**)

Giovan Battista di Jacopo (*see* **Rosso Fiorentino**)

Giovanni da Milano (Como ca. 1325- post 1369)
(room 4)
    Ognissanti Polyptych

Giovanni di Paolo (Siena 1403-1482)
(room 5/6)
    Madonna and Child with Saints

Goya y Lucientes, Francisco (Saragossa 1746 - Bordeaux 1828)
(room 45*)
    <u>Portrait of Maria Teresa de Vallabriga on Horseback</u>
    <u>Portrait of the Countess of Chinchòn</u>

Granacci, Francesco (Florence 1477-1543)
(room 25)
    <u>Joseph Presents his Father and Brothers to the Pharaoh</u>
    Joseph Being Taken to Prison

Greco (El) (Candia 1541 - Toledo 1614)
(room 35*)
  Saints John the Evangelist and Francis

Guardi, Francesco (Venice 1712-1793)
(room 45*)
  Caprice with an Arch and Pier
  Caprice with Bridges over the Canal

Guercino (Cento 1591 - Bologna 1666)
(room 43*)
  Country Concert

Holbein, Hans, the Younger (Augsburg ca. 1497 - London 1543)
(room 22)
  Portrait of Sir Richard Southwell
  Self-portrait
  Portrait of a Man, known as Thomas More

Italian school (16th century)
(room 33*)
  Man in Armour
  Fortune

Jacopo del Casentino (ca. 1290 - Florence post 1358)
(room 4)
  Madonna Enthroned with Angels and Saints

Jacopo del Sellaio (Florence 1442-1493)
(room 9)
  The Banquet of Ahasuerus

Jacopo di Cione (Florence ca. 1330-1398)
(room 4)
  Saint Matthew and Stories from his Life
  (Jacopo di Cione and Orcagna)

Jordaens, Jacob (Antwerp 1593-1678)
(room 41*)
  Portrait of a Woman, known as "Jordaens' Mother"

Landini, Jacopo (*see* **Jacopo del Casentino**)

Lemberger, Georg (Landshut ca. 1490 - Magdeburg ? ca. 1540)
(room 20)
  Saint George Freeing the Princess

Leonardesque painter
(room 23)
  Leda

Leonardo da Vinci (Vinci 1452 - Amboise 1519)
(room 15)
  Annunciation
  Adoration of the Magi
  Baptism of Christ (Leonardo and Verrocchio)

Licinio, Bernardino (Pescante ca. 1490- ca. 1565)
(room 34)

  Nude (attr.)

Ligozzi, Jacopo (Verona 1547 - Florence 1626)
(room 33*)
  Sacrifice of Isaac

Lingelbach, Johannes (Frankfurt 1622 - Amsterdam 1674)
(room 44*)
  Rest after the Hunt

Liotard, Jean-Etienne (Geneva 1702-1789)
(room 45*)
  Maria Adelaide of France in Turkish Dress

Lippi, Filippino (Prato 1457 - Florence 1504)
(room 8)
  Adoration of the Child (being restored)
  Saint Jerome
  Signoria Altarpiece ("Pala degli Otto")
  Adoration of the Magi
  Portrait of a Young Man (attr.)

Lippi, Filippo (Florence ca. 1406 - Spoleto 1469)
(room 8)
  Madonna and Child with Four Saints
  Annunciation, Saint Anthony Abbot and Saint John the Baptist
  Coronation of the Virgin
  Predella of the Barbadori Altarpiece
  Adoration of the Child with Saints Joseph, Gerome, Mary Magdalen and Hilary
  Adoration of the Child and Saints
  Madonna and Child with Angels

Longhi, Alessandro (Venice 1733-1813)
(room 45*)
  Portrait of a Lady
  Portrait of a Magistrate

Longhi, Pietro (Venice 1733-1813)
(room 45*)
  The Confession

Lorenzetti, Ambrogio (Siena 1285- ca. 1348)
(room 3)
  Four Stories from the Life of Saint Nicholas
  Presentation in the Temple
  Madonna and Child with Saints

Lorenzetti, Pietro (Siena ca. 1280- 1348 ?)
(room 3)
  Madonna and Child Enthroned
  Beata Umiltà Altarpiece

Lorenzo di Alessandro da Sanseverino (Sanseverino Marche records 1468 -1503)
(room 19)
  Pietà

Lorenzo di Credi (Florence ca. 1459-1537)
(rooms 15, 19)
    Adoration of the Shepherds
    Venus
    Annunciation

Lorenzo di Pietro (*see* **Vecchietta**)

Lorenzo Monaco (Siena? ca. 1370 - Florence ca. 1425)
(room 5/6)
    Coronation of the Virgin
    Adoration of the Magi (Lorenzo Monaco and
    Cosimo Rosselli)

Lorrain (Nancy 1600 - Rome 1682)
(room 43*)
    Port with Villa Medici

Lotto, Lorenzo (Venice ca. 1480 - Loreto ca. 1556)
(room 34)
    Portrait of a Youth
    Susanna and the Elders
    Holy Family with Saints Jerome, Anne and
    Joachim

Lucas van Leyden (Leyden 1489-1533)
(room 22)
    Christ Crowned with Thorns (attr.)

Luccan school (mid 13th century)
(room 2)
    Crucifix with Stories of the Passion

Luciani, Sebastiano (*see* **Sebastiano del Piombo**)

Luini, Bernardino (Luino ca. 1460- post 1532)
(room 23)
    Herodias

Luteri, Giovan Battista (*see* **Dossi, Dosso**)
    Crocifissione

Maineri, Francesco (Parma, records 1489-1506)
(room 23)
    Christ Carrying the Cross

Maler zu Schwaz, Hans (Schwaz, records 1500-1510)
(room 20)
    Portrait of Ferdinand of Castille

Mantegna, Andrea (Isola di Carturo 1431 - Mantua 1506)
(room 23)
    Madonna of the Quarries
    Triptych: Adoration of the Magi, Circumcision,
    Ascension
    Portrait of Cardinal Carlo de' Medici

Martini, Simone (Siena ca. 1284 - Avignon 1344)
(room 3)

(Simone Martini and Lippo Memmi)
    Annunciation and Two Saints

Masaccio (San Giovanni Valdarno 1401 - Rome 1428)
(room 7)
    Madonna and Child
    Madonna and Child with Saint Anne
    and Five Angels (Masaccio and Masolino)

Masolino da Panicale (San Giovanni Valdarno ca. 1383 - 1440)
(rooms 5/6, 7)
    Madonna dell'Umiltà
    Madonna and Child with Saint Anne
    and Five Angels (Masolino and Masaccio)

Master of the Bardi Saint Francis (active between 1240 and 1270)
(room 2)
    Saint Francis Receives the Stigmata

Master of the Baroncelli Portraits (Flanders 15th century)
(room 22)
    Portraits of Pierantonio Baroncelli and Maria
    Bonciani

Master of Greve (13th century)
(Room of San Pier Scheraggio)
    Madonna and Child

Master of Hoogstraeten (Hoogstraeten, active ca. 1490-1530)
(room 22)
    Madonna and Child with Saints Catherine and
    Barbara

Master of Mary Magdalen (active at the end of the 13th century)
(room 2)
    Saint Luke the Evangelist

Master of Saint Cecilia (active in Florence ca. 1300-1320)
(room 4)
    Saint Cecilia altar frontal

Master of San Martino alla Palma
(Room of San Pier Scheraggio)
    "Madonna della Ninna"

Master of San Torpè (active until ca. 1320)
(room 2)
    Madonna and Child

Master of the Virgo inter Virgines (Delft, active ca. 1470-1500)
(room 22)
    Crucifixion

Mazzola, Francesco (*see* **Parmigianino**)

Mazzolino, Ludovico (Ferrara ca. 1480-1528)
(room 30)
    <u>Adoration of the Shepherds</u>
    Massacre of the Innocents
    Circumcision
    <u>Madonna and Child with Saints</u>

Meldolla, Andrea (*see* **Schiavone**)

Meliore di Jacopo (records in Florence in 1260)
(room 2)
    The Redeemer and Four Saints

Memling, Hans (Seligenstadt ca. 1435 - Bruges 1494)
(room 22)
    <u>Madonna and Child Enthroned with Two Angels</u>
    Portrait of a Man
    Saint Benedict
    Portrait of a Man
    <u>"Mater Dolorosa"</u>
    Portrait of Benedetto Portinari
    <u>Portrait of a Man</u>

Memmi, Lippo (? ca. 1290 - ? ca. 1347)
(room 3)
    <u>Annunciation and Two Saints</u> (Lippo Memmi and Simone Martini)

Merisi, Michelangelo (*see* **Caravaggio**)

Metsu, Gabriel (Leyden 1629 - Amsterdam 1667)
(room 44*)
    Lady and a Knight

Michelangelo (Caprese, Arezzo 1475 - Rome 1564)
(room 25)
    <u>Holy Family with the Young Saint John (Tondo Doni)</u>

Micheli, Andrea (*see* **Vicentino**)

Molenaer, Jan Miense (Haarlem ca. 1609-1668)
(room 44*)
    Tavern Scene

Morandini, Francesco (*see* **Poppi**)

Moroni, Giovan Battista (Albino ca. 1530 - Bergamo 1578)
(room 34)
    Portrait of Pietro Secco Suardo
    Portrait of the Poet Giovanni Antonio Pantera
    Portrait of a Scholar

Nardo di Cione (Florence ca. 1320- ca. 1365)
(room 4)
    <u>Crucifixion</u>

Nattier, Jean Marc (Paris 1685-1766)
(room 45*)

Marie Zephirine of France

Negretti, Jacopo (*see* **Palma il Vecchio**)

Netscher, Caspar (Heidelberg 1639 - Hague 1684)
(room 44*)
    The Cook

Niccolò dell'Abate (Modena ca. 1509 - France post 1571)
(room 33*)
    Portrait of a Youth

Niccolò di Bonaccorso (Siena, records 1372-1388)
(room 3)
    Presentation of the Virgin in the Temple

Nicola di Guardiagrele (Abruzzo, records late 14th- mid 15th century)
(room 5/6)
    Madonna and Child with Angels

North Italian Painter (16th century)
(room 34)
    Portrait of Teofilo Falengo

Oliverio, Alessandro (first half of the 16th century)
(room 31)
    Portrait of a Man

Orcagna (Florence ca. 1320-1368)
(room 4)
    <u>Saint Matthew and Stories from his Life</u>

Pace, Gian Paolo (Venice, records 1528-1560)
(room 32)
    Portrait of Giovanni dalle Bande Nere

Pacino di Bonaguida (14th century; workshop of)
(room 4)
    Crucifixion and Saints

Pagani, Gregorio (Florence 1558-1605)
(room 35*)
    Pyramus e Thisbe

Palma il Vecchio (Bergamo 1480 c. - Venice 1528)
(room 28)
    <u>Resurrection of Lazarus</u>
    Holy Family with the Young Saint John and Saint Mary Magdalen
    Judith

Palmezzano, Marco (Forlì ca. 1460-1539)
(room 19)
    Crucifixion

Paolo di Dono (*see* **Paolo Uccello**)

Paolo Uccello (Florence 1397-1475)
(room 7)

The Battle of San Romano

Parmigianino (Parma 1504 - Casalmaggiore 1540)
(room 29)
    Madonna and Child with Saints, known
    as the "Madonna di San Zaccaria"
    Portrait of a Man
    Madonna and Child with Angels, known
    as the "Madonna of the Long Neck"

Pedrini Giovanni (or Giovanni Pietro Rizzi)
(*see* **Giampietrino**)

Pencz, Georg (Nuremburg ca. 1500 - Leipzig 1550)
(room 22)
    Portrait of a Seated Youth

Perin del Vaga (Florence 1501 - Rome 1547)
(room 27)
    Tarquin Founds the Temple of Jove on the Capitol
    Justice of Seleucus

Perréal, Jean (? ca. 1435 - ? 1530)
(room 33*)
    Portrait of a Lady

Perugino (Città della Pieve ca. 1448 - Fontignano
1523)
(rooms 15, 19)
    Madonna and Saints
    Pietà
    Agony in the Garden
    Crucifix with Saints
    Portrait of Francesco delle Opere
    Portrait of a Man
    Portrait of Don Biagio Milanesi
    Portrait of Baldassarre Vallombrosano

Pesellino (Florence 1422-1457)
(room 8)
    Predella with Stories of Saints

Piazzetta, Giovanni Battista (Venice 1682-1754)
(room 45*)
    Susanna and the Elders

Piero della Francesca (Borgo San Sepolcro 1410/20-
1492)
(room 7)
    Portraits of the Duke and Duchess of Urbino

Piero del Pollaiolo (Florence ca. 1443 - Rome 1496)
(room 9)
    Charity
    Faith
    Justice
    Prudence
    Hope
    Temperance (being restored)
    Portrait of Gian Galeazzo Maria Sforza
    Altarpiece with Three Saints (Piero and Antonio

del Pollaiolo)

Piero di Cosimo (Florence ca. 1462-1521)
(rooms 15, 19)
    Incarnation
    Perseus Frees Andromeda
    Immaculate Conception with Six Saints

Piero di Giovanni (*see* **Lorenzo Monaco**)

Piero di Lorenzo (*see* **Piero di Cosimo**)

Pino, Paolo (Venice, active in the mid 16th century)
(room 34)
    Portrait of a Man, known as the "Portrait
    of Doctor Coignati"

Pippi, Giulio (*see* **Romano, Giulio**)

Pisan school (late 13th century)
(room 2)
    Crucifix with Stories of the Passion

Ponte (da), Jacopo (*see* **Bassano, Jacopo**)

Ponte (da), Leandro (*see* **Bassano, Leandro**)

Pontormo (Pontorme, Empoli 1494 - Florence 1556)
(rooms 18, 27)
    Madonna and Child with the Young Saint John
    Portrait of Cosimo the Elder
    Leda and the Swan (attr.)
    The Expulsion from Earthly Paradise
    Portrait of a Musician
    Saint Antony Abbot
    Portrait of Maria Salviati
    Nativity of Saint John
    Supper at Emmaus
    Madonna and Child with Saint Jerome,
    Saint Francis and Two Angels
    Martyrdom of Saint Maurice and the
    Theban Legion (Pontormo and Bronzino)

Poppi (Poppi 1544 - Florence 1597)
(room 33*)
    The Three Graces

Porta (della), Bartolomeo (*see* **Fra' Bartolomeo**)

Pot, Hendrick Gerritsz (Haarlem ca. 1585 -
Amsterdam 1657)
(room 44*)
    The Miser

Pourbus, Frans, the Elder (Bruges ca. 1542 -
Antwerp 1580)
(room 33*)
    Portrait of Viglius von Aytta

Predis (de'), Giovanni Ambrogio (Milan ca. 1455-
post 1508)

(room 23)
> Portrait of a Man

Preti, Mattia (Taverna 1613 - Malta 1699)
(room 43*)
> Vanity

Puligo (Florence 1492-1527)
(room 26)
> Portrait of Pietro Carnesecchi

Pynas, Jacob (Haarlem 1585 - Delft post 1648)
(room 44*)
> Mercury and Erse

Raphael (Urbino 1483 - Rome 1520)
(rooms 18, 26)
> Saint John the Baptist in the Desert (R. and workshop)
> Portrait of a Man, known as that of Francesco Maria della Rovere
> Portrait of Elisabetta Gonzaga
> Self-portrait
> Portrait of Leo X with Cardinals Giulio de' Medici and Luigi de' Rossi
> Portrait of Julius II (R. and workshop)
> Portrait of Guidobaldo da Montefeltro
> Madonna of the Goldfinch
> Portrait of Perugino (attr.)

Raibolini, Francesco (*see* **Francia**)

Rembrandt Harmenszoon van Rijn (Leyden 1606 - Amsterdam 1669)
(room 44*)
> Self-portrait as a Young Man
> Self-portrait as an Old Man
> Portrait of an Old Man

Reni, Guido (Bologna 1575-1642)
(rooms 36-40)
> Madonna of the Snow

Ricciarelli, Daniele (*see* **Daniele da Volterra**)

Riccio, Domenico (*see* **Brusasorci**)

Ridolfo del Ghirlandaio (Florence 1483-1561)
(room 18, 25)
> Portrait of a Man
> The Nun (attr.)
> Portrait Cover (attr.)

Robusti, Domenico (*see* **Tintoretto**)

Robusti, Jacopo (*see* **Tintoretto**)

Romano, Giulio (Rome ca. 1499 - Mantua 1546)
(room 18)
> Madonna and Child

Rosa, Salvator (Naples 1615 - Rome 1673)
(room 43*)
> Landscape with Figures

Rosselli, Cosimo (Florence 1439-1507)
(room 5/6)
> Adoration of the Magi (Cosimo Rosselli and Lorenzo Monaco)

Rossi (de'), Francesco (*see* **Salviati, Cecchino**)

Rosso Fiorentino (Florence 1495 - Fontainebleau 1540)
(rooms 18, 27)
> Musician Angel
> Portrait of a Young Woman
> Madonna and Child with Saints (Spedalingo Altarpiece)
> Moses Defends the Daughters of Jethro
> Portrait of a Young Man Dressed in Black

Rubens, Pieter Paul (Siegen 1577 - Antwerp 1640)
(room 42*)
> Judith and Holophernes
> Henry IV at the Battle of Ivry (being restored)
> Bacchus Astride a Barrel
> Portrait of Isabella Brandt
> Self-portrait
> Triumphal Entrance of Henry IV into Paris (being restored)

Ruysch, Rachel (Amsterdam 1664-1750)
(room 44*)
> Fruits and Insects

Salviati, Cecchino (Florence 1510 - Rome 1563)
(rooms 18, 27, 33*)
> Charity
> Christ Carrying the Cross
> Artemisia Mourning Mausolus
> Adoration of the Shepherds

Samacchini, Orazio (Bologna 1532-1577)
(room 33*)
> The Chastity of Joseph (attr.)
> Susanna Bathing (attr.)

Savoldo, Giovanni Girolamo (Brescia ca. 1480 - Venice? 1548)
(room 34)
> Transfiguration

Scarsella, Ippolito (*see* **Scarsellino**)

Scarsellino (Ferrara ca. 1550-1620)
(room 33*)
> The Judgement of Paris

Schalcken, Godfried (Made 1643 - Hague 1706)
(room 44*)
> Pygmalion

Schiavone (Sebenico ca. 1500 - Venice 1563)
Portrait of a Man in a Fur Cloak (not on display)

School of Fontainebleau
(room 33*)
Two Women Bathing

Sebastiano del Piombo (Venice 1485 - Rome 1547)
(room 28)
Death of Adonis
Portrait of a Woman

Seghers, Daniel (Antwerp 1591-1661)
(room 41*)
Garland of Flowers with Marble Bust

Seghers, Hercules Pietersz (Haarlem ca. 1590 - Amsterdam ca. 1638)
(room 44*)
Mountain Landscape

Signorelli, Luca (Cortona ca. 1445-1523)
(rooms 15, 19)
Crucifix with Mary Magdalen
The Trinity, the Virgin and Two Saints
Three predella panels
Holy Family
Madonna and Child with Allegorical Figures
Allegory of Fertility and Abundance

Simone dei Crocefissi (Bologna doc. 1355-1399)
(room 3)
Nativity

Sodoma (Vercelli 1477 - Siena 1549)
(room 23)
Christ at the Column

Spinelli, Giovan Battista (doc. ca. 1630-1660)
(rooms 36-40)
David is Celebrated by the Jewish Women
David Placates Saul's Anguish with a Harp

Starnina, Gherardo (Florence ca. 1354-1413)
(room 5/6)
Madonna and Child

Steen, Jan (Leyden 1626-1679)
(room 44*)
The Luncheon

Strozzi, Bernardo (Genoa 1581 - Venice 1644)
(rooms 36-40)
Saint Catherine of Alexandria
Saint Cecilia

Suss von Kulmbach, Hans (Kulmbach ca. 1480 - Nuremburg 1522)
(room 20)
Episodes from the Lives

of Saints Peter and Paul (8 panels)

Sustermans, Justus (Antwerp 1597 - Florence 1681)
(room 41*)
Portrait of Galileo Galilei

Theotokópulos, Domenico (*see* **El Greco**)

Tiepolo, Giovanni Battista (Venice 1696 - Madrid 1770)
(room 45*)
Reginald Abandons Armida
Reginald Looks at Himself in the Shield of Ubaldo
Erecting a Statue in Honour of an Emperor

Tintoretto (Robusti, Domenico) (Venice 1560-1635)
The Miracle of Saint Augustine (attr. - not on diplay)

Tintoretto (Robusti, Jacopo) (Venice 1518-1594)
(room 32)
Portrait of a Man
Adam and Eve Before God
Portrait of a Man with a Red Beard
Portrait of Jacopo Sansovino
Leda and the Swan
Portrait of a Venetian Admiral
Christ at the Well of the Samaritan
The Samaritan at the Well
Portrait of a Man

Tisi, Benvenuto (*see* **Garofalo**)

Titian (Pieve di Cadore ca. 1488 - Venice 1576)
(room 28)
Venus of Urbino
Portrait of a Knight of Malta
Portrait of Bishop Ludovico Beccadelli
Saint Margaret
Portrait of Eleonora Gonzaga della Rovere
Flora
Portrait of Francesco Maria della Rovere
Portrait of a Man, known as "The Sick Man"
Portrait of Sixtus IV (workshop)

Tura, Cosmè (Ferrara 1432-1495)
(room 21)
Saint Dominic

Ubaldini, Domenico (*see* **Puligo**)

Ubertini, Francesco (*see* **Bachiacca**)

Van Clève, Joos (Antwerp ca. 1485- ca. 1540)
(rooms 20, 22)
Portrait of a Man
Portrait of a Woman

Van den Hoecke, Jan (Antwerp 1611 - Brussels ? 1651)
(room 41*)

Hercules Between Vice and Virtue
Triumphal Entrance of Cardinal Prince Ferdinand of Spain into Antwerp

Van der Goes, Hugo (Gand ca. 1440 - Rouge Cloitre)
(room 10/14)
Portinari Triptych

Van der Werff, Adriaen (Kralingen 1659 - Rotterdam 1722)
(room 44*)
Adoration of the Shepherds

Van der Weyden, Rogier
Entombment (not on display)

Van Dyck, Anthony (Antwerp 1599 - London 1641)
(room 41*)
Portrait of Sustermans' Mother
Portrait of Marguerite of Lorraine, Duchess of Orléans
Portrait of Jean de Montfort
Portrait of Charles V on Horseback

Van Huysum, Jan (Amsterdam 1682-1749)
(room 44*)
Vase of Flowers

Van Mieris, Frans, the Elder (Leyden 1635-1681)
(room 44*)
The Dutch Charlatan
The Artist and his Family
Two Old Men at the Table

Vanni, Andrea (Siena 1332-1414)
(room 3)
Madonna and Child

Vannucci, Pietro (*see* **Perugino**)

Van Orley, Bernaert (Brussels ca. 1488-1541)
(room 22)
Portrait of a Man and his Wife

Van Poelenburg, Cornelis (Utrecht 1586-1667)
(room 44*)
Mercury and Batto

Van Ruysdael, Jacob (Haarlem ca. 1628 - Amsterdam ? 1682)
(room 44*)
Landscape with Shepherds and Peasants

Van Valckenborch, Martin (Louvain 1535 - Frankfurt 1612)
(room 33*)
Country Dance

Vasari, Giorgio (Arezzo 1511 - Florence 1574)
(rooms 18, 33*)

Portrait of Lorenzo the Magnificent
Allegory of the Immaculate Conception
The Prophet Elisha
Vulcan's Forge
Adoration of the Shepherds

Vecchietta (Castiglion d'Orcia ca. 1412 - Siena 1480)
(room 5/6)
Madonna Enthroned with Saints

Velàzquez, Diego Rodriguez de Silva y (Seville 1599 - Madrid 1660)
(room 41*)
Self-portrait
Equestrian Portrait of Philip IV of Spain

Venetian school (16th century)
(room 31)
Portrait of a Man
Portrait of an Artist

Veneto-Friulian painter (16th century)
(room 29)
Portrait of a Woman

Veronese (Verona 1528 -Venice 1588)
(room 31)
Holy Family with Saint Barbara and the Young Saint John
Martyrdom of Saint Justine
Saint Agatha Crowned by Angels
Venus and Mercury present their Son Anteros to Jove
Annunciation
Esther and Ahasuerus
Madonna Enthroned

Verrocchio (Florence 1453 - Venice 1488)
(room 15)
Baptism of Christ (Verrocchio and Leonardo)

Vicentino (Vicenza 1542 - Venice 1617)
(room 31)
Visitation

Vivarini, Bartolomeo (Venice doc. 1450-1499)
(room 21)
Saint Louis of Toulouse

Vouet, Simon (Paris 1590-1649)
(room 43*)
Annunciation

Zucchi, Jacopo (Florence 1541? - Rome ? ca. 1590)
(room 33*)
Age of Iron
Age of Silver
Age of Gold
Rest During the Flight into Egypt

LIST BY PERIOD AND GEOGRAPHICAL ZONE

EMILIAN AND LOMBARD PAINTING OF THE 15TH C:	room 23
EMILIAN PAINTING OF THE 16TH C:	rooms 29, 30
FLEMISH PAINTING OF THE 15TH AND EARLY 16TH C:	rooms 10/14, 22
FLORENTINE PAINTING OF THE 14TH C:	room 4
FLORENTINE PAINTING OF THE 15TH C:	room of San Pier Scheraggio, rooms 5/6, 7, 8, 9, 10/14, 15
FLORENTINE PAINTING OF THE 16TH C:	rooms 15,18, 25, 26, 27, 33
FLORENTINE PAINTING OF THE 17TH C:	rooms 35, 36-40
FRENCH PAINTING:	rooms 33, 43, 45
GERMAN PAINTING OF THE 15TH C:	rooms 20, 22
ITALIAN LATE GOTHIC PAINTING:	room 5/6
NEAPOLITAN PAINTING OF THE 17TH C:	room 43
NORTH EUROPEAN PAINTING OF THE 17TH C:	rooms 41, 44
ROMAN PAINTING OF THE 17TH C:	room 43
SIENESE PAINTING OF THE 14TH C:	room 3
SPANISH PAINTING OF THE 17TH AND 18TH C:	rooms 35, 41, 45
TUSCAN PAINTING OF THE 13TH C:	room 2
UMBRIAN PAINTING OF THE 15TH C:	rooms 15, 19
VENETIAN PAINTING OF THE 15TH C:	rooms 5/6, 21, 23
VENETIAN PAINTING OF THE 16TH C:	rooms 28, 31, 32, 35
VENETIAN PAINTING OF THE 17TH AND 18TH C:	rooms 35, 36-40

LIST OF WORKS BY ROOM

ROOM 2
Room of the 13th century and Giotto

Bonaventura Berlinghieri (workshop of), _Madonna and Child with Saints and Crucifixion_
Cimabue, _Santa Trinita Madonna_
Agnolo di Bondone known as Giotto, _Ognissanti Madonna_
Agnolo di Bondone known as Giotto, _Badia Polyptych_
Duccio di Boninsegna, _Rucellai Madonna_
Master of the Bardi Saint Francis, _Saint Francis Receives the Stigmata_
Master of Mary Magdalen, _Saint Luke the Evangelist_
Master of San Torpè, _Madonna and Child_
Meliore di Jacopo, _The Redeemer and Four Saints_
Florentine school (mid 13th century), _Madonna and Child_
Luccan school (mid 13th century), _Crucifix with Stories of the Passion_
Pisan school (late 13th century), _Crucifix with Stories of the Passion_

ROOM 3
Room of 14th-century Sienese painting

Pietro Lorenzetti, _Madonna and Child Enthroned with Angels_
Pietro Lorenzetti, _Beata Umiltà Altarpiece_
Ambrogio Lorenzetti, _Four Stories from the Life of Saint Nicholas_
Ambrogio Lorenzetti, _Presentation in the Temple_
Ambrogio Lorenzetti, _Madonna and Child with Saints_
Niccolò di Bonaccorso, _Presentation of the Virgin in the Temple_
Simone dei Crocefissi, _Nativity_
Andrea Vanni, _Madonna and Child_
Simone Martini and Lippo Memmi, _Annunciation and Two Saints_

ROOM 4
Room of 14th-century Florentine painting

Bernardo Daddi, _Madonna and Child with Saints Matthew and Nicholas_
Bernardo Daddi, _Madonna and Child Enthroned with Angels and Saints_
Bernardo Daddi, _San Pancrazio Polyptych_
Taddeo Gaddi, _Madonna and Child Enthroned with Angels and Saints_
Jacopo Landini, known as Jacopo del Casentino, _Madonna Enthroned with Angels and Saints_
Giotto di Stefano known as Giottino, _San Remigio Pietà_
Giovanni da Milano, _Ognissanti Polyptych_
Saint Cecilia Master, _Saint Cecilia altar frontal_
Nardo di Cione, _Crucifixion_
Pacino di Bonaguida (workshop of), _Crucifixion and Saints_
Andrea Orcagna - Jacopo di Cione, _Saint Matthew and Stories from his Life_

ROOM 5/6
Room of International Gothic

Jacopo Bellini, _Madonna and Child_
Gentile di Niccolò, known as Gentile da Fabriano, _Adorationof the Magi_
Gentile di Niccolò, known as Gentile da Fabriano, _Four Saints from the Quaratesi Polyptych_
Agnolo Gaddi, _Crucifixion_
Giovanni di Paolo, _Madonna and Child with Saints_
Lorenzo Monaco and Cosimo Rosselli, _Adoration of the Magi_
Lorenzo Monaco, _Coronation of the Virgin_
Gherardo Starnina, _Madonna and Child_
Beato Angelico, _Thebaid_
Masolino da Panicale, _Madonna dell'Umiltà_
Nicola di Guardiagrele, _Madonna and Child with Angels_

ROOM 7
Room of the Early Renaissance

Beato Angelico, _Coronation of the Virgin_
Beato Angelico, _Madonna and Child with Saints_
Domenico Veneziano, _Santa Lucia dei Magnoli Altarpiece_
Piero della Francesca, _Portraits of the Duke and Duchess of Urbino_
Paolo Uccello, _The Battle of San Romano_
Masaccio, _Madonna and Child_
Masaccio and Masolino, _Madonna and Child with Saint Anne and Five Angels_

ROOM 8
The Lippi Room

Filippo Lippi, _Madonna and Child with Angels_
Filippo Lippi, _Madonna and Child with Four Saints_
Filippo Lippi, _Adoration of the Child and Saints_
Filippo Lippi, _Coronation of the Virgin_
Filippo Lippi, _Adoration of the Child with Saints Joseph, Jerome, Mary Magdalen and Hilary_
Filippo Lippi, _Annunciation, Saints Antony Abbot and John the Baptist_
Filippo Lippi, _Predella of the Barbadori Altarpiece_
Francesco di Stefano, known as Pesellino, _Predella with Stories of Saints_
Alessio Baldovinetti, _Annunciation_
Alessio Baldovinetti, _Madonna and Child with Saints_
Filippino Lippi, _Adoration of the Magi_
Filippino Lippi, _Signoria Altarpiece ("Pala degli Otto")_
Filippino Lippi, _Saint Jerome_
Filippino Lippi, _Adoration of the Child_ (being restored)
Filippino Lippi (attr.), _Portrait of a Young Man_

ROOM 9
The Pollaiolo Room

Sandro Botticelli, *Fortitude*
Sandro Botticelli, *The Return of Judith*
Sandro Botticelli, *The Discovery of the Body of Holophernes*
Piero del Pollaiolo, *Charity*
Piero del Pollaiolo, *Faith*
Piero del Pollaiolo, *Justice*
Piero del Pollaiolo, *Prudence*
Piero del Pollaiolo, *Hope*
Piero del Pollaiolo, *Temperance* (being restored)
Piero del Pollaiolo, *Portrait of Gian Galeazzo Maria Sforza*
Jacopo del Sellaio, *The Banquet of Ahasuerus*
Antonio del Pollaiolo, *Hercules and Antaeus*
Antonio del Pollaiolo, *Portrait of a Lady*
Antonio del Pollaiolo, *Hercules and the Hydra*
Antonio and Piero del Pollaiolo, *Altarpiece with Three Saints*

ROOM 10/14
The Botticelli Room

Sandro Botticelli, *Madonna of the Rose Garden*
Sandro Botticelli, *Madonna of the Magnificat*
Sandro Botticelli, *Madonna and Child*
Sandro Botticelli, *The Birth of Venus*
Sandro Botticelli, *Pallas and the Centaur*
Sandro Botticelli, *Madonna of the Pomegranate*
Sandro Botticelli, *Calumny*
Sandro Botticelli, *Annunciation*
Sandro Botticelli, *Primavera (Spring)*
Sandro Botticelli, *Adoration of the Magi*
Sandro Botticelli, *Portrait of a Man with a Medal of Cosimo the Elder*
Sandro Botticelli, *Saint Ambrose Altarpiece*
Sandro Botticelli, *Saint Augustine*
Sandro Botticelli, *Saint Mark Altarpiece*
Sandro Botticelli, *San Barnaba Altarpiece*
Domenico Bigordi, known as Ghirlandaio, *Madonna Enthroned with Saints*
Domenico Bigordi, known as Ghirlandaio, *Madonna and Child with Angels and Saints*
Domenico Bigordi, known as Ghirlandaio, *Adoration of the Magi*
Hugo van der Goes, *Portinari Triptych*

ROOM 15
The Leonardo Room

Leonardo da Vinci, *Annunciation*
Leonardo da Vinci, *Adoration of the Magi*
Verrocchio and Leonardo da Vinci, *Baptism of Christ*
Perugino, *Madonna and Saints*
Perugino, *Pietà*
Perugino, *Agony in the Garden*
Perugino, *Crucifix and Saints*
Piero di Cosimo, *Incarnation*
Piero di Cosimo, *Immaculate Conception with Six Saints*
Luca Signorelli, *Crucifix with Mary Magdalen*
Luca Signorelli, *The Trinity, the Virgin and Two Saints*
Luca Signorelli, *Three predella panels*
Lorenzo di Credi, *Adoration of the Shepherds*

ROOM 16
Room of the Geographical Maps

Caravaggio, *Sacrifice of Isaac*
Caravaggio, *Bacchus*

ROOM 18
The Tribune

Paintings

Alessandro Allori, *Portrait of Bianca Cappello*
Carlo Caliari, *Original Sin*
Carlo Caliari, *The Creation of Eve*
Carlo Caliari, *The Expulsion from Paradise*
Carlo Caliari, *The Family of Adam*
Andrea del Sarto, *Portrait of a Woman with the Young Petrarch*
Agnolo Bronzino, *Portrait of Bartolomeo Panciatichi*
Agnolo Bronzino, *Portrait of Lucrezia Panciatichi*
Agnolo Bronzino, *Portrait of Bia, illegitimate daughter of Cosimo I*
Agnolo Bronzino, *Portrait of a Man with a Lute*
Agnolo Bronzino, *Portrait of Eleonora of Toledo with her Son Giovanni*
Agnolo Bronzino, *Portrait of Giovanni de' Medici as a Child*
Agnolo Bronzino, *Portrait of Cosimo I*
Agnolo Bronzino, *Portrait of a Woman*
Agnolo Bronzino, *Portrait of Maria de' Medici*
Agnolo Bronzino, *Portrait of Francesco I de' Medici*
Agnolo Bronzino, *Annunciation*
Franciabigio, *Madonna of the Well*
Ridolfo del Ghirlandaio, *Portrait of a Man*
Rosso Fiorentino, *Musician Angel*
Giulio Romano, *Madonna and Child*
Raphael, *Saint John the Baptist in the Desert*
Cecchino Salviati, *Charity*
Cecchino Salviati, *Christ Carrying the Cross*
Pontormo, *Madonna and Child with the Young Saint John*
Pontormo, *Portrait of Cosimo the Elder*
Pontormo (attr.), *Leda and the Swan*
Pontormo, *The Expulsion from Earthly Paradise*
Giorgio Vasari, *Portrait of Lorenzo the Magnificent*
Giorgio Vasari, *Allegory of the Immaculate Conception*
Giorgio Vasari, *The Prophet Elisha*
Daniele da Volterra, *Massacre of the Innocents*

ROOM 19
Room of Perugino and Signorelli

Lorenzo Costa, *Saint Sebastian*
Girolamo Genga, *Martyrdom of Saint Sebastian*
Lorenzo di Credi, *Venus*
Lorenzo di Credi, *Annunciation*
Francesco Raibolini, known as Francia, *Portrait of Evangelista Scappi*
Lorenzo di Alessandro da Sanseverino, *Pietà*
Marco Palmezzano, *Crucifixion*
Perugino, *Portrait of Francesco delle Opere*
Perugino, *Portrait of a Man*
Perugino, *Portrait of Don Biagio Milanesi*
Perugino, *Portrait of Baldassarre Vallombrosano*
Piero di Cosimo, *Perseus Frees Andromeda*

Luca Signorelli, _Holy Family_
Luca Signorelli, _Madonna and Child with Allegorical Figures_
Luca Signorelli, _Allegory of Fertility and Abundance_

ROOM 20
Room of Dürer and German Artists

Lukas Cranach the Elder, _Adam_ (being restored)
Lukas Cranach the Elder, _Eve_ (being restored)
Lukas Cranach the Elder (workshop of), _Portraits of Martin Luther and Catherine Bore_
Lukas Cranach the Elder (workshop of), _Portrait of a Young Woman_
Lukas Cranach the Elder (workshop of), _Portraits of Frederick III the Wise and Johann I, Electors of Saxony_
Lukas Cranach the Elder (workshop of), _Portraits of Martin Luther and Philipp Melanchthon_
Lukas Cranach the Younger, _Portrait of Lukas Cranach the Elder_
Hans Baldung Grien, _Adam_ (from Dürer)
Hans Baldung Grien, _Eve_ (from Dürer)
Hans Maler zu Schwaz, _Portrait of Ferdinand of Castille_
Georg Lemberger, _Saint George Freeing the Princess_
Albrecht Dürer, _Madonna and Child with a Pear_
Albrecht Dürer, _The Apostle James_
Albrecht Dürer, _Adoration of the Magi_
Albrecht Dürer, _Portrait of the Artist's Father_
Albrecht Dürer, _The Apostle Philip_
German school of the 16th century, _Open Book_
German school of the 16th century, _Crucifixion with Mary Magdalen and the Patrons_
Hans Suss von Kulmbach, _Episodes from the Lives of Saints Peter and Paul_
Joos van Clève, _Portrait of a Man_
Jan Brueghel the Elder, _Calvary_ (from Dürer)
Hans Burgkmair, _Portrait of a Man_

ROOM 21
Room of Giambellino and Giorgione

Giovanni Bellini, _Sacred Allegory_
Giovanni Bellini, _Portrait of a Young Man_
Giovanni Bellini, _Lamentation over the Dead Christ_
Vittore Carpaccio, _Prophet_
Vittore Carpaccio (attr.), _Sibyl_
Vittore Carpaccio (attr.), _Group of Soldiers and People in Oriental Dress_
Giorgione da Castelfranco, _Portrait of a Man in Armour with Equerry_
Giorgione da Castelfranco, _The Judgement of Solomon_
Giorgione, _Moses Undergoes Trial by Fire_
Cosmè Tura, _Saint Dominic_
Giovanni Battista Cima da Conegliano, _Madonna and Child_
Bartolomeo Vivarini, _Saint Louis of Toulouse_
Lorenzo Costa, _Portrait of Giovanni Bentivoglio_

ROOM 22
Room of Flemish and German Renaissance Artists

Albrecht Altdorfer, _Saint Florian Takes Leave of the Monastery_
Albrecht Altdorfer, _Martyrdom of Saint Florian_
Hans Holbein the Younger, _Portrait of Sir Richard Southwell_

Hans Holbein the Younger, _Self-portrait_
Hans Holbein the Younger, _Portrait of a Man_, known as that of Thomas More
Master of the Baroncelli Portraits, _Portrait of Pierantonio Baroncelli and Maria Bonciani_
Lucas van Leyden (attr.), _Christ Crowned with Thorns_
Master of Hoogstraeten, _Madonna and Child with Saints Catherine and Barbara_
Gerard David, _Adoration of the Magi_
Gerard David, _Deposition_
Hans Memling, _Madonna and Child Enthroned with Two Angels_
Hans Memling, _Portrait of a Man_
Hans Memling, _Saint Benedict_
Hans Memling, _Portrait of a Man_
Hans Memling, _"Mater dolorosa"_
Hans Memling, _Portrait of Benedetto Portinari_
Hans Memling, _Portrait of a Man_
Georg Pencz, _Portrait of a Seated Youth_
Bernaert van Orley, _Portrait of a Man and his Wife_
Master of the Virgo inter Virgines, _Crucifixion_
Joos van Clève, _Portrait of a Man_
Joos van Clève, _Portrait of a Woman_

ROOM 23
Room of Mantegna and Correggio

Alessandro Araldi, _Portrait of Barbara Pallavicino_
Boccaccio Boccaccino, _Gypsy_
Giovanni Antonio Boltraffio, _Narcissus at the Well_
Vincenzo Foppa, _Madonna and Child with an Angel_
Correggio, _Adoration of the Child_
Correggio, _Rest During the Flight into Egypt_
Correggio, _Madonna and Child in Glory_
Bernardino Luini, _Herodias_
Bernardino de' Conti, _Portrait of a Man_
Giovanni Ambrogio de' Predis, _Portrait of a Man_
Giovanni Pedrini known as Giampietrino, _Saint Catherine of Alexandria_
Francesco Maineri, _Christ Carrying the Cross_
Leonardesque painter, _Leda_
Sodoma, _Christ at the Column_
Andrea Mantegna, _Madonna of the Quarries_
Andrea Mantegna, _Triptych: Adoration of the Magi, Circumcision, Ascension_
Andrea Mantegna, _Portrait of Cardinal Carlo de' Medici_

ROOM 24
Room of the Miniatures

Housed in this room are numerous examples of the Medici collection of miniatures and small portraits in ebony frames, including copies of celebrated masterpieces by Raphael, Andrea del Sarto and other masters of the 16th century.

ROOM 25
Room of Michelangelo and Florentine Artists

Mariotto Albertinelli, _Visitation_
Mariotto Albertinelli, _Predella with Scenes from the Life of Christ_
Ridolfo del Ghirlandaio (attr.), _The Nun_
Ridolfo del Ghirlandaio (attr.), _Portrait Cover_

Fra' Bartolomeo, *Portia*
Fra' Bartolomeo, *The Virgin Appears to Saint Bernard*
Fra' Bartolomeo, *Annunciation, Nativity and Circumcision*
Francesco Granacci, *Joseph Being Taken to Prison*
Francesco Granacci, *Joseph Presents his Father and Brothers to the Pharaoh*
Alonso Berruguete, *Salomé with the Head of John the Baptist*
Michelangelo, *Holy Family with the Young Saint John (Tondo Doni)*

ROOM 26
Room of Raphael and Andrea del Sarto

Andrea del Sarto, *Madonna of the Harpies*
Andrea del Sarto, *Portrait of a Woman with a Basket of Spindles*
Andrea del Sarto, *Vallombrosa Altarpiece*
Andrea del Sarto, *Saint James*
Raphael, *Portrait of a Man*, known as *Francesco Maria della Rovere*
Raphael, *Portrait of Elisabetta Gonzaga*
Raphael, *Self-portrait*
Raphael and workshop, *Portrait of Julius II*
Raphael, *Portrait of Guidobaldo da Montefeltro*
Raphael, *Madonna of the Goldfinch*
Raphael (attr.), *Portrait of Perugino*
Raphael, *Portrait of Leo X with Cardinals Giulio de' Medici and Luigi de' Rossi*
Puligo, *Portrait of Pietro Carnesecchi*
Francesco di Cristofano, known as Franciabigio, *Portrait of a Young Man*
Francesco di Cristofano, known as Franciabigio, *Madonna of the Well*

ROOM 27
Room of Pontormo and Rosso Fiorentino

Agnolo Bronzino, *Pygmalion and Galatea*
Agnolo Bronzino, *Panciatichi Holy Family*
Agnolo Bronzino, *Lamentation of Christ*
Francesco Ubertini, known as Bachiacca, *Christ before Caiaphas*
Francesco Ubertini, known as Bachiacca, *Deposition*
Francesco Ubertini, known as Bachiacca, *Predella with Scenes from the Life of Saint Acasius*
Mirabello Cavalori (attr.), *Madonna and Child with Saints*
Cecchino Salviati, *Adoration of the Shepherds* (presently on loan)
Giovan Battista di Jacopo, known as Rosso Fiorentino (attr.), *Portrait of a Young Woman*
Pier Francesco di Jacopo Foschi, *Portrait of a Man*
Pontormo (attr.), *Portrait of a Musician*
Pontormo, *Portrait of Maria Salviati*
Pontormo, *Saint Antony Abbot*
Pontormo, *Supper at Emmaus*
Pontormo, *Nativity of Saint John*
Pontormo and Bronzino, *Martyrdom of Saint Maurice and the Theban Legion*
Domenico di Giacomo di Pace, known as Beccafumi, *Escape of Clelia and the Roman Virgins from the Camp of Porsenna*
Domenico di Giacomo di Pace, known as Beccafumi, *Holy Family with the Young Saint John*

Domenico di Giacomo di Pace, known as Beccafumi, *Self-portrait*
Rosso Fiorentino, *Moses Defends the Daughters of Jethro*
Rosso Fiorentino (attr.), *Portrait of a Young Man Dressed in Black*
Rosso Fiorentino, *Madonna and Child with Saints (Spedalingo Altarpiece)*
Rosso Fiorentino, *Portrait of a Young Woman*
Pietro Bonaccorsi, known as Perin del Vaga, *Tarquin Founds the Temple of Jove on the Capitol*
Pietro Bonaccorsi, known as Perin del Vaga, *Justice of Seleucus*

ROOM 28
Room of Titian and Sebastiano del Piombo

Sebastiano Luciani, known as Sebastiano del Piombo, *Death of Adonis*
Sebastiano Luciani, known as Sebastiano del Piombo, *Portrait of a Woman*
Titian, *Portrait of a Man* known as *"The Sick Man"*
Titian, *Flora*
Titian, *Venus of Urbino*
Titian, *Portrait of a Knight of Malta*
Titian, *Portrait of Eleonora Gonzaga della Rovere*
Titian, *Portrait of Francesco Maria della Rovere*
Titian, *Portrait of Bishop Ludovico Beccadelli*
Titian, *Saint Margaret*
Titian and workshop, *Portrait of Sixtus IV*
Jacopo Negretti, known as Palma il Vecchio, *Resurrection of Lazarus*
Jacopo Negretti, known as Palma il Vecchio, *Judith*
Jacopo Negretti, known as Palma il Vecchio, *Holy Family with the Young Saint John and Saint Mary Magdalen*

ROOM 29
Room of Dosso and Parmigianino

Francesco Mazzola, known as Parmigianino, *Madonna and Child with Saints* known as the *"Madonna di San Zaccaria"*
Francesco Mazzola, known as Parmigianino, *Portrait of a Man*
Francesco Mazzola, known as Parmigianino, *Madonna and Child with Angels* known as the *"Madonna of the Long Neck"*
Amico Aspertini, *Adoration of the Shepherds*
Giovan Battista Luteri, known as Dosso Dossi, *Rest During the Flight into Egypt*
Giovan Battista Luteri, known as Dosso Dossi, *Witchcraft (Allegory of Hercules)*
Giovan Battista Luteri, known as Dosso Dossi, *The Virgin Appears to Saints John the Baptist and John the Evangelist*
Giovan Battista Luteri, known as Dosso Dossi, *Portrait of a Warrior*
Benvenuto Tisi, known as Garofalo, *Madonna and Child with Saints Martin and Dorothy*
'Friulian friend of Dosso', *Allegorical Figure*
'Friulian friend of Dosso', *Portrait of a Man*
Veneto-Friulian painter (16th century), *Portrait of a Woman*
Emilian school (16th century), *Portrait of a Youth*

ROOM 30
Room of 16th-century Emilian Artists

Benvenuto Tisi, known as Garofalo, *Adoration of the Shepherds*
Benvenuto Tisi, known as Garofalo, *Annunciation*
Benvenuto Tisi, known as Garofalo, *Saint Jerome*
Ludovico Mazzolino, *Madonna and Child with Saints*
Ludovico Mazzolino, *Circumcision*
Ludovico Mazzolino, *Adoration of the Shepherds*
Ludovico Mazzolino, *Massacre of the Innocents*

ROOM 31
The Veronese Room

Paolo Caliari, known as Veronese, *Esther and Ahasuerus*
Paolo Caliari, known as Veronese, *Martyrdom of Saint Justine*
Paolo Caliari, known as Veronese, *Holy Family with Saint Barbara and the Young Saint John*
Paolo Caliari, known as Veronese, *Venus and Mercury*
Paolo Caliari, known as Veronese, *Annunciation*
Paolo Caliari, known as Veronese, *Saint Agatha Crowned by Angels*
Paolo Caliari, known as Veronese, *Virgin Enthroned*
Andrea Micheli, known as Vicentino, *Visitation*
Domenico Riccio, known as Brusasorci, *Bathsheba*
Venetian school (16th century), *Portrait of a Man*
Venetian school (16th century), *Portrait of an Artist*
Alessandro Oliverio, *Portrait of a Man*

ROOM 32
The Tintoretto Room

Jacopo Robusti, known as Tintoretto, *Portrait of Jacopo Sansovino*
Jacopo Robusti, known as Tintoretto, *The Samaritan at the Well*
Jacopo Robusti, known as Tintoretto, *Adam and Eve before God*
Jacopo Robusti, known as Tintoretto, *Portrait of a Venetian Admiral*
Jacopo Robusti, known as Tintoretto, *Portrait of a Man with a Red Beard*
Jacopo Robusti, known as Tintoretto, *Portrait of a Man*
Jacopo Robusti, known as Tintoretto, *Portrait of a Man*
Jacopo Robusti, known as Tintoretto, *Christ at the Well of the Samaritan*
Jacopo Robusti, known as Tintoretto, *Leda and the Swan*
Paris Bordon, *Portrait of a Knight*
Paris Bordon, *Portrait of a Man in a Fur Coat*
Jacopo da Ponte, known as Jacopo Bassano, *Two Dogs*
Jacopo da Ponte, known as Jacopo Bassano, *Annunciation to the Shepherds*
Jacopo da Ponte, known as Jacopo Bassano, *Judas and Tamar*
Gian Paolo Pace, *Portrait of Giovanni dalle Bande Nere*
Leandro da Ponte, known as Leandro Bassano, *The Concert* (attr.)
Venetian school (late 16th century), *Portrait of an Artist*

ROOM 34
Room of 16th-century Lombard Artists

Lorenzo Lotto, *Holy Family with Saints Jerome, Anne and Joachim*
Lorenzo Lotto, *Susanna and the Elders*

Lorenzo Lotto, *Portrat of a Youth*
Bernardino Licinio (attr.), *The Nude*
Paolo Pino, *Portrait of a Man* known as the *Portrait of Doctor Coignati*
Sebastiano Florigerio, *Portrait of Raffaele Grassi*
North Italian painter (16th century), *Portrait of Teofilo Folengo*
Giovan Battista Moroni, *Portrait of Pietro Secco Suardo*
Giovan Battista Moroni, *Portrait of a Scholar*
Giovan Battista Moroni, *Portrait of the Poet Giovanni Antonio Pantera*
Giovanni Girolamo Savoldo, *Transfiguration*
Giulio Campi, *Portrait of Galeazzo Campi*
Giulio Campi (attr.), *Portrait of a Musician*
Bernardino Campi (attr.), *Portrait of a Man*
Camillo Boccaccino (attr.), *Head of an Old Man*
Girolamo Figino, *Madonna and Child with Saints Margaret and Mary Magdalen*
Sofonisba Anguissola (attr.), *Portrait of a Man*

ROOMS 36-40
Vestibule of Buontalenti

Bernardo Strozzi, *Saint Catherine of Alexandria*
Bernardo Strozzi, *Saint Cecilia*
Guido Reni, *Madonna of the Snow*
Giovan Antonio Fumiani, *The Stoning of Zachariah*
Giovan Battista Spinelli, *David is Celebrated by the Jewish Women*
Giovan Battista Spinelli, *David Placates Saul's Anguish with a Harp*

ROOMS TEMPORARILY CLOSED TO THE PUBLIC

33 - The 16th-century Corridor
35 - The Room of Barocci and the Tuscan Counter-Reformation
41 - The Rubens Room
43 - The Caravaggio Room
44 - The Room of 17th-century Flemish Artists
45 - The Room of the 18th Century
- Room of San Pier Scheraggio:
  Andrea del Castagno, *Dante Alighieri*
  Andrea del Castagno, *Giovanni Boccaccio*
  Andrea del Castagno, *Francesco Petrarch*
  Andrea del Castagno, *Pippo Spano*
  Andrea del Castagno, *Niccolò Acciaioli*
  Andrea del Castagno, *Farinata degli Uberti*
  Andrea del Castagno, *The Cumaean Sibyl*
  Andrea del Castagno, *Queen Esther*
  Andrea del Castagno, *Queen Tomyris*
  Master of San Martino alla Palma, *"Madonna della Ninna"*
  Master of Greve, *Madonna and Child*
  Corrado Cagli, *The Battle of San Martino*

NB: *we have reported the list of the works on display in the Room of San Pier Scheraggio only, since, although closed to the public, it is arranged in a certain way.*

379

*Finished printing in the
month of September 1999 by the
Centro Stampa Editoriale Bonechi
Sesto Fiorentino - Firenze*